Adoption with Contact
Implications for policy
and practice

Acknowledgements

The study from which this publication derives would not have been possible without the contribution of the 60 or so participants in adoption – the adoptive and birth parents and their children. They shared their experiences willingly, many of them expressing the hope that other adoption participants would benefit from what they had shared. From all of them, especially the children and young people, I learned a great deal, and hope I have adequately conveyed their "expert" perspectives.

I especially wish to thank also

- Members of self help and voluntary organisations concerned with children and their families: British Agencies for Adoption and Fostering; Family Rights Group; The Grandparents Federation; National Foster Care Association; Natural Parents Support Group; National Organisation for the Counselling of Adoptees and Parents; Parent to Parent Information on Adoption Services; and Parents Aid, Harlow.
- Jane Rowe and June Thoburn, who generously allowed me to build o their research and made suggestions about the direction of the stud June also offered help with the analysis.
- The voluntary agency representatives who gave their time to prov information about their agency policy and practice.

In addition, I am grateful for the assistance received from colleagues Barnardo's, supervisors at Cranfield University, Sheila Smith and Shaila Shah at BAAF and friends and family members, especially Paul, Roz and Niko.

The author

Joan Fratter has had both local authority and voluntary agency experience in child care, initially in Liverpool Children's Department and subsequently in Barnardo's. Currently she is a senior social worker in Positive Options, a Barnardo's project based in North London which offers a social work service to families affected by HIV.

This publication is based on research Joan undertook between 1985 and 1995 for a PhD in the School of Social Policy, Cranfield University.

Inter-departmental Review of Adoption Law

Background Paper Number 1: *International Perspectives*, DoH, 1990.
Background Paper Number 2: *Review of Research Relating to Adoption*, DoH, 1990.
Background Paper Number 3: *Intercountry Adoption*, DoH and Welsh Office and Scottish Office, 1992.

Discussion Paper Number 1: *The Nature and Effect of Adoption*, DoH, 1990.
Discussion Paper Number 2: *Agreement and Freeing*, DoH and Welsh Office, 1991.
Discussion Paper Number 3: *The Adoption Process*, DoH and Welsh Office, 1991.
Discussion Paper Number 4: *Intercountry Adoption*, DoH and Welsh Office and Scottish Office, 1992.

Review of Adoption Law: Report to Ministers of an Interdepartmental Working Group, DoH and Welsh Office, 1992
Adoption: The future, CM 2288, Department of Health, the Welsh Office and the Lord Chancellor's Department, HMSO, 1993.

Adoption – A service for Children (Adoption Bill – a consultative document), DoH and Welsh Office, 1996.

Adoption with Contact

Implications for policy and practice

Joan Fratter

Published by
British Agencies for Adoption & Fostering
(BAAF)
Skyline House
200 Union Street
London SE1 0LX

Charity registration 275689

British Library Cataloguing in Publication Data
A catalogue record for this book is available from the British Library

ISBN 1 873868 37 5

Designed by Andrew Haig & Associates
Typeset by Avon Dataset Ltd, Bidford on Avon
Printed by Russell Press (TU), Nottingham

Contents

Foreword

The continued maintenance of links between members of the birth family and the adopted child is a recent development. As a result, openness in adoption has been one of the main issues dominating adoption policy and practice over the last ten or so years. The mid-1980s were to mark a decided shift away from the earlier "clean break" approach that had been characteristic of adoption practice over many decades. Since then, positions have sometimes been polarised between the defenders of the status quo and proponents of openness and contact. The arguments for and against contact have been rehearsed many times over, usually ending with a plea for more evidence. The White Paper, *Adoption: The Future* published in 1993 gave cautious support to the move towards greater openness and the recent draft Adoption Bill published in March 1996 makes provision for this change in policy. Whilst all these debates were taking place, empirically based evidence to inform the discussion was thin on the ground. Some of the evidence was inferred from related studies as those involving custody and step-parenting, but obviously the issues are not exactly the same.

Examples of more open forms of adoption involving babies were not uncommon both here and particularly in the USA, but a more decided shift towards this position was taken by New Zealand in the early 1980s. The debate in Britain, though, as different from either in New Zealand or the US, has focused mostly around issues of contact concerning children placed when older as part of the so called "permanency movement". In fact, it is surprising that though the "permanency movement" had its origins in the US, there has been almost total silence there on the issue of contact between older placed children and their birth families.

Anecdotal and other evidence emerging from some adoption studies in the UK, where contact was only peripheral to other key issues being pursued, was suggesting that older placed children could not be expected to give up past meaningful attachments to a parent, sibling or grandparent, as exclusion seemed to threaten the stability of the placement. In fact, such an expectation, it was argued, appeared to be making the child's attachment to the adoptive parent(s) difficult, if not impossible.

In the absence of substantive empirical evidence for or against adoption with contact, it was appropriate that the official response had to be a cautious one. Joan Fratter's study which is described in this publication, is possibly the first of its kind to focus exclusively on the adoption of children with special needs, most of them beyond the toddler stage, at the time of placement. Some form of contact had been planned or developed out of these arrangements. The study covered 32 children placed in 22 families and the interviews with adoptive parents, birth parents and adopted children (who were old enough to be interviewed) took place between about 1987 and 1994. The credibility and reliability of the study were greatly enhanced by the follow-up interviews with the main protagonists and with a long enough gap to allow for more than first experiences and impressions to be shared.

This is a painstaking study to which Joan Fratter has brought a dispassionate and much needed level-headed approach. It was difficult not to be impressed by the careful and methodical examination and sifting of the material, separating facts from opinion, in the attempt to establish the contribution of contact to the general welfare of the children involved. A further strand to this pioneering study was the way in which the author successfully pieced together the policy and practice lessons emerging from her study.

It has to be recognised that these are early days yet and bigger studies will eventually be needed before more firm conclusions can be drawn on the subject. However, this excellent study provides a firm base from which to begin to look at adoption with contact, especially when it involves the placing of older children.

The management of adoption with contact, and its aftermath, is emerging as one of the main challenges facing adoption workers. Whilst the findings support the move towards more open forms of adoption, not surprisingly perhaps, the author herself urges caution stressing the importance of considering each case separately to ensure first and foremost that it is based on a child-centred approach.

Professor John Triseliotis
Senior Research Fellow
International Social Sciences Institute
The University of Edinburgh

Introduction

The study from which this publication is derived was concerned with issues of contact in relation to children unable to live with members of their family of origin. It was begun in 1985 in a context in which "permanency planning" policies in most statutory and voluntary agencies required that children under twelve years of age be placed for adoption if restoration to the birth family was unlikely to be achievable within prescribed time limits; and, furthermore, that contact with birth relatives should be terminated in order to facilitate a secure adoption. These policies were likely to be implemented irrespective of the quality of the child's relationship with birth relatives and of his or her ethnic and cultural background. Having been working as a fieldworker for many years in family placement, both in a local authority and a voluntary agency, I found it difficult to reconcile with my practice experience the widely held view that continuing contact was incompatible with achieving permanence, and furthermore that only adoption provided a secure enough placement. "Practitioner research" was undertaken at Cranfield University in order to explore these issues.

The fieldwork was conducted in two stages. The first stage, undertaken in 1987, explored how a child's need for contact could be accommodated within a family placement outside the family of origin. Interviews were conducted with voluntary adoption agency representatives and with adoptive parents with experience of contact after adoption. These indicated that contact (in a variety of forms) need not impede the additional developmental tasks of adoptive parents and adopted children and indeed in some respects could be beneficial. The findings are reported in two BAAF publications: the agency interviews as part of the survey conducted by Thoburn and Rowe[1] (reported in Fratter *et al*, 1991) and the interviews with adoptive parents in Mullender.[2]

Stage 2 was undertaken in 1991 and focused on how the principle underpinning the Children Act 1989 of promoting contact between children and their families could be applied to children being placed for adoption. There were further interviews with the adoptive parents, some four years after the first interviews, together with interviews with some of their adopted children and with a few of the birth parents who were part of the same family network. These are reported and discussed in the chapters which follow. The M Phil and the Ph D thesis respectively, which describe fully each stage of the research, are available from Cranfield University and Barnardo's.

The term "openness" is used by the author to describe a range of options which depart from the exclusive, closed model of adoption. Thus openness in adoption represents a continuum of possibilities, ranging from an initial exchange of non-identifying information via the agency to ongoing contact in some form negotiated directly by members of the birth and adoptive families. "Contact" encompasses a variety of forms of communication between the parties in adoption, both direct and indirect. While the study was in progress, there were considerable changes in legislation, policy and practice in the UK regarding openness and contact in permanent placements outside the family of origin.

The extreme form of permanency planning as practised in the early 1980s recalled the philosophy of rescue which had characterised the activities of Victorian philanthropists. Within workhouses, parents and their children were separated and contact was severely restricted between children who were placed in voluntary homes or who were boarded out and their relatives.[3,4] The belief that the welfare of a deprived child was best served by his or her being prevented from having contact with relatives remained largely unchallenged.

Even after the setting up of children's departments in 1948, policy and practice focused on the child as separate from his or her parents. Eventually, disillusion grew about the effects of "a fresh start" approach which led to rootless young people leaving care with no sense of identity or family base. The Children and Young Persons Act 1963 recognised in Section 1 the importance of offering a service to families as a whole. However, the high expectations of the benefits to children and their families of a service aimed at prevention and reunification were not fulfilled.

The Children Act 1975 strengthened the powers of local authorities in relation to children in care and led to concern that the Act focused on "rescue" without ensuring the allocation of resources to enable families to remain together or to be reunited. The Act provided support, philosophically and legally, for the development of permanency planning outside the family of origin (although the concept as originated in the USA in the early 1970s had demonstrated that additional resources could enable children to leave foster care to be returned home to their relatives). Following implementation of the Act, there was an increase in the assumption of parental rights, termination of children's contact with their birth relatives and contested adoptions. The theories of Goldstein, Freud and Solnit[5,6] highlighted the importance of an exclusive relationship with an adoptive parent to avoid a child being adversely affected by having to relate to more than one set of parents. Practitioners and policy makers in the UK came to regard an exclusive adoptive relationship as the cornerstone of permanency planning, to be achieved within pre-determined timescales. Long-term fostering was regarded as appropriate only in exceptional circumstances.

Whether or not a child was permitted to remain in contact with birth relatives and the type of permanent placement sought, were determined not by individual circumstances but by agency policy and social worker attitudes. Little account was taken of the poverty affecting many parents separated from their children or of issues of power, class and race. Transracial adoption was regarded as more beneficial to children than foster care with a family which reflected the child's ethnic origins. Until the implementation in October 1991 of the Children Act 1989, parents and other relatives (and children and young people) had very restricted rights to challenge local authority decisions regarding contact. While the provisions of the Children Act 1989 have undoubtedly affected judicial and social work attitudes to contact, the legislation itself was informed by growing awareness during the 1980s of the importance of more openness and less secrecy for all participants in adoption.

McWhinnie[7], Kornitzer[8] and Triseliotis[9] had demonstrated the importance to adopted people of knowledge of their origins and the right to birth records. The implementation in 1976 of Section 26 of the Children Act 1975, permitting adopted adults to obtain a copy of their original birth entry, highlighted for adoption practitioners engaged in counselling the significance of the family of origin for many adopted people. In addition, personal accounts by adopted people in the UK and elsewhere of their search for members of their family of origin demonstrated their need for a sense of personal history and identity. Much of the greater understanding which now exists about the emotional and psychological experiences of participants in adoption has derived from the first-hand accounts and the studies of reunions between adopted people and their birth relatives in adulthood.

The complexity of the role of adoptive parents gained greater recognition. Kirk[10] described the 'institutional contradictions of adoptive kinship' and agencies increasingly offered preparation for adoptive parenting, especially regarding disclosure.[11] The benefits of adoptive parents having direct information about their children's birth relatives and, in some cases, "permission" to parent, have become widely recognised. Thus greater openness has not been as threatening to adoptive parents as it was once assumed to be. Positive outcomes have been described of preplacement meetings.

Until relatively recently, birth parents' participation in adoption had been largely unacknowledged and poorly understood. There is now recognition of the lifelong sense of loss experienced by many birth parents. Self-help groups have provided a channel for birth parents to describe their experiences, which have also been portrayed in poetry and personal accounts. However, practice developments which have enabled birth parents to participate more fully in the adoption process have derived primarily from perceptions of the needs of the child, not of the birth parent.

While attitudes concerning the possibility of greater openness in adoption have changed significantly in the UK since the early 1980s, there remains considerable uncertainty about the maintenance of contact, particularly face-to-face contact, after adoption. I hope that the findings from this small-scale study will provide some useful information for practitioners, as well as highlighting where further research, particularly longitudinal studies, is needed.

Joan Fratter
July 1996

References

1. Fratter J, Rowe R, Sapsford D, and Thoburn J, *Permanent Family Placement: A decade of experience*, BAAF, 1991.

2. Mullender A (ed), *Open Adoption: The philosophy and the practice*, BAAF, 1991.

3. Barnardo S, and Marchant J, *Memoirs of the late Dr Barnardo*, Hodder and Stoughton, 1907.

4. Barnardo T J (ed), *Night and day: A record of Christian missions and practical philanthropy*, collected pamphlets, Vol X, J R Shaw & Co, 1886.

5. Goldstein J, Freud A, and Solnit A J, *Beyond the Best Interests of the Child*, Free Press, 1973

6. Goldstein J, Freud A, and Solnit A J, *Before the Best Interests of the Child*, Burnett Books, 1980.

7. McWhinnie A M, *Adopted Children: How they grow up*, Routledge and Kegan Paul, 1967.

8. Kornitzer M, *Adoption and Family Life*, Putnam, 1968.

9. Triseliotis J, *In Search of Origins*, Routledge and Kegan Paul, 1973.

10. Kirk H D, *Adoptive Kinship: A modern institution in need of reform*, Toronto: Butterworth, 1981, Canada.

11. Triseliotis J, *Adoption Services in Scotland: Recent research findings and their implications*, Scottish Office, Central Reseach Unit Papers, 1992.

1 Adoption and contact

There would seem to be little dissension from the assertion of Baran and Pannor that many of the psychological problems which may affect adopted people, adoptive parents and birth parents 'are directly related to the secrecy or anonymity of the closed, traditional system of adoption'.[1] Most studies indicate that the more modest forms of openness in adoption, involving birth parents in the choice of adoptive parents and pre-placement meetings, for example, are on the whole beneficial to all parties in adoption.[2] Indeed a few adoption agencies in the UK, in response to the needs of adoption consumers, have included these alternatives to the closed adoption model for a number of years.[3] However, there is much less certainty among practitioners and policy makers about the circumstances in which adoption with some form of continuing contact should be planned.

Agency placements from the 1950s onwards in the UK discouraged any forms of openness, and the possibility of continuing contact with a birth relative was scarcely considered until the mid-1980s. Previously, adoption with contact seems to have occurred in agency placements mainly when children had been adopted by foster carers. Raynor[4] and Lambert *et al*[5] described a few such placements, and Triseliotis and Russell anticipated the need for more open or "inclusive" adoption:

> 'Planned permanency, through adoption or fostering, need not of course exclude interested parents or other relatives from playing a continuing part. Though this is an area in which practice experience is still very limited, it is bound to assume greater significance with the increasing number of older children being placed. Provision may have to be made in suitable cases for access to children by parents and relatives who still have meaningful bonds with them . . . The very few children who retained some contact with a member of their family in our sample derived considerable satisfaction from it.'[6]

However, while adoption with continuing contact by birth parents or other relatives would seem in some respects to be a logical progression from the move towards greater openness, its development has been controversial. Baran and Pannor, advocates of "open adoption" in the US since the early 1970s, recalled that they had not perceived 'how threatening change was to the institution of adoption'.[7]

I ADOPTION WITH CONTACT IN RELATION TO KEY CONCEPTS

Because of the comparatively low incidence of adoption with contact in the UK and in most Western societies, there are no long-term research studies currently available which examine adoption with different types of contact in a range of situations. The literature therefore draws on small scale studies, personal accounts, anecdotal evidence and speculation based on experience of the closed model. Those studies undertaken outside the UK mainly relate to the placements of infants voluntarily relinquished and placed with adoptive parents of the same racial background. The accounts by people directly affected are illuminating, although they cannot be generalised.

Adopted children

Pannor and Baran stated that of the parties directly involved in adoption, 'the benefit of open adoption to the child is probably the most significant'.[8] The potential effects of adoption with contact are here considered in relation to attachment and identity.

The development of attachment

Attachment theory derives from the work of John Bowlby, whose publications over a period of forty years have been widely read by child care workers from many disciplines. In 1951, the World Health Organisation published *Maternal Care and Mental Health*, and Bowlby continued to develop and modify his work until his death in 1991.[9] The development of attachment theory by Bowlby and others, particularly Ainsworth, has been summarised by Bretherton.[10] Attachment theory has been particularly influential in the understanding of child development and of psychotherapeutic intervention with children.

Goldstein *et al*, basing their work on clinical experience in the US and in the UK, drew on psychoanalytic theory in referring to 'the need of every child for unbroken continuity of affectionate and stimulating relationships with an adult'.[11] The emphasis in both attachment theory and psychoanalytic theory on the importance of a child's early relationship with a caregiver has been particularly influential since the early 1970s in adoption theory and practice. A secure attachment is seen to promote trust in adults, a sense of self-worth, resilience to handle stress in the future and self-confidence regarding the environment.

Attachment theory, with its emphasis on the importance of the early relationship with one caregiver, normally the mother, has been criticised as being culturally biased. Pennie and Best have described how the strengths of black families have been undervalued and undermined:

> 'To black people, the meaning of bonding is very different to that which is held by society in general and social workers in particular. Bonding between black children and parents is seen as multidimensional while in the British context it is seen as mono-dimensional, i.e. the close relationship between parents and child within the nuclear family.
>
> There is little difference between biological and psychological parenting among black families. Both are seen as symmetrical, therefore adequate parenting can be provided by the extended family without any real conflict between the natural parent and the substitute parents. This is a common historical feature of black family life.
>
> Multiple mothering is a healthy and accepted pattern of family organisation among black people.'[12]

More recent discussions of attachment theory have given greater weight to "the issue of cultural diversity":

> 'Thus, at a general level, sensitive responsiveness (of a caregiver) is likely to be a precursor to security of attachment across cultures. However, at a more specific level, in terms of descriptions of the pre-

cise patterns of mothering involved, antecedents of secure attachment may well *differ* between cultures . . .'[13]

In addition to the limitation in relation to adoption practice deriving from the cultural bias of attachment theory, it has also been acknowledged that there has been little systematic research into siblings as attachment figures.[14,15] The significance of separating brothers and sisters prior to adoption placement and not maintaining contact between them after placement has received little attention in the adoption literature until recently.

It is of great relevance in adoption practice to consider how far a child's capacity to attach is damaged by disrupted attachments early in life or by the lack of opportunity to develop attachments. Prospective studies have shown that the patterns of attachment observed in one-year-olds tend to persist, in part because the caregiver's way of relating to the child tends to continue unchanged and in part because each pattern tends to be self-perpetuating.[16] During a child's first two or three years, the pattern of attachment can change in accordance with the caregiver's behaviour. Nevertheless, 'as a child grows older, the pattern becomes increasingly a property of the child himself, which means that he tends to impose it, or some derivative of it, upon new relationships such as with a teacher, a foster mother, or a therapist'.[17]

Schaffer, in a review of the research on attachment in adoption, found no research relating to children placed over the age of seven but concluded that up to that age, children placed from an institution could be successfully integrated into a family, although some behaviour problems and difficulties were found subsequently.[18]

A study by Smith and Sherwen in the USA of the relationship of adoptive mothers and their children indicated that 'children adopted over a certain age may have problems in attaching to adoptive parents . . . age four seemed to be an important age – before four, the adoptive mother-child bonding process seemed very similar to the biological bonding process'.[19] However, Smith and Sherwen added that 'viable attachment relationships *can* and do occur, albeit with more work and a willingness to overcome problems'.[20]

This is one of a number of studies which suggest that in the placement of older children it may be more realistic to hope for a "good enough" attachment which will provide a loving and lasting relationship rather than the concept described in attachment theory.[21,22] It is important that a sufficient degree of attachment exists to enable the adopted child to separate from the adoptive parents and achieve independence in a way that is not disruptive – without a biological tie to connect, an adopted child may have a fear of leaving and/or may equate leaving with disloyalty.[23]

Schaffer asserted, having reviewed literature from the UK and the US, that children could attach themselves to more than one set of carers at the same time.[24] Triseliotis, having described the sadness of three adopted children whose contact with birth relatives had been severed, posed the hypothesis, although the sample group was very small, that 'severing children's meaningful emotional links with members of their birth families limits their capacity for full attachment to their new families'. He added that 'when a child's existing links to a birth parent or relative are severed on placement with a new family, the feelings involved are not eradicated but driven "underground". Furthermore such feelings can jeopardise the stability of the placement.'[25]

Barth and Berry studied a large number of placements in the US which had a high risk of disruption, including some situations in which children had maintained contact with birth relatives:

> 'Older children have multiple attachments. When they are adopted, they struggle with the significance of that event for the continuity of other attachments. If those attachments are positive but not strong, children and adoptive families may be able to incorporate them with little effect on their own relationship. Open adoption provides such opportunities. If the attachment to birth or prior foster parents is more intense, then efforts to facilitate disengagement may be necessary.'[26]

Thus, it has been increasingly recognised that expectations regarding the potential of an adopted child to attach need to take into account her or his age and pre-placement experiences and that continuing contact with birth relatives (or other significant others) is not necessarily an obstacle to the development of attachment. Practitioners in the UK have been particularly wary of continuing face-to-face contact in the placement of babies and young children, fearing confusion on the part of the child and interference with attachment. However, Schaffer asserted that 'when stability and quality of relationships are satisfactory, children's well-being is not put at hazard by multiple-care arrangements . . . children are able to sort out the differing roles of people at much earlier ages than they had been given credit for'.[27]

Referring specifically to adoption with contact, Triseliotis suggested that a visiting birth parent is 'less likely to become a close attachment figure and more likely to be like a visiting aunt or friend to the child who also happens to be a biological parent'.[28]

The development of identity

Awareness of the additional complexities for adopted people in developing a sense of identity began to grow during the 1960s.[29,30,31] Prior to this, adoption practitioners had encouraged adoptive parents to regard adoption as an emotional as well as a legal transplant. Thus, as described by Raynor, there was an emphasis in adoption practice on "matching" so as to minimise the perception of difference.[32]

Triseliotis, whose 1973 study was so significant in increasing understanding of the importance to adopted people of knowledge of origins, has written extensively about identity in adoption.[33]

In 1983, Triseliotis highlighted three key areas as contributing to identity building in adoption: the warmth and security offered by the adoptive family; knowledge of origins; and the attitudes of people in the community.[34] This study drew on these key areas in constructing the interview schedules. More recently, Triseliotis has suggested that while the quality of parenting appeared to be the most important factor in identity building for white children adopted within a broadly similar ethnic and cultural context, as children move towards adulthood, community attitudes may 'assume much greater importance, and if hostile and rejecting can prove devastating to the self'.[35]

While the importance of identity has been acknowledged in the literature, the practice of severing any form of birth family contact regardless of individual circumstances would suggest that in the recent past a sense of identity was seen as less important than a sense of permanence, whereas a placement should seek to encompass both.

Life story work has been developed in the UK and the US as a means of helping a child make sense of her or his past.[36,37] Hunter concluded in relation to children placed after infancy 'that insufficient acknowledgement and work is spent on their shattered life histories . . . A child may separate from his birth parents but they will be found within him, in his identifications and expectations, in his continuation of the interrupted business between them.'[38]

Harper, a psychotherapist, commented on the basis of a small preliminary study in Australia of 25 adopted children and a matched control group of children who had not been adopted that:

> 'All children are concerned with a sense of belonging and the need to know that they are related to and are like someone else, an extension of another as it were. For adopted children, for whom the biological bond is broken, belonging is qualitatively different because the continuity of a shared genetic existence is not there, and shared experience takes its place. But it is obvious that these shared experiences, even over a long period of time, do not compensate for the loss of the continuity of existence through the generations. The need to know who they are remains a potent question translated by the young ones into "What does she look like? Does she look like me?" and by the older ones into, "What does she look like? Do I look like her?"[39]

Brinich asserted that 'the normal ambivalence of parent–child relationships is modified and amplified in adoptive relationships', in which there is an implicit sense of rejection and loss for the adopted child.[40] Knowing that she or he is wanted by the adoptive parents (chosen)

> '. . . is inseparable from the fact that he was unwanted by his biological parents. It is my experience that adopted children have to wrestle with this message of opposites throughout their development – a burden which most non-adopted children are spared . . . When adopted children learn of their adoption they do not lose real people; but they do lose aspects of an important fantasy regarding their relationship with their parents. They lose the fantasy that they are loveable no matter what. They lose the fantasy that parents remain parents no matter what.'[41]

With reference to adolescents being assessed for treatment, Brinich described how adoption may affect two major tasks for adolescents – identity formation and separation from parental figures:

> 'Are unconscious identifications with rejected aspects of the biological parents active in the symptoms presented? Are adopted adolescents able to separate from their parents in appropriate ways without feeling that their separation is an act of disloyalty?'[42]

The potential additional pressures on children transracially adopted are widely acknowledged. Referring to the psychological well-being of a black child in a racist society, Small stated that:

> 'The child should be psychologically satisfied with the self as being of a specific racial and ethnic group and this is accepted and positively reinforced by those with whom the child interacts. A healthy racial and ethnic identity must, therefore, be one with which the child is happy, and which is accepted by the adoptive parents, extended family and society rather than rejected or related to negatively. In short, there should be harmony with self.'[43]

Banks commented that many parents and children as well as professionals may choose the route of denial of a black identity for children with one white and one black parent. However:

> 'In order to be viable an identity must be psychologically comforting and socially valid or approved. Those who claim their children are "free to choose" hold a sadly mistaken idea of what the labelling game is about. The choice does not exist. It is but an illusion of a misunderstanding of racist social reality.'[44]

The tasks in identity formation which are regarded as particular to adopted people – drawing on the connection with two families and understanding the circumstances of the implied rejection in a way which does not diminish self-esteem – would seem likely to be even more complex in transracial adoption in a racist society. However, there is a range of views as to how far racial and ethnic identity are significant in the achievement of self-esteem. Gill and Jackson, in a study of adopted black children described the young people as having high self-esteem, even though 'they saw themselves as "white" in all but skin colour'.[45] In a later review of the literature regarding the development of identity in black children (those brought up with their birth families as well as those transracially adopted) Tizard and Phoenix argued that 'Self-esteem and racial identity may derive from different contexts and relationships, and a negative attitude to one's race may not necessarily be associated with low self-esteem.'[46]

McRoy concluded from a review of the literature on transracial adoption that:

> 'Children who develop positive racial and ethnic self-feelings have families who acknowledge the significance of ethnic identity. The child receives subtle and perhaps not so subtle messages about his/her racial identity from friends, family and society. Families who deny the significance of nationality and ethnic background are failing to prepare their children for a world which believes these are important.'[47]

Most intercountry adoptive placements in the UK, and in Northern Europe and other Western societies, are transracial or transcultural. There are differing views about the effects on children's psychological development, particularly on their self-esteem. Bagley's review of studies of adopted people from different ethnic groups in several countries suggests that the extent to which a particular minority ethnic group is marginalised within a society affects the development of identity, because of the importance of community attitudes to self-esteem.[48] Tizard concluded from a review of the literature that in the estimated 20 to 25 per cent of intercountry placements in which problems occurred there was reason to believe that this was a consequence of 'their early experiences or their situation as adopted children, rather than from the experience of intercountry adoption'.[49] Triseliotis highlighted the need for further studies which followed the progress of children through adolescence and into adulthood.[50]

Kay, an adopted woman of Nigerian/Scottish descent adopted by a white Scottish couple, is quoted as saying of the children from Latin America and Eastern Europe adopted by Western European and North American families that it 'will be interesting to see in twenty years' time what those children are saying about their experience. What will they know of their own culture, their past? How alienated and displaced will they feel?'[51] (Kay's poetry gives a powerful and moving account of transracial adoption.[52])

There is virtually no empirical data about the impact of continuing contact on identity, nor indeed is there any consensus as to what constitutes a "good" or "poor" sense of identity and how this can be measured. A self-assessment may result in a different analysis from that reached by another person. Most of the literature is speculative or anecdotal. The view of the adopted person is conspicuously absent. Greater openness, possibly including contact, is suggested as a means of counteracting the disadvantages of the closed model of adoption. Most of the literature available is from the USA.

"Adoption-with-connection" is the term used by Colon to describe continuing contact through "visitation", which he believes would 'appear to be a good choice for the older child'. Writing from the perspective of having been fostered as a child in the US, Colon adopts as a central premise that the child's 'experience of biological-familial continuity and connection is a basic and fundamental ingredient of his sense of self, his sense of personal significance, and his sense of identity'.[53] In describing the possibility of maintaining links, he writes: 'Necessarily, the thread of connection to one's biological family may need at times to be very thin indeed – dormant perhaps, but never broken. Later, when conditions are favorable, the dormant ties can be reactivated.'[54]

Pannor and Baran were early advocates in the US of greater openness and anticipated benefits in terms of identity:

> 'Open adoption can enable adoptees to learn the true circumstances that led to their adoption in contrast to the romantic stories, untruths and distortions that have been told or have been imagined. It would help them to better understand that placing a child for adoption is probably one of the hardest decisions parents can make. Open adoption would also diminish the feeling of many adoptees that an existing block to the past may, in fact, create a block to the future as well. The secrecy that has enveloped adoptions, fostering both "good" and "bad" illusions for adoptees, would be lessened, if not eliminated . . . The need to be connected with one's biological and historical

past is an integral part of one's identity formation.'[55]

Silber and Dorner, who studied a number of placements with contact from infancy, claimed: 'They do not have to be confused by, or obsessed with, unanswered questions or fantasies. They accept the relationship with their birthparents as extended family members as natural and normal . . . The resulting heightened comfort level with adoption nurtures feelings of self-esteem and entitlement within both families."[56]

McRoy summarised the rationale behind the development in the US of departures from the "traditional confidential adoption process":

> 'Research on adoptees . . . has shown that adopted children seem to lack a sense of biological connection and continuity and may feel a need to search for their biological parents . . . For the adopted adolescent, questions about birth parents and origins play an important role in the identity-formation process . . . advocates of open adoption believe that knowledge of one's past is a basic human need and emotional problems may result when this knowledge is denied.'[57]

Although the author is not aware of any published studies which examine the effects of continuing contact on the identity development of a child who is transracially or transculturally adopted, it seems likely that well-managed contact would be beneficial. McRoy, in her review of transracial adoption, found that:

> 'Adoptive families who seek and have ongoing contact with persons of the same ethnic background as their adopted child, model for the child acceptance, not only of their minority child, but of others who have the same ethnic background as their child. The child in this situation views others like him and no longer feels so very different from everyone. The child also learns more about and from persons of his or her own ethnic background. They find they no longer have to deny their heritage – instead they become bi-cultural and accept both worlds.'[58]

Dutt and Sanyal suggested that professionals working within a Eurocentric framework should learn from the experiences of black communities:

> 'Black families have for decades looked after children who are not their own, and continue to now. The process is open and stems from

> the belief that where birth families are experiencing difficulty in caring for their children, then those children can be cared for by someone else. It is based on shared understanding, equal partnership and commitment. The children are fully aware of the arrangements and do not feel insecure or undermined, and do not have to deal with any divided loyalties.'[59]

While there are some very enthusiastic advocates of adoption with contact, it has to be acknowledged that most of the literature currently supporting this form of openness is concerned with infants voluntarily relinquished and, in the US, with independent or "co-operative" adoption arrangements in which the birth parents have been involved in the selection of the adoptive family. Concerns have been expressed about developing openness beyond the provision of full information to adoptive parents and birth parents at the time of placement; a pre-placement meeting between the two families; and later exchange of information via the agency. In the USA, Ferguson warned about the potentially damaging effects of adoption with contact[60] and the National Committee for Adoption has campaigned against this degree of openness.[61]

In the UK, the consultation papers and the Review of Adoption Law Published in 1992, led to a considerable amount of lobbying against the possibility of contact after adoption becoming more common. An 'Open Space' programme on BBC2 in June 1992, produced by Nicola Jennings, attracted a great deal of media attention. In a *Guardian* article, she saw the encouragement of continuing contact as a 'new trend' which 'may place the needs of the birth parents above those of the child'.[62] While the White Paper was awaited McWhinnie, interviewed in *The Independent*, pointed out that the outcomes for children of continuing face-to-face contact were unknown, thereby making open adoption 'an experiment in people's lives . . . These relationships require great maturity on the part of the adults in the child's life to prevent the child becoming a pawn'.[63]

At the time of writing, there is limited reliable data to guide practitioners regarding the effects of adoption with contact on the child's emotional and psychological development and how far personal contact can confer benefits which are not available through written information or photographs.

Adoptive parents

The key concepts discussed in this section are "entitlement" and attachment. While the provision by adoptive parents of a close and nurturing attachment to the child was identified by Triseliotis as the most important contribution to the growing child's sense of identity and self-esteem, entitlement is considered first because, as the literature demonstrates,[64] problems regarding entitlement can interfere with the adoptive parent's ability to become attached.

Entitlement

One dictionary definition of "entitlement" is 'the right to have something'.[65] This term in relation to a child is not an altogether happy one, with its connotation of ownership. Other terms such as "validation"[66] and "confirmation"[67] have been used instead. However, as the term is so well understood in adoption literature, it is used for the present discussion. Entitlement embraces a sense of security, of being in control and feeling comfortable in discussing adoption-related issues. It is linked with the concept of loss and with the development of identity as an adoptive parent.

Raynor, the writer who was largely responsible for the acceptance in the UK of the concept of entitlement, attributed it to Jaffee and Fanshel.[68] In analysing the additional complexities of adoptive parenthood she believed the key question was:

> 'whether or not an adoptive family considered themselves to be a "real" family with the right to parent the child, whether they had feelings of "entitlement". It is this basic issue which creates the extra dimension that separates adoptive from ordinary families (though step-parent families face some of the same questions). Entitlement encompasses an interlocking web of feelings about parenthood, self-worth, genealogy, heredity, fertility and some deep-seated attitudes towards giving and receiving.'[69]

Winkler *et al* focused on the loss experienced by all participants in adoption (as practised in Australia and the USA) and described adoption as a 'life course experience'. Developing the concept of entitlement, they wrote:

> 'One result of the role handicap sometimes felt by adoptive parents is the belief that they do not have the right to parent – that they are not entitled to be parents. On some levels, they feel that they have stolen their child from birth parents.'[70]

The problems which could arise from lack of entitlement were identified by Raynor:

> 'Parents who had little feeling of entitlement to their child – for whatever reason – were often incapable of disciplining him. Such people felt they had little right to the child, that in spite of the legal ties that bound them to him there were stronger ties which still bound him to his birth mother, and if they overstepped by denying him anything he wanted or by disciplining him in other ways he might withdraw his love for them and seek his other mother.'[71]

There is limited empirical evidence as to whether contact after adoption is likely to diminish or enhance a sense of entitlement. Raynor herself, who interviewed a small number of adoptive family members who had had some experience of contact after adoption with the birth mother, found that the effects were mixed. In a small-scale study of "open adoptions" in the USA, Belbas explored whether the relationship which develops between the adoptive parents and the birth family can be characterised as "empathic" and if so, whether that makes it more or less difficult for the adoptive parents to feel entitled to the child or to feel confident as the child's psychological parent. She concluded that all the adoptive parents in her study 'were found to be empathic toward their child's biological parent' and that:

> '. . . in terms of trusting the bond, none of the parents felt openness and empathy adversely affected the ties they had with their children . . . None of the parents in any group felt having contact made them worry about whether or not the child loved them, and none hesitated to say "there is no doubt in our minds that we are our children's real parents".'[72]

In another US study, McRoy found that most adoptive parents expressed some satisfactions concerning their arrangements, regardless of level of openness. She quoted an adoptive parent in an open arrangement: 'My friendship with the birth mother has helped me resolve my own issues around infertility and given me permission to parent.'[73]

Loss through infertility is a factor in the lives of many adoptive families. Brebner *et al* asserted that 'both adoptive father and adoptive mother should be mainly free of the traumatic aspects of infertility in order to assume the identity of adoptive parents'.[74] Silber and Dorner described contact as helpful in relation to grief arising from infertility.[75]

The few studies and the limited experience of adoption with contact in the UK do not confirm the reality of the threat to adoptive parents' security from contact. Moreover, none of the adoptive parents who had initiated or maintained contact following a contested adoption application, referred to interference by birth relatives as a disadvantage of contact, although historically this has been one of the reasons most commonly put forward for secrecy.[76]

Attachment

"Bonding" is the term usually used in clinical psychology to describe the parent–child (mostly the mother–child) relationship: 'This usage is tacitly in agreement with those who hold that this is not an attachment because a mother does not normally base her security on her relationship with her child.'[77] The literature on bonding is almost exclusively concerned with the development of the relationship between a caregiver and an infant, although it is no longer believed that there is necessarily a critical period very early in an infant's life after which bonding is likely to be problematic.[78,79] However, in the adoption field the term is usually applied to the placement of very young children. Hoopes quotes Singer's observations about the development of adoptive mother–infant relationships:

> 'What seems to be more important is the emergence of caretaking confidence and competence on the part of the parent, and a general caretaking atmosphere that is warm, consistent and contingent on the needs of the infant. To the extent that adoptive parents develop these characteristics and provide this type of environment, there is little reason to believe their attachment relationships with their young infants will differ markedly from nonadoptive parents.'[80]

As in many aspects of adoption literature, the adoptive father's relationship is not discussed here – and indeed Ainsworth acknowledges that the research on the bond of father to child in birth families is limited.[81]

The term "attachment" rather than "bonding" is usually preferred, particularly in the UK, in discussion of adoptive relationships of older-placed children. Schaffer found the research evidence about the ability of adoptive parents to develop a close relationship with adopted children reassuring: 'It is a history of social interaction, not kinship, that breeds attachment.'[82] Ward stated that: 'People with a broad recognition of kinship can more readily nurture adopted children, since they do not see kinship as strictly limited to the biological nuclear family, the extended family or the clan.'[83]

Smith and Sherwen described circumstances which can promote attachment by an adoptive mother. "Deterrents to bond formation" included negative and destructive or detached or rejecting behaviour on the part of the child.[84] Grotevant and McRoy identified factors that may reduce adoptive parents' ability to be 'optimally responsive' to their infant:

> '. . . unresolved parental ambivalence concerning infertility; parental tentativeness in interacting fully with the infant in order to protect against loss, should the agency or birthparents not permit the adoption to be finalized; lack of support typically available to biological parents, such as childbirth preparation classes and hospital-based programs; and attributions that the child is "different" and therefore "not ours" '.[85]

Concerns have been expressed by some commentators about the potentially damaging effects to the "bonding" process of greater openness: 'Open records adoption, which may entail having the biological parent in the infant's life, may disrupt the adoptive parent's ability to form and maintain an ongoing healthy attachment to the child.'[86]

Dominick's large-scale study in New Zealand indicated that adoptive parents' fears were generally unfounded.[87] She concluded that a large proportion of the adoptive parents who had had contact with the birthparent(s) of their child found that this had enhanced their relationship with the child and their feelings of security as parents. Beek interviewed a small number of adopters involved in contact arrangements with birth parents in England. Their overall experience was that they 'found face-to-face contact to be beneficial and enriching to their adoptive family life'.[88]

The effects of contact on attachment were explored in the interviews with adoptive parents undertaken in the present study.

Birth parents

The two most powerful themes identified in the literature in relation to birth parents are the experience of loss and the persistence of unresolved grief; and the shame, guilt and powerlessness resulting in poor self-esteem. The few studies available regarding greater openness and the impact on birth parents indicate that the opportunity to be more involved in the adoption arrangements may assist the grieving process and enhance self-esteem.

There are even fewer studies and personal accounts available regarding the effects on birth parents of contact after adoption, whether in the form of occasional or regular exchange of information or personal contact through letters, telephone calls and face to face meetings. In Dominick's New Zealand study only two birth parents were having direct contact with the adoptive parents at the time of the interview (only one face-to-face), although 16 were having indirect contact through an intermediary.[89] Rockel and Ryburn interviewed a small number of birth parents in New Zealand who were in touch with their children,[90] and Ryburn subsequently re-interviewed some of them about five years later.[91] In both these studies the birth parents had "voluntarily" relinquished their child.

In the USA, Sorich and Siebert followed up for a period of six years a group of birth parents who had received continuing information from adoptive parents through a "sharing" arrangement.[92] A small number of birth relatives and adoptive parents who described their experiences of co-operative adoption had been party to the arrangements for periods of five years or less.[93] Baran *et al* cited a placement with contact which was described by the social worker as genuinely satisfying to all the parties.[94] In a later publication, Baran and Pannor showed how open adoption, in the case of voluntary relinquishment of infants, can benefit birth parents.[95] Silber and Speedlin, whose observations are drawn from a small number of cases, were also confident about the benefits of contact after adoption.[96]

Adjusting to loss

Many birth parents, describing their experience of continuing pain and awareness of loss, have expressed the view that information and perhaps contact after adoption would assist by providing them with news of their child's progress and reassurance about the appropriateness of their decision for the child's well-being. However, this view has sometimes been criticised on theoretical grounds. Dominick, and Sorich and Siebert refer to authors who maintained that a more open adoption, and especially continuing contact (whether face-to-face or through direct or indirect links), could adversely affect birth parents by "reminding" them of their loss and causing more pain and regret; preventing their completing the mourning process; and tempting them to consider tracing their child and possibly misusing the knowledge they have.

The lack of research evidence and the need to rely on "theoretical formulations" was highlighted by Curtis who quoted opposing viewpoints found in the literature:

> 'Open adoption allows biological mothers to mourn and work through the loss of their children because they do not have to worry (in fantasy) about the children's well-being.
>
> 'Closed adoption allows biological mothers to mourn and work through the loss of their children because they cannot rely upon unrealistic fantasies of reunion.'[97]

Curtis commented: 'Obviously, at least one of these statements should not serve as a general guideline for practice in clinical child welfare.'[98]

Burnell asserted that information and perhaps contact can assist adjustment:

> 'Despite "openness" in adoption, the central issue remains the same. Information exchange and contact do not lessen the sense of loss for birth parents or children, but do appear to help some, at certain points in their lives, to make sense of it and provide some certainty

about what has happened to the other family members since their separation. All the feelings felt by those in a closed adoption remain the same in open adoptions. Information can, however, sometimes provide a more concrete reminder of a separation and loss without which, for parents and children alike, adoption and all that it entails can take on a dreamlike and unreal quality. But it is this "concreteness" of the loss and the limitations of the relationship that provide the framework within which all parties can adjust to their new and changing relationship, including adoptive parents. By providing information and sometimes limited contact, the loss is not removed but in a paradoxical way made manifest and so easier to adjust to.'[99]

A birth mother maintaining contact with her daughter described these mixed emotions:

'I don't want to give the impression that this hasn't been painful for me. I have suffered a loss, that is the loss of my daughter, and I will live with that for the rest of my life . . . But I feel great joy that I can watch her grow and have an opportunity to develop a relationship with her.'[100]

Silber and Dorner asserted that 'in open adoption birth parents work through the normal feelings of grief in a healthier manner, and they are more at peace with their decision. Being active in the child's life helps them each time feelings of grief resurface at different stages.'[101]

Self-esteem

There is limited literature on this point and some of the observations which follow derive from experiences of a closed adoption. Studies indicate the need of birth parents to explain to their child the reasons for adoption; to have some sense of how the child regards their action and to hope for "forgiveness"; and to make a contribution to the child, whether through providing information or reassuring the child that she or he was not rejected. Baran and Pannor suggested that open adoption can reduce birth parents' feeling of powerlessness and enable them to make a contribution to their child's life:

'When a birth mother helps choose the adoptive family and participates in the placement of her child, she knows that she is giving up her child and that it is not being snatched from her. She is part of the decision process, not a victim of a powerful institution. Her availability to the adoptive family and her existence to the child is of immeasurable value to all of them, including herself.'[102]

Sawbridge explained that it can be a "healing" process for parents of older children, including those who have lost their children involuntarily, to compile records of the child's past. She added:

> 'Many birth parents could be helped to do something like this, and to express some of the love and sorrow they feel, instead of being left thinking that all they had been able to show the child had been anger or abuse . . . for the birth parents who have made, or have had made for them, the hardest decision any human being has to make, the road ahead is a rough and uphill one. Instead of punishing them yet more, should we not be finding ways of helping them to live with their loss, and maybe even to go on contributing, in however small a way, to the success of adoption?'[103]

White questioned the purpose of a contact arrangement made when a child is young: 'To what extent does contact sought by a parent reflect reluctance to come to terms with the loss of a child? Does the contact merely continue the pain?'[104]

In practice there may be a fine line between a situation in which contact enables a birth parent to give agreement to an adoption application appropriately (because he or she wishes to be reassured about the child's well-being and to make a contribution, for example) and one which has an element of "bargaining", compromise, or an avoidance of a difficult planning decision. In the latter, the necessary spirit of co-operation between the adults may be absent.

The potential impact of contact on the three parties personally involved in adoption has been considered separately for the sake of clarity. This is not to suggest (as is the case in some of the literature) that the needs and wishes of adopted child, birth parent and adoptive parent are necessarily incompatible or in conflict, nor that each party is unaware of or indifferent to the feelings of the others.

The limited amount of literature available on adoption with contact has been considered above in relation to some key concepts in adoption. Other aspects are briefly considered below.

Potential impact on recruitment of adopters

Adoption with contact has been regarded as potentially most problematic and least beneficial to adoptive parents. For example, the pilot study of McRoy *et al* in the US concluded that the 'benefits to adoptive parents seem less clear. The greatest benefit is that it gives them a realistic picture of the birth parent and prevents stereotyping.'[105] It has therefore been suggested that adoption with contact may have implications for recruitment, particularly in the UK, where the majority of domestic agency placements are of older children and children with special needs. White questioned whether in asking adoptive parents to take on additional tasks 'we will overburden them and bring about the disruption of the placement' and whether there will be 'difficulty in finding suitable adopters when they recognise the complexity of the task they are being asked to undertake'.[106]

However, Parent to Parent Information on Adoption Services (PPIAS), the self-help organisation of adoptive parents, conducted a questionnaire in 1990 about attitudes to open adoption. The responses indicated that:

> 'In general adopters are favourably disposed to the idea of adopted children having some sort of contact with birth families . . . Several people said that they had changed in favour of more openness through their awareness of the changing needs of their children as they grew up; others had been made more aware of the birth mother's needs . . . If there is a unified theme emerging, it would seem to be a plea for flexibility, and for individual circumstances to be taken very much into account when determining the amount, frequency and type of contact.'[107]

To date there have been only anecdotal accounts as to how far seeking an adoptive family who would consider contact limits an agency's choice of placement for a child, apart from the agency survey conducted as part of this study in 1987.[108]

The range of views

A recent contribution to the debate on openness contained several contributions which highlight the potential risks of continuing contact, for example, where children have been subjected to sexual or other forms of abuse; where siblings placed together have different reactions to contact; where parents' needs cannot be disentangled from those of the child; and following a contested case.[109] Vyas described concerns regarding greater openness for members of some Asian communities in Britain.[110] White put forward the possibility that 'information provided in a photo or report could be used by the parent or other member of the birth family to seek out the child in a way which may be disruptive to the placement'.[111]

Other concerns expressed about continuing contact include the fact that some adoptive parents who have agreed in good faith to exchange information before their child was placed 'have found it unexpectedly difficult when the time comes'.[112] In relation to adoptive parents of babies, Kaniuk commented that they 'are often extremely highly motivated to become parents and are vulnerable to agreeing to something which they do not truly feel comfortable about implementing'.[113] There have certainly been accounts of adoptive parents reneging on informal arrangements in Australia.[114]

Ryburn explored the extent of contact after adoption with birth relatives among adoptive parents in the UK (PPIAS members) who had experienced a contested adoption. He found, surprisingly, that there had been contact in 42 per cent of the 74 cases considered. A particularly relevant finding was that although nearly all the adoptive parents who had contact could perceive disadvantages, 'none mentioned interference by birth relatives as one of these disadvantages'.[115] Burnell, drawing on the experience of the Post-Adoption Centre in London, asserted that:

> 'Adoptive parents can encompass the birth family. This we have experienced both with adoptive parents in closed adoptions having to encompass the birth family in fact and fantasy, and with adoptive parents of adolescents initiating contact by consent, and in more contemporary adoptions with contact.'[116]

Burnell added that the complexity of adoption is not resolved by either the "open" or "closed" model and that four dimensions of adoption are significant in all adoptions: continuity, co-operation, mediation and openness. He highlighted the importance of co-operation between birth parents and adoptive parents and of the availability of mediation.[117]

The experience of adoption with contact outside the UK

Most of the literature regarding the experience of adoption with contact relates to infant placements outside the UK. Van Keppel has described the process involved in drawing up negotiated adoption agreements in Australia, which formalise the issues of continued information exchange and contact, if desired, between birth parents and adoptive parents.[118] There is considerable emphasis on mediation, agreement and flexibility.

Etter reported on a follow-up study in the US some four years after adoption of 56 "open adoption" placements of infants. Birth parents and adoptive parents had 'designed their own adoptions, using mediation techniques within a structure that provided protection for both sides'.[119] The high level of compliance with the agreement for contact and of satisfaction with openness on the part of both birth and adoptive parents was attributed to the provision of *choice* regarding the degree of openness "*before* matching"; *thorough preparation*; and the *written agreement* (original emphasis). Etter's findings suggested that:

> 'For this group at least, adoptive and biological parents can handle both planning successful open adoptions and living with them afterward. A plethora of adoption practices designed to protect individuals from one another may be unnecessary and even counterproductive. Certainly, sealed records and secrecy can create great harm in the name of protection.'[120]

Gross, on the basis of a review of the (mainly US) literature on openness and a small-scale follow up study of birth parents and adoptive parents involved with an agency with a commitment to open practice, concluded that 'openness is working . . . and every indication suggests that more and more adoptive and biological families are entering into open arrangements'.[121] However, she acknowledged that 'we cannot foresee what the children's response will be, nor can we be sure that the positive evaluation of those early years will endure'.

Flexibility is a dimension which emerges from the studies of Rockel and Ryburn[122] and Ryburn[123] in New Zealand, and of McRoy in the US.[124] They have found that the nature and frequency of contact is subject to change over time. Silber and Dorner, writing in the context of the US where non-agency adoptions are commonly practised, asserted that in open adoption the adoptive parents and birthparents are 'completely in control and in charge of the adoption experience, rather than the control being in the hands of agencies or other intermediaries'.[125]

There have been two large-scale studies outside the UK which include a wider range of children placed, including older children, and which have some information regarding contact. Bagley summarised a Danish study, published in 1976, of 216 adopted people placed between 1924 and 1947. Bagley noted the finding that about one-fifth of the adopted people, especially those placed later, had some contact with a birth parent after adoption: 'Such contact was associated with better satisfaction with the adoption process, as reported by the adult adoptees.'[126]

A more recent study of 1,396 adoptions in California has been reported by Berry.[127] Anglo-American children and adoptive parents were over-represented in adoptions with post-placement contact. Two thirds of the children had been infants aged under one year at placement. The sample included adoption by relatives and placements arranged through public and private agencies and placements independently arranged. Berry points out that independent adoptions 'have become an avenue for biological parents to achieve more openness and control in adoptive placement'. The most significant factor linked with adoptive parents feeling comfortable with contact was their feeling they had some control of contact. Other key predictors of comfort included: the child's absence of a history of abuse; the directness of contact; and the adoptive parents having talked to the birth parents prior to placement.

Berry reported that 81 per cent of adoptive parents planning for contact had adopted children less than one year old. In the UK, by contrast, contact is much more likely to be maintained in the permanent placement of older children and in such cases, is emerging as a protective factor.[128,129,130] While there are no statistics available, it appears that planning for continuing contact, particularly face-to-face contact, in the placement of very young children is still unusual in the UK.

Contact in re-formed families

Like adoption, assisted conception and step-parenting as a means of creating families, place particular pressures on those involved because of society's attitudes. Walby and Symons drew parallels between the stigma affecting adoption and assisted conception and the consequent desire for secrecy: 'If such families were seen as different but as valid and acceptable as "natural" families, the need for secrecy would disappear'.[131] Robinson asserted that step-families are 'often evaluated on a deficit model, in which they are compared unfavourably to nuclear families'.[132] This was expanded upon by Robinson and Smith: 'The reaction to the suspicion that a step-family is an inferior, even dangerous kind of family may lead to ignoring the facts and pretending that a step-family is not different from the traditional nuclear family of two parents and their children'.[133] Kirk questioned whether the Shared Fate theory which he had developed in relation to adoptive families also applied to other families confronted by "culturally-based deviance."[134]

The experience of contact with the non-custodial (or non-resident) parent after divorce is sometimes cited as offering some similarities to contact with birth relatives after adoption.[135] Goldstein *et al* advocated a "clean break" approach after divorce as well as after adoption: the custodial parent should have the right to determine whether or not the non-custodial parent should have contact.[136] However Schaffer, having reviewed a number of studies, concluded that 'children adjust better to the step-family if they have a continuing relationship with the non-custodial parent'. The research 'gives no support to the idea that a clean break with the non-custodial parent is an essential precondition for establishing a good relationship with the step-parent, nor need one fear that the new relationship will inevitably destroy the old one'.[137]

In considering what makes contact work well after divorce, most studies point to the importance of a child-centred approach, with the adults being able to be co-operative. James and Wilson found there were access difficulties where the custodial parent was hostile. The involvement of a new partner with either spouse 'apparently did not affect attitudes towards access or the incidence of access difficulties at all'.[138] Schaffer found that the situation 'most conducive to children's welfare is one where there is only minimal overt conflict between the parents and maximal agreement as to methods of child rearing'.[139] Johnson highlighted as features of "good quality" contact the recognition by the "residence" parent of the child's need for the other parent; amicable, civil handovers and a negotiating process that provided flexibility.[140] Following divorce and re-marriage there is the potential for rivalry and jealousy but, as in adoptive situations, the child needs to receive permission and approval in relation to continuing contact.

De'Ath highlighted the potential strengths of the step-family:

> 'It is just possible that the step-family which survives the pressures of the early stages – the needs of children for continuity of contact with both their parents, sharing responsibilities and allowing previous connections to exist – provides a model for family life which is needed in a complex multicultural society, where differences are not only allowed but respected.'[141]

The hope that diversity in family structures will come to be regarded as equally valid and respected, rather than being viewed as somehow second best and "deficient", may seem over-optimistic to those who are currently living in untypical families, particularly in the current political climate in the UK. However, much greater openness about and within adoption has been developing since the mid-1970s, and Hill has highlighted how the influence of other cultures and changing concepts of parenthood have contributed to this:

> 'After a long period during which the Western model has been widely imposed elsewhere, we have recently witnessed a reverse process whereby this dominant legal form is now being challenged by some of those different traditions . . . much adoption practice remains based on a particular view of adoption as a total transfer of parenthood. This in turn is related to conceptions of so-called normal parenthood . . . Western adoption has been dominated by the idea of the complete break – that an adopted child completely and permanently severs ties with the original parents . . . Whilst this concept of adoption as the total transfer of parenthood is reflected in the legal situation in many countries, it seems to be an excessively narrow view of the psychological and sociological realities of both adoptive and non-adoptive parenthood . . . many forms of non-western adoption have included

some continuing role for the original parents as a normal expectation . . . At the very least, birth parents have a part to play (whether directly or symbolically) in an adopted person's evolving sense of identity.'[142]

In the next section, the legal aspects of openness and adoption with contact are considered.

II PERMANENCY AND OPENNESS IN THE 1990s

Legal aspects of openness and contact

As practice in the adoption field changed rapidly after 1975, the courts had been criticised for not keeping abreast of developments. Adcock and Levy commented in 1979 that 'judicial views have been slower to change'. They were referring to the reluctance of courts to make adoption orders in contested cases and to 'sever the blood relationship'.[143] Subsequently, as social work practice in the mid-1980s began to move away from the belief that parental contact would invariably need to be terminated, members of the judiciary struggled in some instances to reconcile the possibility of continuing contact with birth relatives with the accepted concept of adoption.

Adoption with a condition of access

The 1958 Adoption Act had provided for the possibility of conditions being attached to an adoption order in section 7(3). At the time of writing section 12(6) of the Adoption Act 1976 enables a court to impose "such terms and conditions" as it thinks fit, which could include a condition regarding contact. However, it has been clarified through case law that a section 8 contact order under the Children Act 1989 would be a preferred means of providing legally for contact after adoption if this were deemed appropriate.

Prior to the implementation of the Children Act 1989, section 12 (6) appears to have been applied sparingly in relation to contact. An important consideration was that any condition imposed should not impinge on the autonomy of adoptive parents, a principle set out by Cairns LJ in 1976 (Re S): 'Clearly no condition should be imposed which would be regarded as detracting from the rights and duties of the adoptive parents.'

The legal situation with regard to contact and adoption became more complex when the legislation giving limited rights to parents in relation to access (HASSASSA Act, 1983) was implemented in January 1984. There was a number of reported cases in which a parent had applied to a juvenile court for an access order while adoption or freeing proceedings were pending in a county court.

With the increase during the 1980s in the number of contested adoption applications where access was a key issue, there appeared to be some variation in the attitude of judges, although generally it was stated that a birth parent would not be found to be withholding consent unreasonably if continuing access were judged to be of benefit to the child in a county court. Furthermore, a ruling in the House of Lords (re C, 1988) clarified that in appropriate (albeit exceptional) circumstances, a condition of access could be imposed.[144]

The strength of the principle that a condition should not be attached to an adoption order without the agreement of the adoptive parents was highlighted by a Court of Appeal judgement in January 1992 (re D (a minor)). Adoptive parents successfully appealed against a condition that they send photographs once a year to the birth mother. The guardian *ad litem* had been opposed to the condition, arguing that 'it would possibly be harmful to the child in that it would reduce the adopters' sense of security and undermine their morale'.[145] Murch *et al*, in their 'Pathways to Adoption' research project, found that orders for adoption with access were very rare (less than one per cent): 'These findings tend to reinforce a "traditional" approach to adoption in that, once the order has been made, the child severs connections with members of its birth family.'[146] However, there was some evidence of informal contact in rather more cases, more frequently with siblings than with other relatives.

The effects of the Children Act 1989 in relation to contact

The Children Act 1989 ("the Act"), implemented in October 1991 in England and Wales, represented a major shift in philosophy from the "child-saving" emphasis of the 1975 Children Act. The Act focuses on support to families and children in need, highlighting the importance of working co-operatively with parents and of ensuring that children can grow up with their own families, as long as this is consistent with their welfare. While the achievement of the overall objective has, in some areas, been limited by insufficient resources and the attitudes of social workers, there is evidence that in others, local authorities and social workers have 'taken the principle of partnership with families and endeavoured to make it work in practice'.[147] The Family Rights Group has been working with a small number of local authorities in a pilot project to develop a system of family conferences, modelled on New Zealand practice.[148]

A key principle in the Act is the importance of maintaining contact between families and children being looked after by local authorities. Further legislation regarding contact was necessary in the face of policy and practice which continued to pay little attention to promoting contact, despite earlier legislation and research evidence of its value for children's well-being and sense of identity. Inadvertent barriers and termination of contact had characterised practice, particularly in relation to children who were placed with alternative families on a permanent basis.[149,150,151]

The Act introduced the new concept of "contact" to replace "access". Although contact is not defined in the Act, it is described in Guidance[152] as being wider than face-to-face meetings (para 6.9). Schedule 2, para 15(1), requires local authorities to promote contact between all children looked after and their birth parents and a wide range of other relatives and significant people, as long as this is consistent with the child's welfare. In all contact decisions the welfare of the child is the paramount consideration. Among other important principles in the Act, the acknowledgement that delay in determining an issue is likely to prejudice the welfare of the child is a relevant one in the context of contact and permanent placement, given the number of placements in which courts have had in the past to endorse a *fait accompli* – an adoption application in respect of a child who has spent a long time in an alternative family without birth family contact.

Under section 34, a local authority must allow a child who is subject of compulsory proceedings reasonable contact with his or her birth parents and relatives and reach agreement with them about a plan for contact prior to a hearing. The court has a duty to consider the arrangements for contact and invite parties to comment. A local authority wishing to refuse contact must apply to the court for authorisation to do so (section 34 (4)) or may refuse contact as a matter of urgency if essential for the child's welfare for no longer than seven days (section 34 (6)). Where a local authority and a birth parent cannot agree what is reasonable contact, the court can prescribe the form and frequency of contact (section 34 (3)). A child can apply for an order for contact under section 34.

Section 8 orders can be considered in any family proceedings, including proceedings under the Adoption Act 1976. This enables a birth parent to apply for a contact order in a freeing as well as an adoption hearing. A child may apply for leave to make an application for a section 8 order. The court may only grant leave 'if it is satisfied that he has sufficient understanding to make the proposed application' (section 10 (8)).

Prior to the development of case law, concerns had been expressed by some adoptive parents as to whether birth parents or other relatives would seek to re-establish contact through section 8 with their children who had been adopted. However, it was clarified in the court of appeal in November 1992 that a father of children who had been freed for adoption was not entitled to apply for a section 8 order without leave of the court, ie. he was not a "parent" within the meaning of section 10 of the Act.[153]

There are two safeguards against the possibility of an adoption being undermined as a result of applications by former parents or relatives to apply for leave to make a section 8 application: one through legislation and the other through case law. Section 10 (9) specifies the factors to be taken into account in reaching a decision as to whether or not to grant leave. And the court ruling In re S (a minor) (judgement 18.02.93) determined that adoptive parents should not be notified of an application unless the judge sees sufficient merit in the application to have a hearing regarding leave.

A particularly significant effect of the Act has been to redress a previous imbalance between the local authority and a parent. Firstly, section 100 removed the right of local authorities to use wardship in all but exceptional cases. Wardship – available to local authorities but not to parents – could in the past be used to frustrate orders made in favour of parents by lower courts. Secondly, the interpretation of the Act in case law has ended the judicial position which obtained from 1981 (A *v* Liverpool City Council) whereby a court could not overturn a local authority's decision to refuse contact, if to do so would interfere with long-term plans made by the authority.[154,155]

The potential of the Act to promote contact in permanent placements is illustrated by the observation in the Guidance:

> 'Contacts, however occasional, may continue to have a value for the child even when there is no question of returning to his family. These contacts can keep alive for a child a sense of his origins and may keep open options for family relationships in later life.'[156]

This contrasts with the implication in the Code of Practice,[157] that contact should be terminated if there is no possibility of restoration. However, Jackson, drawing on the experience of the Family Rights Group, reported in 1993 that:

> '. . . contact is often cut and eventually terminated if a decision has been made that a child will not return home. The benefit of contact is being lost. Family Rights Group's experience shows few local authorities are setting up face-to-face post-adoption contact.'[158]

The Adoption Contact Register

The Adoption Contact Register was set up in England and Wales in May 1991 following the insertion of a new provision in the Adoption Act 1976 (section 51A). As a result of Schedule 10, para 21, of the Children Act 1989, the Registrar General maintains a register of adopted people and of birth relatives (aged 18 and over) who have asked for their details to be placed on the Register. A relative is defined in para 21 (13) (a) as 'any person (other than an adoptive relative) who is related to the adopted person by blood (including half-blood) or marriage'. The Registrar General will pass on to the adopted person who has registered with him the name and address (or contact address) of a birth relative who has registered. The birth relative will not be given reciprocal information, but only told that her or his name and address have been passed on to the adopted person. The Post Adoption Centre, the National Organisation for the Counselling of Adoptees and Parents (NORCAP) and the Natural Parents Support Group (NPSG) will provide intermediary and counselling services and their address may be used for registration. There is no provision for the exchange of non-identifying information through the Register.

The Adoption Contact Register is an important, although many would argue limited, official recognition of the need to facilitate contact between adopted people and their birth relatives. The Register does not provide for relatives to express a wish for no contact and counselling is not part of the process (although the leaflet explaining the working of the Register, (ACR 110, Department of Health, 1991) gives information about the availability of counselling). By contrast, the Birth Link Register, established in Scotland by the Adoption Counselling Centre in Edinburgh in the early 1980s, provides that a counsellor will get in touch with each party if both an adopted person and a birth relative have registered a wish for contact. The counsellor will explore with the parties the best way to begin the reunion process. Identifying information is not exchanged until both parties are ready. The register enables birth relatives to record a wish for no contact and this would be conveyed to the adopted person by a counsellor.

Research in Scotland[159] indicated that contact registers are not the main avenue to reunion: a 'useful but rather passive method of signalling a willingness to make contact if this is also desired by the other party'. Organisations such as NORCAP and NPSG campaigned prior to the introduction of the Register for a more pro-active service for birth relatives, both to remedy an imbalance and alleviate stress and also, more pragmatically, to prevent the need for birth relatives, or those acting on their behalf, to trace adopted children using the Adopted Children's Register.

NORCAP urged the Department of Health to encourage agencies to take the initiative in contacting adoptive families when a member of the birth family seeks news or contact, in accordance with the duty under section 1 of the Adoption Act 1976 to provide a comprehensive service. The increasingly common practice of tracing adopted children was given wide publicity in March 1994 when a London borough sought a court order requiring the Registrar General to make a blank entry in the Adopted Children's Register in respect of an adopted boy aged six. This legal action was an attempt to prevent the child being traced by his birth mother who had tried to abduct him in the past. The activities of tracing agencies were highlighted. The Court of Appeal judgement was that the Registrar General was required by legislation to make a full entry but he was ordered not to disclose information without the leave of the court.[160,161]

The Adoption Bill[162] does not address the issue of the unevenness of agency responses to requests for information or contact by birth relatives, which NORCAP and NPSG believe contributes to members of birth families using tracing agencies or searching themselves via the public records at St Catherine's House.

The Review of Adoption Law

The Review of Adoption Law[163] was part of an extensive consultation process about legislative changes in England and Wales. There was a separate process in Scotland: *The Future of Adoption Law in Scotland* was published in 1993.

The interdepartmental working group had been set up in July 1989 and produced a series of four discussion papers and three background papers between September 1990 and January 1992. A wide range of proposals was explored in the discussion papers, some quite radical in relation to contact. The first paper, *The Nature and Effect of Adoption*, generated anxiety on the part of adoptive parents particularly because of a perception that there might be retrospective ongoing contact by birth parents.[164]

The working group recognised that existing legislation was geared to baby placements in a context of secrecy, there having been no fundamental changes since 1926. In particular, there was insufficient flexibility to provide legal security without adoption, and children and their birth parents had limited opportunities to participate in the process. Murch *et al*[165] had identified some uncertainty among the practitioners they interviewed as to whose responsibility it was to ascertain the child's wishes and feelings and to explain adoption to the child.

Following comments on the discussion papers, the Review was also published as a consultation document. Among 45 recommendations, it proposed that adoption as a legal concept should continue to involve the severing of legal links between a child and her or his birth relatives and the irrevocable transfer of parental responsibility to adoptive parents (R1). The Family Rights Group expressed regret that the document did not propose any amendment to the nature and legal effect of adoption:

> 'In particular, we question whether the severance of legal links with the birth family is a prerequisite for establishing a permanent relationship with a new family. In our view it is not and this is confirmed by research findings; and we question why children should have such severance, which has life-time implications, imposed upon them, when permanence could also be achieved without such severance.'[166]

The Children's Legal Centre has consistently proposed that adoption should be abolished and replaced by a continuum of residence orders:

> 'This would replace the proprietorial concept of adoption with that of responsibility and caring for children. It should also provide greater flexibility so that the different placement needs of children are met in appropriate circumstances allowing for the security that adoption provides at present.'[167]

Recognising that adoption was to be retained, the Centre subsequently proposed that 'the status of an adoption order should be expressed so that the adoptive parents acquire parental responsibility after the making of an adoption order with birth parents retaining, but not being able to exercise, their parental responsibility.'[168]

The Review proposed increasing the range of permanence options by introducing an addition to the residence order. This would enable carers to be *inter vivos* guardians, having parental responsibility until the child reached the age of 18 (R5). Such an option could potentially be suitable particularly for older children and children from minority ethnic groups, for whom the UK concept of adoption is not culturally acceptable.

As one of the major deficits in existing legislation concerns the child's involvement in the process, there was general approval of the recommendation that a child aged 12 years and over should automatically have party status, with the right to legal representation. Children under 12 could be added as a party by the courts (R34). Inevitably, there has been some dispute about the arbitrariness of this age limit, and the Children's Legal Centre proposed that all children involved in adoption proceedings should have party status.

It was further recommended that a child aged 12 or over should give agreement to the making of an adoption order (R11). This elicited a mixed response.[169,170,171] The main concern was that a child would, in effect, be asked to make a choice between being a legal member of her or his birth or adoptive family in a way which might be experienced, at that time or later, as a rejection of the birth family. An alternative suggestion was that the child have the right of veto. Reactions to recommendations 34 and 11 illustrate the debate about how far children should or can be involved in life-determining decisions. Hinchliffe asserted that 'just because we see childhood as a dependent state, the need of children for protection and support should not mean that their perceptions and opinions become devalued, marginalised or moulded to fit'.[172]

The Review proposed further increasing the child's participation through imposing a duty on agencies to take into account children's wishes and feelings (R24). Services to birth families were to be strengthened through the allocation of a separate social worker to birth parents (R27) and the provision of an adoption service to meet the needs not only of children, parents and adopters, but also of the relatives of children who have been or may be adopted (para 29.2). The Review proposed that birth parents should be consulted as to the kind of family they would prefer and have a right to put their views to the adoption panel (paras 28.2 and 28.3). The grounds for dispensing with parental agreement were to be less censorious (R13). The recommendation that freeing be abolished and replaced by a placement order, as a means of avoiding a *'fait accompli'* adoption application (R16), attracted support for the principle but concern about the detail.

The Review indicated cautious support of the development of greater openness. Reference was made in para 4.3 to the possibility of meetings between birth parents and prospective adoptive parents. In para 5.1, following a reference to contact as 'any form of communication or meeting between an adopted child and a parent, sibling, grandparent, other relative, or some other relevant person, for instance a former foster carer', the Review stated:

> 'Although adoption involves the severance of all legal ties with one's birth family, there is no inherent reason why this should preclude the possibility of some contact being maintained, nor should it preclude the possibility that there is no contact at all.'

Most important of the factors determining the appropriateness of a particular form of contact would be 'the wishes, feelings and welfare of the child; the willingness of the adoptive parents; and the ability of those with whom the child is to have contact to recognise and respond to the child's needs' (para 5.2). It was stated that experience indicates that contact 'may cause difficulties, particularly where the adoption was contested, and should always be handled with great care and sensitivity'. There was acknowledgement in para 5.3 of the child's potentially changing needs in relation to contact.

The White Paper on adoption, published just over a year later, was regarded as having a less child-focused perspective on contact and other issues.

Adoption: the Future

The White Paper on adoption (Cm 2288) was introduced in November 1993. Media perceptions were that the government was seeking to end 'political correctness' in adoption.[173] Attention was focused on references in the White Paper to "ideology" and "rigidity" in respect of social work practice regarding race and culture, age of prospective adoptive parents and intercountry adoption. The White Paper emphasised the importance of 'commonsense human judgements reflecting the value placed on traditional parenting' and 'commonsense values in such matters as the age of adoptive parents and issues of race and culture in considering the best option for the child' (para 2.6). The implication that older couples were being 'denied the chance' to adopt as a result of social work ideology was widely criticised: Thoburn was one of many commentators to point out that the White Paper 'will not be producing any more babies'.[174]

The "strong presumption" in favour of adoption by married couples was regarded as devaluing the existing and potential contribution as adopters of those living in "non-traditional" families, including single people and gay men and lesbians. In addition, the concession that single parents could be considered in exceptional circumstances for children with special needs could seem to be suggesting that such children are less entitled to (apparently superior) traditional parenting! Jolly and Sandland highlighted the confusion and the misleading nature of the government's approach in the White Paper and presentation of the issues:

> ' "Ideology", or value-judgments, will always be part of adoption law. The White Paper on adoption does not signal the end of ideology – in fact, its views about suitable adopters are determined by the values of the new right and the primacy of the nuclear family.'[175]

Overall, the disappointing features of the White Paper were that it appeared to prioritise the needs of adoptive and prospective adopters in comparison with those of children and their birth families; that the importance to children of acknowledgement of their race, ethnicity and culture was minimised; and that there was no recognition of the importance and the cost of providing post-adoption services – in para 7.4 there was a reference to "cost-neutrality".[176]

Two particularly positive features of the White Paper were the extending of the range of orders available as alternatives to adoption (a Parental Responsibility Order for step-parents and inter-vivos guardianship for a range of other carers); and the recognition in para 2.6 that 'the permanent legal severance of the relationship between child and birth parents should be justified by *clear and significant advantage to the child* (original emphasis) compared with less permanent options'.

Representatives of organisations set up to support and inform adoptive parents acknowledged that the White Paper focused on the needs of adoptive parents at the expense of considering the needs of the child (see quoted comments of members of PPIAS and of Children First in Transracial Fostering and Adoption, *Community Care*, 09.12.93), and comments of BASW reported in *Professional Social Work* (January, 1994). This is in contrast to the earlier Review of adoption law which stated that eligibility to adopt should be judged 'primarily according to the needs of a particular child rather than by reference to a notional concept of what makes a good adoptive parent' (para 26.3); and which, in acknowledging that adoption cannot meets the needs of all those who are involuntarily childless, referred to the "primary focus" of adoption on the needs of children (para 30.2).

Birth parents and other members of the birth family received very limited attention in the White Paper in comparison with adoptive parents. The Review recommendations regarding a separate worker for birth parents and the emphasis on a service to all birth relatives were omitted, as was R30 which would have given agencies the power to contact an adopted person over the age of 18 for permission to pass on identifying details. The disappointment and dismay felt by birth parents were reflected in the presentation made by Doreen Ward of the Natural Parents Support Group to the All Parliamentary Committee on Children's Affairs:

> 'We feel that the White Paper does little to help adopters recognise the good in birth parents, its 'not so hidden' message seems to be that birth parents are marginal to the adoption story and have nothing to offer that is positive and of value'.[177]

With regard to contact with birth relatives, the White Paper implied that it may have a negative impact – there was no recognition of the possibility of beneficial effects:

> 'In suitable cases a degree of such contact may well be desirable. However, the Government considers that once an adoption order is made, the most important objective is to support the new family relationship.'[178]

The statement in para 4.15 that the wishes of adoptive parents in relation to contact will after placement be given "greater weight" than those of the child was written, according to Richards,[179] 'with the needs of adopters to the forefront'.

Even openness with regard to sharing of information after adoption was viewed as potentially threatening:

> 'The natural wish of some birth parents to know who has adopted their child, to have information about the child's progress and perhaps some opportunity for continuing contact must often be balanced with the need to avoid undermining the full development and stability of the child's relationship with the new legal parents, or the reasonable wishes and feelings of the adoptive parents themselves.'[180]

The Government proposed to ensure that by regulation, the courts and adoption agencies would 'assess the most suitable arrangements for contact between the birth family and the child after his adoption'(para 4.16).[181] Agencies would have to make arrangements to keep open the possibility of voluntary contact; consult birth parents and 'objectively counsel' them about being kept informed about their child's progress where there is no contact; and counsel prospective adoptive parents about the 'advisability or otherwise' of contact (para 4.23).[182] The effect of such agency involvement is likely to depend not solely on the individual circumstances of a proposed placement but on the attitudes of workers to contact and their perception of the availability of adoptive parents who are willing to maintain contact, as Stage 1 of the present study demonstrated.[183,184,185]

Draft Adoption Bill

The final phase of the consultative process reviewing adoption legislation in England and Wales (*Adoption – A service for children*) was published in March 1996.[186] Amendments to adoption law in Scotland are included in the Children (Scotland) Act 1995. The paramountcy of the child's welfare, in childhood and later, has been welcomed. However, in comparison with *Review of Adoption Law*, published in 1992, the draft Bill, like the White Paper *Adoption: The future*, seems weighted more towards the needs of adoptive parents than of children and their families of origin. The draft Bill does not achieve the objective, set out in the introduction, of taking account of the Children Act 1989. In particular, the omission of specific reference to the child's religious, racial, cultural and linguistic needs has been widely criticised.[187]

Like the White Paper, the draft Bill does not require the allocation of a separate worker for birth parents, nor allow joint applications by unmarried couples, nor emphasise the importance and additional costs of providing a comprehensive post-adoption service. There is no requirement that adoption agencies assist birth relatives who are seeking information about an adopted person. Provision for inter-vivos guardianship, which would have extended the range of alternative orders, has not been included. The new ground for dispensing with parental agreement is likely to be open to differing interpretations and to value judgements: 'The court must not make any order under this Act unless it considers that making the order would be better than not doing so' (1(5)). The

White Paper had referred to 'clear and significant advantage to the child'.

There is limited reference to contact in the draft Bill. What little there is seems to be in conflict with the philosophy of the Children Act 1989 and research findings published by the Department of Health about the importance of maintaining contact.[188,189]

Clause 27(4) states that prospective adoptive parents with whom the child is placed are not required to allow the child to have contact except under a contact order. There appears to be an assumption that contact will necessarily be unwelcome to adoptive parents and potentially jeopardise the placement.

Following a three month period of consultation, further work has to be undertaken on the Bill prior to its introduction into Parliament.

Current attitudes and practice developments

Attitudes to greater openness

With the implementation of the Children Act 1989, and in the light of research findings about contact as a protective factor in permanent family placement, concepts of permanence are being reconsidered in the literature, although social work attitudes may prove resistant to change. The Department of Health review of research concluded: 'Concepts of permanence should be broadened to include the possibility of continued family contact through open adoption or permanent fostering'.[190]

Triseliotis[191] explored the concept of permanence within a framework which recalls that set out by Jordan in 1981. The concept of permanence in children's lives is examined 'from prevention to restoration and permanence (where necessary) outside the family of origin'. Where permanence is to be achieved through permanent foster care or adoption, such arrangements 'need not result in the child losing meaningful links with members of its original family'. However, contact has long been regarded as a disposable aspect of a child's needs and, as outlined above, the draft Adoption Bill tends to perpetuate the view that contact is necessarily destabilising.

France[192] described the international instruments which have implications for adoption law and practice in the UK and in other jurisdictions. There is a slightly different emphasis in the approaches taken on the question of openness of adoption. There seems no doubt that since this study was begun, there have been considerable developments in the UK in the direction of greater openness, including involving birth parents to some degree in the choice of adoptive parents, arranging pre-placement meetings and sharing non-identifying information. "Letter-box" schemes set up by agencies for the indirect exchange of information after adoption seem to be becoming relatively common. As far as direct contact in some form is concerned, views and experience are more mixed. Murch *et al*[193] sought the views of practitioners about contact continuing after adoption: 'It was clear . . . that open adoption was a subject of great concern to them but one with which they found it difficult to grapple. Some had very clear views for or against but most expressed a great deal of ambivalence.'

Other jurisdictions

Information about developments in relation to openness and contact in other European countries is relatively limited. Most of the literature available in the UK about adoption in other countries concerns that in comparable jurisdictions, mainly the USA but also Canada and Australia and, particularly in relation to openness, New Zealand.

Baran and Pannor[194] reported that the American Adoption Congress adopted a policy statement supporting 'the policy of open adoption as standard practice'. Their definition of open adoption 'will permit adoptees, birth parents and adoptive parents to make decisions about the kind and extent of relationships they desire'. Rompf[195] reported the finding of a public opinion survey in May and June 1991 which found that 'most adults appear to be in favour of open adoption'. This was particularly so in the case of African Americans. However there are dissenting views and Caplan,[196] asserting that the 'open adoption envisioned by Baran and Pannor has been shaped by the cause of the birth mother', described the concerns of the National committee for Adoption that open adoption diminishes 'the sense of entitlement to be a full and independent adoptive parent'.

In Canada, as in the USA, it appears that private placements may be preferred by birth parents where these are allowed because they 'have more control over the adoption process, including greater initial choice about the adoptive parents and more opportunities for access later'.[197]

Butler[198] highlighted legislative changes in Australia which were more sensitive to Aboriginal and Islander communities and France[199] stated that in most jurisdictions in Australia there are provisions 'addressing the question of adoptions involving the Aboriginal community'. Van Keppel[200] reported the 'increasingly popular practice' in Western Australia of ongoing contact (non-identifying or identifying) between birth parents, adoptive parents and their children. However, birth parents were said to have 'no, or at best little, influence in the decision-making process and no control over whether or not agreed arrangements are honoured by adoptive parents and, indeed, adoption agencies'.

In New Zealand more open placements, including those with ongoing contact, have become an established part of adoption practice.[201,202,203,204,205] Such placements are made through agencies and usually involve infants in uncontested adoptions. Ryburn[206] recalled that adoption placements in New Zealand were open until "restrictive" legislation was passed in 1955 and that Maori beliefs informing their models of caring for children have influenced recent pakeha adoption. Ancestral origins are regarded as 'the foundation of identity, both public and private'.

Accounts of New Zealand adoption practice have had some influence in the UK, although reservations have been expressed as to how far that model of adoption can be applied in the UK, where the majority of adoption placements concern older children, some of whose parents may not have requested an adoption placement.[207]

Agency practice in the UK

As far as contact once an adopted person reaches 18 is concerned, the Contact Register arrangements which pertain in England and Wales, and the more extensive arrangements in Scotland, have been described above.

Much more varied in the UK is agency practice related to making contact with an adopted adult on behalf of a birth relative, and tracing either birth relatives or an adopted person at the request of another party. Agencies in England and Wales which undertake to contact an adopted person or her or his adoptive family following an approach by a birth relative can justify doing so on the basis of the Local Authority Circular LAC(84)3. This includes reference to giving a natural parent information about the child's progress as one of the circumstances in which an agency can disclose information from case records in accordance with Regulation 15(2) of the Adoption Agencies Regulations 1983.

However, information from NORCAP and NPSG indicates that many agencies are not prepared to assist birth relatives in this way.[208] In comparison with the operation of legislation in comparable jurisdictions regarding information after the adopted person had reached 18, legislation in England and Wales, but not in Scotland, is on the whole more restrictive and unlikely to be more permissive with the forthcoming adoption legislation, despite positive reports of agency intervention in this area.[209]

Given the limited experience of greater openness and of adoption with contact in the UK, it is difficult to assess the demands on agency time and skills which further developments will entail. Clearly arrangements for indirect contact will require not just administrative resources but possibly counselling and mediation skills in some instances. There is as yet limited knowledge of the incidence of contact orders in respect of adopted children and the implications in terms of post-adoption support. Furthermore, the pattern of contact and how it is experienced by participants is likely to change over time. Most of the adoptive parents interviewed in the present study were negotiating contact direct, without social worker input, although some mentioned that they valued the possibility of contacting the agency if they felt the need to do so.

Drawing on their experience in the USA, Pannor and Baran[210] emphasises the likely need of 'the best skills and knowledge of adoption professionals'. However, there is limited information about ongoing contact in relation to older children. It seems likely that the need for post-placement support will depend at least in part on the pre-placement preparation offered to all parties and particularly on expectations having been clarified.

A further area in which the need for post-adoption support is likely to increase is intercountry adoption. The Department of Health established an overseas adoption helpline in May 1992 to provide information and advice to prospective adopters and professionals. The Government participated, along with representatives of 75 countries, in the Hague Conference on Private International Law on Inter-Country Adoption which in May 1993 drew up a Convention on international co-operation in intercountry adoption.[211] The measures contained in the draft Adoption Bill, if enacted, will enable the UK to ratify the Hague Convention, and seek to ensure that children adopted through intercountry adoption will be subject to the same safeguards as those involved in domestic adoptions.

III SUMMARY

Stage 1 of the present study set out to explore whether foster care could meet a child's need for permanence and whether contact could be accommodated within an adoption placement. By the time the findings were published in 1989, agencies were beginning to develop alternatives to the closed model of adoption. These developments came about as a result of a number of factors: the increasingly-heard voice of self-help and advocacy groups; greater understanding of the need of some adopted people for information and contact as a result of counselling undertaken in connection with access to birth records; the recognition of some birth parents' wish for news of their adopted child and for an opportunity to contribute after adoption; adoptive parents' need for first hand information and in some cases for "permission" to parent; the changing profile of children awaiting placement; the impact, albeit limited, of the 1983 legislation on access; and the dissemination of research findings about the importance of contact to the self-esteem and well-being of children separated from their families. Currently, contact seems to be emerging from research studies as a factor making disruption of a permanent family placement less likely. In addition, agencies have been encouraged to explore more open models of adoption by the experience of families and workers in New Zealand and some states in the USA where birth parents relinquishing babies and young children are commonly being given identifying information and the opportunity of continuing contact.

However, while the importance of ending the secrecy which has characterised adoption practice in England and Wales since 1949 is generally accepted, there remains ambivalence among some practitioners and adoption participants about adoption with contact being instituted in other than very limited circumstances. In part, reservations on the part of a few practitioners may derive from their reluctance to relinquish the power which the closed model confers. And the adversarial nature of many adoption placements is thought likely to limit the possibility of birth relatives and adoptive parents planning co-operatively, although Ryburn's findings suggest otherwise.[212] Furthermore, there have been no large scale longitudinal studies of the impact of various forms of ongoing or occasional contact on the adopted person at different developmental stages. Most studies have obtained the views only of the adoptive and birth parents over a relatively short time scale, and generally they involve the placements of infants in New Zealand and the USA. There are only anecdotal accounts of contact following the adoption of older children and those with special needs, including children whose birth parents had opposed adoption.

Stage 2 of the present research provided an opportunity to explore, albeit with a small number of families, some of the current concerns about adoption with contact.

References

1. Baran A, and Pannor R, 'Open adoption', in Brodzinsky D M, and Schechter M D (eds), *The Psychology of Adoption*, Oxford University Press, p 318, 1990.
2. Fratter J, Rowe J, Sapsford D, and Thoburn J, *Permanent Family Placement*, BAAF, 1991.
3. See 2 above.
4. Raynor L, *The Adopted Child Comes of Age*, Allen and Unwin, 1980.
5. Lambert L, Buist M, Triseliotis J, and Hill M, *Freeing Chidren for Adoption*, BAAF, 1990.
6. Triseliotis, J, and Russell J, *Hard to Place: The outcome of adoption and residential care*, Heinemann/Gower, p 197, 1984.
7. See 1 above, p 316.
8. See 1 above, p 330.
9. Bowlby J, *Maternal Care and Mental Health*, World Health Organisation, Geneva, 1951; 'The making and breaking of affectional bonds', in *Working*

with Children, BAAF, 1986; *The making and breaking of affectional bonds*, Tavistock, 1979; *A Secure base*, Routledge, 1988.

10. Bretherton I, 'The roots and growing points of attachment theory', in Parkes C M, Stevenson-Hinde J and Marris P (eds), *Attachment Across the Life Cycle*, Routledge, 1991.

11. Goldstein J, Freud A and Solnit A J, *Beyond the Best Interests of the Child*, Free Press, p 6, 1973.

12. Pennie P, and Best F, *How the Black Family is Pathologised by the Social Services Systems*, Association of Black Social Workers and Allied Professionals, p 2, 1990.

13. Hinde R A, and Stevenson-Hinde J, 'Perspectives on attachment', in Parkes C M, Stevenson-Hinde J, and Marris P (eds), *Attachment Across the Life Cycle*, Routledge, pp 60–62, 1991.

14. Kosonen M, 'Sibling relationships for children in the care system', *Adoption & Fostering*, 18:3, pp 30–35, 1994.

15. Wedge P, and Mantle G, *Sibling Groups and Social Work*, Avebury, 1991.

16. Bowlby J, *A Secure Base*, Routledge, p 126, 1988.

17. See 16 above, p 127.

18. Schaffer H R, *Making Decisions about Children*, Blackwell, p 45, 1990.

19. Smith D W, and Sherwen L N, *Mothers and their Adopted Children – The bonding process*, Tiresias Press, New York, p 172, 1988, USA.

20. See 19 above, p 173.

21. Scottish Office, *Adoption and Fostering: The outcome of permanent family placements in two Scottish local authorities*, p 33, 1991.

22. Thoburn J, *Success and Failure in Permanent Family Placement*, Avebury/Gower, p 59, 1990.

23. Howe D, 'Assessing adoptions in difficulty', *British Journal of Social Work*, 22, pp 1–15, 1992.

24. See 18 above, p 83.

25. Triseliotis J, 'Maintaining the links in adoption', *British Journal of Social Work*, 21, pp 401–414, 1991.

26. Barth R P, and Berry M, *Adoption and Disruption: Rates, risks and responses*, Aldine de Gruyter, New York, p 171, 1988, USA.

27. See 18 above, pp 83–84.

28. Triseliotis J, 'Open adoption: the evidence examined', in Adcock *et al*, (eds), *Exploring Openness in Adoption*, Significant Publications, pp 40–41, 1993.

29. Kornitzer M, *Adoption and Family Life*, Putnam, 1968.

30. McWhinnie A M, *Adopted Children: How they grow up*, Routledge and Kegan Paul, 1967.

31. Sants H J, 'Genealogical bewilderment in children with substitute parents', *British Journal of Medical Psychology*, 1964, reprinted in Association of British Adoption and Fostering Agencies, *Child Adoption*, 1978.

32. See 4 above.

33. Triseliotis J, *In Search of Origins*, Routledge and Kegan Paul, 1973.

34. Triseliotis J, 'Identity and security in adoption and long-term fostering', *Adoption & Fostering*, 7:1, pp 22–31, 1983.

35. Triseliotis J, 'Inter-country adoption', *Adoption & Fostering*, 15:4, p 51, 1991.

36. Ryan T, and Walker R, *Life Story Work*, BAAF, 1993.

37. Sawbridge P (ed), *Parents for Children*, BAAF, 1983.

38. Hunter M, 'Working with the past', *Adoption & Fostering*, 17:1, pp 31–36, 1993.

39. Harper J, 'What does she look like? What children want to know about their birth parents', *Adoption & Fostering*, 17:2, p 29, 1993.

40. Brinich P, 'Adoption, ambivalence and mourning: clinical and theoretical inter-relationships', *Adoption & Fostering*, 14:1, pp 6–17, 1990.

41. See 40 above, pp 10–12.

42. See 40 above, p 13.

43. Small J, 'Ethnic and racial identity in adoption within the United Kingdom', *Adoption & Fostering*, 15:4, p 63, 1991.

44. Banks N, *Social Work Today*, 10 September 1992.

45. Gill O, and Jackson B, *Adoption and Race*, Batsford, p 130, 1983.

46. Tizard B, and Phoenix A, 'Black identity and transracial adoption', *New Community*, 15:3, p 427, 1989.

47. McRoy R G, 'Significance of ethnic and racial identity in intercountry adoption within the United States', *Adoption & Fostering*, 15:4, p 59, 1991.

48. Bagley C, *International and Transracial Adoptions*, Avebury, 1993.

49. Tizard B, 'Intercountry adoption: a review of the evidence', *Journal of Child Psychology and Psychiatry*, 32:5, p 755, 1991.

50. See 35 above.

51. *The Observer*, 20 October 1991.

52. Kay J, *The Adoption Papers*, Bloodaxe Books, 1991.

53. Colon F, 'Family ties and child placement', in Sinanoglu P A, and Maluccio A N (eds), *Parents of Children in Placement*, Child Welfare League of America, p 241, 1981, USA.

54. See 55 above, p 265.

55. Pannor R, and Baran A, 'Open adoption as standard practice', *Child Welfare*, Vol LXIII, no 3, p 247, 1984.

56. Silber K, and Dorner P M, *Children of Open Adoption and their Families*, Corona Publishing Company, San Antonio, Texas, p 66, 1990, USA.

57. McRoy R G, 'American experience and research on openness', *Adoption & Fostering*, 15:4, p 100, 1991.

58. See 47 above.

59. Dutt R, and Sanyal A, 'Openness in adoption or open adoption – a Black perspective', *Adoption & Fostering*, 15:4, p 114, 1991.

60. Ferguson H K, 'Open adoption', *Adoption & Fostering*, no 104 (1981 no 2), pp 45–46, 1981.

61. Caplan L, 'A reporter at large, an open adoption II', *The New Yorker*, 28.05.90, 1990, USA.

62. *The Guardian*, 27 May 1992.

63. *The Independent*, 22 June 1993.

64. See 34 above.

65. *Collins Dictionary of the English Languarge*, 1979.

66. Ward M, 'Parental bonding in older-child adoptions', *Child Welfare*, Vol LX, January 1981, USA.

67. Ryburn M, 'Openness and adoptive parents', in Mullender A (ed), *Open Adoption: The philosophy and the practice*, BAAF, 1991.

68. See 4 above, p 104.

69. See 4 above, p 103.

70. Winkler R C, Brown D W, Van Keppel M, and Blanchard A, *Clinical Practice in Adoption*, Pergamon Press, p 73, 1988.

71. See 4 above, p 109.

72. Belbas N F, 'Staying in touch: empathy in open adoptions', *Smith College Studies in Social Work*, Vol 57, no 3, pp 195–196, 1987.

73. See 57 above.

74. Brebner C M, Sharp J D, and Stone F H, *The Role of Infertility in Adoption*, BAAF, p 67, 1985.

75. See 56 above.

76. Ryburn M, 'Contact after Contested Adoptions', *Adoption & Fostering*, 18:4, pp 30–37, 1994.

77. Ainsworth M D S, 'Attachments and other affectional bonds across the life cycle', in Parkes C M, Stevenson-Hinde J and Marris P (eds), *Attachment across the Life Cycle*, Routledge, p 40, 1991.

78. See 77 above, pp 39–40.

79. See 18 above, p 57.

80. Hoopes J L, 'Adoption and identity formation', in Brodzinsky D M, and Schechter M D (eds), *The Psychology of Adoption*, Oxford University Press, p 151, 1990.

81. See 77 above.

82. See 18 above, p 72.

83. See 66 above, p 25.

84. See 19 above, p 87.

85. Grotevant H D, and McRoy R G, 'Adopted adolescents in residential treatment: the role of the family', in Brodzinsky D M, and Schechter M D (eds), *The Psychology of Adoption*, Oxford University Press, p 173, 1990.

86. See 19 above, p 175.

87. Dominick C, *Early Contact in Adoption*, Research series no 10, Wellington, NZ: Department of Social Welfare, Head Office, Research Section, p 191, 1988, New Zealand.

88. Beek M, 'The reality of face-to-face contact after adoption', *Adoption & Fostering*, 18:2, pp 39–43, 1994.

89. See 87 above.

90. Rockel J, and Ryburn M, *Adoption Today: Change and choice in New Zealand*, Heinemann Reed, Auckland, 1988, New Zealand.

91. Ryburn M, *Open Adoption: Research, theory and practice*, Avebury, 1994.

92. Sorich C J, and Siebert R, 'Towards humanizing adoption', *Child Welfare*, Vol LXI, no. 4, pp 207–216, 1982, USA.

93. Rillera M J, and Kaplan S, *Co-operative Adoption: A handbook*, Westminster Ca, Triadoption Publications, 1985, USA.

94. Baran A, Pannor R, and Sorosky A O, 'Open Adoption', in Sinanoglu P A, and Maluccio A N (eds), *Parents of Children in Placement*, pp 159–167, Child Welfare League of America, 1981, USA.

95. See 1 above.

96. Silber K, and Speedlin P, *Dear Birthmother: Thank you for our baby*, (second edn, revised), Corona Publishing Co, San Antonio, Texas, 1991, USA.

97. Curtis P A, 'The dialects of open versus closed adoption of infants', *Child Welfare*, Vol LXV, no 5, pp 437–445, 1986, USA.

98. See 97 above, p 443.

99. Burnell A, 'Open adoption: a post adoption perspective', in Adcock M, Kaniuk J and White R (eds), *Exploring Openness in Adoption*, Significant Publications, p 84, 1993.

100. See 93 above, p 41.

101. See 56 above, p 178.

102. See 1 above, p 329.

103. Sawbridge P, 'On behalf of birth parents', in Mullender A (ed), *Open Adoption*, British Agencies for Adoption and Fostering, p 125, 1991.

104. White R, 'Adoption and Contact: the legal framework', in Adcock M, Kaniuk J and White R (eds), *Exploring Openness in Adoption*, Significant Publications, p 102, 1993.

105. McRoy R G, Grotevant H D, and White K, *Openness in Adoption: Consequences and issues – summary*, University of Texas, unpublished paper, (undated, circa 1988), USA.

106. See 104 above, p 103.

107. PPIAS, newsletter no 56, 1990.

108. See 2 above.

109. Adcock M, Kaniuk J, and White R (eds), *Exploring Openness in Adoption*, Significant Publications, 1993.

110. Vyas I, 'Openness in Adoption: Some concerns', in Adcock M, Kaniuk J and White R (eds), *Exploring openness in adoption*, Significant Publications, 1993.

111. See 104 above, p 103.

112. Kaniuk J, 'Openness in adoption: practice issues', in Adcock M, Kaniuk J and White R (eds), *Exploring Openness in Adoption*, Significant Publications, p 15, 1993.

113. See 112 above, p 16.

114. Van Keppel M, 'Birth parents and negotiated adoption agreements', *Adoption & Fostering*, 15:4, pp 81–90, 1991.

115. See 76 above.

116. See 99 above, p 85.

117. See 99 above, 88–89.

118. See 114 above.

119. Etter J, 'Levels of co-operation and satisfaction in 56 open adoptions', *Child Welfare*, Vol LXXII, no 3, pp 257–267, 1993, USA.

120. See 119 above, p 265.

121. Gross H E, 'Open Adoption: a research-based literature review and new data', *Child Welfare*, Vol LXXII, no 3, pp 269–284, 1993, USA.

122. See 90 above.

123. See 91 above.

124. See 57 above.

125. See 56 above, p 173.

126. See 48 above, p 23.

127. Berry M, 'Adoptive parents' perceptions of, and comfort with, open adoption', *Child Welfare*, Vol LXXII, no 3, May–June 1993, pp 231–253, 1993, USA.

128. Borland M, O'Hara G, and Triseliotis J, 'Placement outcomes for children with special needs', *Adoption & Fostering*, 15:2, pp 18–28, 1991.

129. See 2 above.

130. See 15 above.

131. Walby C, and Symons B, *Who am I?: Identity formation and human fertilisation*, British Agencies for Adoption and Fostering, p 114, 1990.

132. Robinson M, 'Making sense of stepfamilies: a guide for practitioners when applying the Children Act 1989 to steprelationships', in *A step in both directions*, The National Stepfamily Association, p 63, 1992.

133. Robinson M, and Smith D, *Step by Step*, Harvester Wheatsheaf, pp 76–77, 1993.

134. Tansey B J (ed), *Exploring adoptive family life, The collected papers of H David Kirk*, Ben-Simon Publications: Washington and British Columbia, 1988. See also Kirk H D, *Shared Fate: A theory and method of adoptive*

relationships, Ben-Simon Publications, British Columbia, 1984, Canada.

135. Triseliotis J, 'Open adoption', in Mullender A (ed), *Open Adoption: The philosophy and the practice*, British Agencies for Adoption and Fostering, 1991.

136. See 11 above, p 38.

137. See 18 above, p 180.

138. James A L, and Wilson K, 'The trouble with access; a study of divorcing families', *British Journal of Social Work*, Vol 14, pp 497, 1984.

139. See 18 above, p 166.

140. Johnson A, 'Practical guide to contact', *Family Law*, Vol 21, pp 536–537, 1991.

141. De'Ath E, Introduction to Robinson M and Smith D, *Step by Step*, Harvester Wheatsheaf, p xvii, 1993.

142. Hill M, 'Concepts of parenthood and their application to adoption', *Adoption & Fostering*, 15:4, pp 16–23, 1991.

143. Adcock M, and Levy A, 'Effecting permanent placement', *Adoption & Fostering*, no 98, pp 29–33, 1979.

144. Cullen D, 're C (a minor) (Adoption) House of Lords, 25.02.88', *Adoption & Fostering*, 12:2, 1988.

145. Cullen D, 're D (a minor), Court of Appeal, 28.01.92', *Adoption & Fostering*, 16:3, p 45, 1992.

146. Murch M, Lowe N, Borkowski M, Copner R, and Griew K, *Pathways to Adoption Research Project Final Report*, Socio-Legal Centre for Family Studies, University of Bristol, 1991.

147. Jackson, *Community Care*, pp 14–15, 9 December 1993.

148. Tunnard J, *Family Group Conferences*, Family Rights Group, 1994.

149. Ryburn M, 'Advertising for permanent placements', *Adoption & Fostering*, 16:2, pp 8–16, 1992.

150. Southwell M, 'Terminating parental access against the wishes of parents: court hearings of access applications to children in local authority care', *Social Work and Social Sciences Review*, 2(1), pp 61–76, 1990–91.

151. Thoburn J, 'What kind of permanence?', *Adoption & Fostering*, 9:4, pp 29–34, 1985.

152. Department of Health, *Children Act Regulations and Guidance, Volume 3, Family Placements*, HMSO, 1991.

153. Cullen D, 'Effect of freeing order', *Adoption & Fostering*, 16:4, p 58, 1992.

154. Lindley B, 'Family contact with children in the public care system', *Legal Action*, October 1993, pp 12–14, 1993.

155. Brasse G, 'Section 34: a Trojan horse?', *Family Law*, pp 55–58, February, 1993.

156. See 152 above, para 6.9.

157. Department of Health and Social Security, *Code of Practice: Access to children in care*, Social Work Service, HMSO, 1983.

158. See 147 above.

159. Lambert L, Borland M, Hill M, and Triseliotis J, 'Using contact registers in adoption searches', *Adoption & Fostering*, 16:1, pp 42–45, 1992.

160. *The Guardian*, 22 March 1994.

161. Cullen D, 'Confidentiality of Adopted Children's Register, re X (a minor)', *Adoption & Fostering*, 18:3, pp 41–42, 1994.

162. Department of Health and Welsh Office, *Adoption – A service for children (Adoption Bill)*, HMSO, 1996.

163. Department of Health and Welsh Office, *Review of Adoption Law: Report to Ministers of an inter-departmental working group: A consultation document*, 1992.

164. Letters, *The Guardian*, 17 December 1990.

165. See 146 above, p 207.

166. Lindley B, PPIAS Newsletter, no 65, 1993.

167. Comments of the Children's Legal Centre to the Inter-Departmental Review of Adoption Law, Children's Legal Centre, February 1991.

168. Wyld N, 'Adoption law reform – The Children's Legal Centre responds from the perspective of children', *Childright*, March 1993, no 94, p 11, 1993.

169. British Association of Social Workers, unpublished comments, 1993.

170. Richards J, 'The slipper doesn't fit but we have only got the ugly sister to work on', *Law and Practice*, Vol 3(1), July 1993, 1993.

171. See 166 above.

172. Hinchliffe M, 'Issues of permanence and contact', *Practitioners Child Law Bulletin*, 5:9, 1992.

173. *The Guardian*, 4 November 1993.

174. *Community Care*, 9 December 1993.

175. Jolly S, and Sandland R, 'Political correctness and the Adoption White Paper', *Family Law*, pp 30–32, January 1994.

176. Thoburn J, *Professional Social Work*, pp 6–7, January 1994.

177. Natural Parents Support Group Newsletter, Spring 1994.

178. *Adoption: The future*, CM 2288, November 1993.

179. Richards J, 'Adoption: The past', *Law and Practice*, 3:2, January 1994.

180. See 178 above.

181. See 178 above.

182. See 178 above.

183. See 87 above.

184. See 119 above.

185. Masson J, and Harrison C, 'Contact point', *Community Care*, Supplement, 28.10.93, pp 5–6, 1993.

186. See 162 above.

187. Cullen D, *BAAF Response to Draft Adoption Bill*, BAAF, 1996.

188. See 152 above.

189. Department of Health, *Patterns and Outcomes in Child Placements: Messages from current research and their implications*, HMSO, 1991.

190. See 189 above, p 36.

191. Triseliotis J, 'The theory continuum – prevention, restoration and perm-

anence', in Marsh P, and Triseliotis J (eds), *Prevention and Reunification in Child Care*, BAAF/Batsford, 1993.

192. France E, *Inter-departmental review of adoption, law, background paper number 1: International perspectives*, Department of Health, 1990.

193. See 146 above.

194. See 1 above, p 318.

195. Rompf E L, 'Open adoption: what does the "average person" think?', *Child Welfare*, Vol LXII, no 3, May–June 1993, pp 219–230, 1993, USA.

196. See 61 above.

197. Hill M, 'Fostering and adoption in Canada: are there lessons for Britain?', *Adoption & Fostering*, 16:4, p 41, 1992.

198. Butler B, 'Adopting an indigenous approach', *Adoption & Fostering*, 13:2, pp 27–31, 1989.

199. See 192 above.

200. See 114 above, p 82.

201. Howell D, and Ryburn M, 'New Zealand: new ways to choose adopters', *Adoption & Fostering*, 11:4, pp 38–40, 1987.

202. See 87 above.

203. See 91 above.

204. Ryburn M, 'Openness in adoption', *Adoption & Fostering*, 14:1, pp 21–26, 1990.

205. Mullender, A (ed), *Open adoption: The philosophy and the practice*, British Agencies for Adoption and Fostering, 1991.

206. See 204 above.

207. See 109 above.

208. See 177 above.

209. Feast J, and Smith J, 'Openness and Opportunities – Review of an intermediary service for birth relatives', *Adoption & Fostering*, 19:3, pp 17–23, 1995.

210. See 55 above.

211. Convention on Protection of Children and co-operation in respect of Intercountry Adoption (the 1993 Hague Convention).

212. See 76 above.

2 The study

This small-scale exploratory study was undertaken in two stages, the first being concerned with the achievement of permanence for children in contact with birth relatives and the second focusing more narrowly on adoption with contact. Fieldwork for the first stage was undertaken from 1985 to 1987. The focus of Stage 1 was an exploration of how a child's need for contact with birth relatives could be accommodated in a permanent family placement outside the family of origin. Further fieldwork, building on the third strand of the first stage, was undertaken in 1991.

The findings of Stage 1 were published in 1991. The first two strands, the interviews with agency representatives regarding their attitudes towards, and experience of, achieving permanence for children in contact with birth parents, were described as part of the Rowe/Thoburn survey.[1]

I BACKGROUND, AIMS AND METHODS

Background

By the time the findings of Stage 1 of the study had been presented in 1989, the policy of invariably terminating a child's contact with birth relatives in order to achieve permanency was beginning to be challenged – as has been described in Chapter 1. Attention was being focused on how the greater awareness of the value of contact and the principle enshrined in the Children Act 1989 of promoting contact between children and their families could be applied to children being placed for adoption.

On the basis of the interviews with agency representatives and adoptive parents in 22 families in 1987, some tentative observations were made about factors which seemed to contribute to adoption with contact being viewed positively by adoptive parents. I had felt justified, in the light of the interviews and the literature and research available from New Zealand, Australia and the USA, in advocating the development by agencies of alternatives to the closed adoption model. When the opportunity arose to extend the study, it seemed appropriate to focus on adoption with contact.

The 1987 study had essentially drawn on the views of only one group of key participants in adoption – the adoptive parents – and at a particular point in their lives. In designing the second stage, I wished to explore what had been the effects of the passage of time – on the pattern of contact and on the adoptive parents' perception of the impact on themselves and their children, and what had been the perceptions of the other key participants – the adopted children and young people and their birth parents – of adoption with contact.

Research aims

In order to explore further the experience of adoption with contact, it was hoped that the adoptive parents in 22 families, first met in 1987, could be reinterviewed and that with their help, some adopted children and young people and birth parents could also be interviewed.

The interviews with adoptive parents in 1987 had suggested that contact need not impede the additional developmental tasks of adoptive parents and adopted children, and, indeed, could in some respects be beneficial. Furthermore, some birth parents were thought by adoptive parents to have been helped by contact. It was therefore the intention to discover what had been the participants' experience of adoption with contact and how the additional perspectives affected the conclusions drawn from the findings of Stage 1.

It was hoped that the observations of key participants would enable some guidelines to be developed for practitioners and confirm or modify the hypothesis put forward on the basis of the first stage of the study that openness of attitude on the part of adoptive parents was more significant than the nature and degree of contact. I was not aware at that time of any other study in the UK focusing specifically on the adopted people's experience of contact.

Methods

The adoptive parents four years on

As interviewing adoptive parents using a semi-structured schedule had been effective during the first stage, in terms of the information received and the ease and receptiveness of respondents, this process was repeated. The issues previously discussed had remained relevant and replication enabled comparisons to be drawn with the responses received four years earlier. Furthermore, analysis of the findings of Stage 1 did not suggest that different questions should be asked. Exploration of the same issues would allow confirmation as to whether the associations observed in 1987 still held true after four years. The interview schedules used in the interviews with adoptive parents in 1987 and 1991, and with birth parents in 1991, and the adopted children interview checklist (1991) are reproduced in the full report of the study.[2]

Contacting the adoptive parents

Adoptive parents in 18 of the 22 families in the original sample were reinterviewed in 1991. Contact was made direct with the adoptive parents in the four families who had been recruited to the study via PPIAS and with the adoptive parents in two families who had been recruited by a local authority social worker. All agreed to be reinterviewed.

Adoptive parents in 16 of the original study families had been recruited through social workers in eight voluntary adoption agencies. The agencies were contacted in 1990 to find out whether they knew of any reason why the adoptive parents should not be approached again and whether there had been any change of address. In retrospect, I am not sure that this was necessary and feel that a direct approach could have been made. In some instances, contacting the agencies led to considerable delay.

Agency workers knew of no reason why an approach should not be made direct to adoptive parents in 14 families and a letter was sent to them. One couple declined to be interviewed; adoptive parents in the other 13 families responded positively to the letter; and I reinterviewed adoptive parents in 12. I chose not to reinterview the adoptive parents in the thirteenth family, having ascertained from correspondence that there had been no changes in contact or in their attitude to contact. (In 1987, there had been an agreement to exchange Christmas cards and pass on any significant family news. The adoptive parents had been aware of no direct impact of this form of contact on their son, who had joined their family as a baby and who had severe learning difficulties. There had been no face-to-face contact since soon after the placement.)

In two instances adoptive parents were not reinterviewed because the agency worker advised against or did not facilitate contact. The adoptive parents whom the agency worker advised me not to contact were described as being under great stress due to problems in the family which were not related to contact by birth parents. Adoptive parents in this family were among the group of six families who had described difficulties or tensions in relation to contact in 1987. I learned from the agency social worker in 1990 that the two adopted young people, by then aged 19 and 22, were both still living in the adoptive home.

In the second case, the agency worker had asked me not to contact the adoptive parents until she had talked to them (they had needed post-adoption input during the previous twelve months because of their children's difficult behaviour). However, despite several reminders, the worker did not clarify the position prior to the end of the fieldwork period. The adoptive parents in this family had also adopted a sibling pair, aged 13 and 15 respectively, in 1990.

The adoptive parents who declined to be reinterviewed had requested, prior to my interviewing them in 1987, that a meeting be arranged between their adopted children, then aged eight and eleven, and their birth mother. This was to have been the first face-to-face contact for more than two years. However, they indicated in their response to my letter in 1990 about a further interview that they felt contact would be "less appropriate" as their children grew older.

The adoptive parents in the four families who were not reinterviewed (the three described above and the adoptive parents in the fourth family whom I had chosen not to reinterview) had between them adopted seven children.

The interview schedule

I was able to draw on my experience of having interviewed the adoptive parents in 1987, particularly in the use of open-ended questions and in providing an opportunity for adoptive parents to raise additional issues and make general comments.

The schedule broadly covered the same areas as those explored in the first stage of the study.[3] However, there was clearly a need to update information regarding family structure, a child's special needs and behaviour difficulties, known changes in the circumstances of birth parents and, particularly relevant, any changes in the pattern of contact. On certain points it was relevant to learn whether adoptive parents had changed their views (for example, regarding the pre-placement meeting with birth parents) and some additional items were included as a result of observations made when I had presented my findings from the 1987 interviews: the quality of the child's attachment to adoptive parents and what difference it had made to the child to have been adopted with continuing contact rather than fostered.

At the conclusion of the interview, if it had not arisen earlier, adoptive parents were asked about the possibility of a meeting with the child or young person and the birth parents.

Interviewing the adoptive parents

Seventeen of the interviews were conducted in person and one by telephone. The interviews with adoptive parents in 16 families took place in their home and one couple was interviewed in the office in which the adoptive mother worked. In 13 families I interviewed both adoptive parents. Two of the adoptive parents were women who were single parents (one widowed, one divorced). In the remaining two families I met only the adoptive mothers because of the work commitments of the adoptive fathers (one of whom I had met in 1987).

The telephone interview was with the adoptive mother only and was undertaken in preference to a personal interview for practical reasons. I had initially reinterviewed an adoptive mother in a second family by telephone, again because of distance. Afterwards, she wrote to ask if I would visit: 'We would like the children, if they wish, to have the opportunity of talking with you – probably in confidence and we would like some help ourselves . . . Hopefully what you learn, too, can be of help to others. We hope this is not an imposition on your time but we believe you phoned at a very opportune moment for our family and we would very much like the benefit of your expertise and experience.' Feeling somewhat apprehensive as to whether I could meet these expectations, I arranged to spend an afternoon with the family on my way home from a holiday!

I was again made very welcome by all the adoptive parents. Most took pleasure in describing their children's progress since the previous interview and some asked whether I would be interviewing them again in another four years! As on the first occasion, some respondents preferred to be led through the schedule while others "told their story" and then commented on specific points which had been omitted.

I met adopted children included in the study while visiting nine families and in all but one instance (concerning a child with severe learning difficulties) I talked with or interviewed the children and young people, at that time or separately. Thus while the interview with the adoptive parents usually lasted between one-and-a-half and two hours, I often spent considerably longer with the family or saw them on more than one occasion.

The interviews were subject to a degree of bias and unreliability. However, reinterviewing provided greater reliability regarding the information about enduring characteristics, including prior history, through cancelling out the mood-of-the-moment factors. It is difficult to assess the effect on reliability of the greater familiarity between the adoptive parents and myself in the second interview. Overall, I hoped that each of the interviews, in 1987 and 1991, was sufficiently reliable to enable me to assess what changes had taken place in the intervening years in the development of relationships, the nature and extent of contact and in the attitudes of the adoptive parents regarding contact.

The views of adopted children and young people

Obtaining the sample

It was apparent at the outset that realistically, adopted children and young people could only be approached regarding an interview with the blessing and assistance of their adoptive parents. The majority were still members of the adoptive household and those who were living independently could only be contacted via their adoptive parents.

The adoptive parents in the 18 families reinterviewed had between them adopted 25 children who, in 1987, had come within the criterion for inclusion in the study in that there had been some contact after adoption with birth parents. The children were from a range of ethnic and cultural backgrounds. The term "black" is used in this context to refer to children whose parents were members of "the more visible" minority ethnic groups[4] and whose appearance indicated that they had not been born to their adoptive parents. However, of these 25 children and young people, there were 12 whose views could not be discovered: four had severe learning difficulties; four were not approached by their adoptive parents; and four declined to be interviewed.

One of the adopted children with severe learning difficulties was aged six in 1991 and three were 15 years or older. Three were black and one white. The youngest child was said to be unable to grasp the complexity of his adoptive status. I interviewed his mother by telephone in 1991. By this time the contact which had been occurring four years earlier had ceased (on the initiative of the birth parents) and the adoptive mother confirmed that although the child was familiar with the word "adoption", he did not have any sense of another (birth) mother and father. Two of the older three children had been adopted by parents in one family (although they were not related) and neither was able to communicate verbally. The third young person had some, very limited language skills but the adoptive parents believed her to be unaware of the full significance of the regular visits by her birth parents and brother and sister. I interviewed the birth parents of two of these young people and possibly could have negotiated to be present during one of their visits to the respective adoptive family. However, although it would have been illuminating in some respects, I judged it would be intrusive and not relevant in terms of the focus of the study – the adopted person's perspective of the difference made by contact.

There were four adopted children or young people, all white, whose adoptive parents did not raise with them the possibility of their being interviewed to share their views about adoption with contact. Two young people were not living as members of the adoptive household at the time of the second interview with their adoptive parents: one, aged 17, had been admitted to what was then termed voluntary care and placed in local authority accommodation because of persistent delinquency and unmanageable behaviour. Her adoptive parents were in regular contact and clearly still regarded her as a member of their family. The second young person, aged 17 in 1991, had left his adoptive home ("run away") shortly after the 1987 interview to return to live with birth relatives. At the time of the reinterview, he was staying with various friends and still in touch through visits and telephone calls with his adoptive family – in fact he telephoned while I was with them. Although the perspective of these young people regarding contact and whether it had created additional emotional pressures for them would have been useful, I respected the judgment of the adoptive parents regarding the inappropriateness of my seeking to meet them at that stage.

The two other adopted people who were not asked by their adoptive parents about a meeting with me were aged eight and ten years respectively.

The eight-year-old girl had been adopted as a baby and I was able to meet her birth mother. Although I was aware from discussions with the social worker and the adoptive parents that their daughter had a good understanding of adoption (in relation to her age), and the adoptive mother went to a great deal of trouble to put me in touch with her birth mother, somehow the possibility of my meeting the girl herself did not emerge: with hindsight I think I could have been more direct. I met the ten-year-old boy and his younger sister in the adoptive home when I visited the adoptive parents by appointment. I had not expected the children to be present. The boy had gone out to play with his friends soon after I arrived. The adoptive parents indicated that they were quite happy for me to interview them in their daughter's presence and in fact she joined in spontaneously and made a very interesting contribution! They described their son as being much less vocal and less comfortable in talking about adoption than his younger sister. They attributed this in part to his personality and in part to the large number of moves he had had prior to placement. In the circumstances, I did not attempt to set up another appointment to meet with him.

The four adopted people who declined to be interviewed ranged in age from 14 to 20 years. Two had met me while I was visiting the adoptive family and were aware that I had interviewed another young person in the household. Both were described as not being able to talk about feelings easily. The other two had not met me, either in 1987 or in 1991, by which time both were living independently. One agreed to meet me after being approached by his adoptive parents, and an appointment was made, but then he changed his mind. The adoptive parents of the fourth young man said they would ask their son to make direct contact with me if he wished to meet me, but I did not hear from him. All four had been having face-to-face contact with birth parents and siblings in 1987 and this had continued in three instances. It was disappointing not to have spoken with these four adopted people. It is difficult to assess whether my being a white woman made a difference (two of the young people were black).

Thus 12 of the 25 adopted children and young people were not interviewed (19 of the original 1987 sample of 32). This limited the usefulness of the findings in that the perspectives of fewer people and from a more restricted range of placements were available.

In addition to the remaining 13 children and young people, I had the opportunity of interviewing a further two non-related adopted brothers of a child who had been included in the 1987 study. They had each had contact with their birth mother between 1987 and 1991. It seemed legitimate to include the two additional young people in the sample because I had been given information about them in 1987 by their adoptive parents; they wished to meet me and were now eligible to be included.

I considered, but did not pursue, the possibility of extending the sample to include children and young people who were having contact with birth parents after adoption but whose adoptive parents had not participated in the 1987 study. I concluded it would have been inconsistent to include them, since one of the objectives of the study was to consider the effects of the passage of time.

The 15 children and young people who were interviewed, of whom ten were white and five black, ranged in age from nine to 21 years. Thirteen had met me when I interviewed their adoptive parents and talked with me on that occasion or subsequently. Two, who were living independently, were approached by adoptive parents initially and subsequently the arrangement for a meeting was negotiated directly with the young person.

While the 15 children and young people who were interviewed were a disparate group, and so were capable of offering a range of perspectives, the size and unrepresentative nature of the sample make generalisation invalid.

The interview as a means of learning about the perspectives of children and young people

After considerable thought and discussion with other practitioners experienced in communicating with children, with a researcher (Catherine Macaskill) and with two of the adoptive parents in the study, I eventually chose the seemingly unadventurous method of the unstructured interview (while keeping in mind other possibilities while I was with the children and young people). It was apparent that because of the location of families over a wide geographical area and the age range (from nine to twenty years) group interviews would not be feasible, even if considered appropriate.

I had initially considered various play techniques which might enable me to create an atmosphere in which to gain an impression about how children regarded contact with birth parents without having to rely on verbal communication, with all its limitations, especially for younger children and those with limited ability to express themselves verbally. However, there were only three children in the age range nine to eleven years (and none younger than that) whom I would potentially be meeting; I was likely to have an opportunity to meet the children only once; and I also had little control as to the circumstances in which this would occur. Clearly, whatever the age of the child or young person I met, I had a responsibility to her or him and to the adoptive parents not to open up painful or distressing areas with which I would not be involved on an ongoing basis. Because of this, the encounters would inevitably need to be conducted at a superficial level.

It would have been illuminating to spend some time helping children and young people to construct a visual representation of their perceptions of adoptive and birth family relationships through a sociogram or ecomap[5] or a family tree or geneogram.[6] However, I knew from previous experience of using these tools that they are time-consuming to construct and not appropriately undertaken with a stranger or relative stranger. (One young person did draw a kind of family tree to explain her half- and step-sibling relationships, which she gave to her adoptive mother.) I always had paper, pencils and felt tips with me in case they would be useful, being aware of the potential of drawing and colouring to help a child express ideas and feelings.[7] However, I only offered plain paper or a selection of pages from the *Anti-Colouring Book*[8] as a means of breaking the ice or, in one case, while I was speaking with a child's adoptive parents in her presence.

Because of the diversity of the children and young people in terms of their age, culture and understanding, a checklist was used for the interviews rather than a semi-structured schedule. In order to allow for comparison of responses, items were included which related to areas in the schedules used with birth and adoptive parents. An attempt was made to allow for issues likely to be specific to adopted people by drawing on the literature and on the New Zealand video, *Adoption in the Eighties*.[9]

By adapting items from the schedule designed for the interviews with adoptive parents, it was possible to see how far the adopted person's perspective differed from or confirmed that of her or his parents and particularly what difference contact was thought to have made in relation to key areas, such as attachment, identity and security. The account given by children and young people of the circumstances leading to adoption was particularly relevant given the suggestion by some commentators that contact can reduce self-blame – 'another manifestation of grief in children'.[10] They were invited to describe how they felt their birth and adoptive parents viewed adoption with contact, whether contact had been maintained throughout the placement or had been occasional or had ceased.

The questions expressed prior to a meeting with their birth mother by children featured in the New Zealand video included what their parent looked like; what kind of job and home she had; and the need for information about other family members. These questions had been relevant only to a few young people I interviewed as most had grown up with this information through ongoing contact. Given the recognition that there may be negative community attitudes towards adoption,[11] it was pertinent to know how open the adopted children and young people felt able to be at school and work about having been adopted. Additional points raised with the adopted people were their recollection about how much they had been consulted about contact; whether it was important for them to stay in touch with brothers and sisters; their thoughts about future contact; and what they thought it would be helpful for children being placed for adoption and for social workers making adoption placements to know about the effects of contact. There was adequate scope for other issues or observations to emerge.

In using the interview as a means to understand the experiences and views of children and young people, it was necessary to prepare for each person individually, drawing on the checklist. Account had to be taken of what might be relevant items for inclusion, given the young person's experience, and also her or his age, gender, ethnic and cultural background and level of understanding. As I had always met the adoptive parents first, I had the opportunity to learn of any difficult areas for the child or young person which would need to be approached particularly sensitively. Given the suggestibility of children and younger teenagers, I avoided leading questions and phrases which might suggest a right or wrong answer and also asked a number of indirect questions.

The meetings with the children and young people were always engaging and rewarding and some teenagers were more reflective and articulate than I had anticipated after speaking with their adoptive parents. It was important to clarify at the outset what the child or young person understood to be the purpose of the meeting. I found that the adoptive parents had always explained this well to their child and had also given her or him an opportunity to refuse to be interviewed – as demonstrated by the fact that in two families one young person agreed while her brother declined to meet me formally. Nonetheless, I reiterated why I had requested a meeting and explained what would happen to any information or feelings shared (in terms of the research) and that I would not disclose to any members of the birth or adoptive family what had emerged. As I met only those young people who had chosen to speak with me, there was a high level of interest and co-operation and some were particularly keen to respond to my invitation that they pass on, through the interview, their ideas, suggestions and advice to adoptive parents and social workers about how to manage contact in the context of adoption.

It had been suggested that it would be useful to consider the degree to which children and young people had become attached to their adoptive parents. However, I did not formally attempt this, bearing in mind the complexities of such measurement [12, 13] and that my focus in relation to attachment was to learn how far, in the view of the adopted people, its development had been affected by contact. "Attachment" has been used in the sense described by Thoburn as relevant to the placement of children with special needs: 'a close, loving and lasting relationship, rather than in the precise sense of psychological literature'.[14] However, in the course of the time I spent with seven families, I was able to observe the interaction of 14 children and young people with their adoptive parents and inevitably made some assessment of the degree of attachment[15] to supplement what had been said by adoptive parents.

I had the advantage of meeting all the children and young people in circumstances in which they seemed comfortable and relaxed: 13 in the adoptive home and two in their own flat. With the exception of the two young people living independently, and two teenage brothers who had been out when I had reinterviewed their adoptive parents, I had the additional advantage of having already met the child or young person in the company of the adoptive parents, often having shared a meal with them. I had sometimes seen photograph albums, watched a family video and been introduced to an assortment of family pets. These factors, together with the preparation by adoptive parents, contributed to the children and young people seeming confident in expressing opinions, comfortable in talking about adoption and not appearing fidgety, bored or distractible. There was spontaneity and good eye contact. Only one young man, whom I met with his older brother, and who was described by his adoptive parents and by former social workers as having been scapegoated and abused within his first family and the more "difficult" in the adoptive placement, "acted the clown" (his brother's words). He walked around the room from time to time, sometimes argued with his brother and swore. I acknowledged that some things were hard to talk about with a stranger and reminded him that he did not have to stay. Having been given permission to leave, he settled down and made some very perceptive and illuminating remarks.

I met 13 children and young people separately from their adoptive parents, although four spoke to me with a sibling or adoptive sibling present. A nine-year-old girl and a young man of 17 offered their viewpoint during and after my discussion with their adoptive parents. Presumably different or additional comments may have been forthcoming if I had spoken with them separately from their adoptive parents. I spoke with eight children and young people immediately after meeting their adoptive parents and with five on a separate occasion. The adoptive parents of the eleven young people whom I met separately in the adoptive home were helpful in providing space and privacy and did not hover or interrupt.

Each interview was handled differently, depending on circumstances and the adopted person's preference regarding structure. Some "told their story" and then responded to specific points, while others, mainly the older young people, preferred to begin with my highlighting issues for their comment. It was necessary to check out how each adopted person referred to members of their birth family: some spoke of their "first" parents. I took notes, with permission. At various points I reflected back what I had heard to check that I had understood correctly and also asked for elaboration if uncertain. In all the discussions with the adopted people, I hope I conveyed my respect for their perspective and an acknowledgment of their having an "expert" view.

The information obtained was derived mainly from what was said but inevitably I was also aware of, and interpreting, non-verbal data, such as gestures, tone of voice, posture and attitudes. In some instances, adopted people vividly conveyed information about their feelings or attitudes outside the context of the interview: for example, I visited an adoptive home in the company of the former social worker on the day after the birthday of a teenage boy. His first words to her, spoken with great excitement, were: 'My mum rang yesterday to wish me a happy birthday!' He was obviously pleased and relieved.

While the interviews, and sometimes their context, seemed very illuminating, they clearly had limitations. It is hard to assess what difference my having met the adoptive parents first might have made to the responses of an adopted person and indeed to what extent adoptive parents had indicated to their child what response they might be expecting her or him to give in discussion with me. And while the adopted person may have felt relaxed in the adoptive home, this setting may also have had an impact on what they were willing to say to me. Moreover, as is general in interviews of children by adults, there was inevitably an imbalance of power and different frames of reference.[16] Furthermore, my responses would have affected both what was said by the children and young people and my interpretation of what I heard and observed. Nonetheless, despite these limitations, the interviews seem to have yielded some useful findings.

The experiences and perspectives of birth parents

Obtaining the sample

The 32 children and young people included in the 1987 study, and the two additional young people I interviewed in 1991, were from 26 birth families. However, I was able to interview birth parents in only four families, a mother and father together, a single father and two single mothers, all white. That such a small proportion of birth parents was interviewed was due in large part to the number of "gatekeepers" involved. Adoptive parents or adopted children and young people advised against, or were unhappy about, my contacting birth parents in twelve families. Birth parents in the remaining ten families were not interviewed because I had not reinterviewed the adoptive parents (in three families); the adopted people had not been interviewed (in four families); a meeting between an adopted young person and his birth parent, after a gap of many years, had not yet taken place; and it was not possible to set up a meeting with birth parents in two families although the adoptive parents and their children were willing to facilitate this.

In seeking to approach birth parents, I decided that it would be necessary to establish that the adoptive parents would have no objection. This was primarily for ethical reasons: the need to respect adoptive parents' feelings and also the recognition that they would be having to deal, directly or indirectly, with any repercussions arising from my contacting birth parents. Adoptive parents were also able to advise me of instances in which, while they had no objection in principle to my contacting them, the circumstances of birth parents made this inappropriate or impossible. The situations which were included within this group included marital tensions which had been focused around the placement of the child for adoption; a recent divorce; uncertainty by adoptive parents as to how a birth mother might respond to a request for an interview; a birth parent's whereabouts being unknown (in two instances); and the psychiatric problems of a birth mother.

Additional gatekeepers were the adopted children and young people: I felt I should be guided by their wishes and views regarding an approach to their birth parents. In six instances, adoptive parents had either not expressed a view or had not objected to the possibility of my contacting birth parents, but the adopted children and young people themselves expressed reservations: in three families, they expressed sensitivity to the fact that their birth parents were upset or ashamed in talking about adoption and three young people were aware that their birth parents would have liked more contact than they themselves wanted. Birth parents in a further four families were lost to the sample because I had not been able to interview the adopted young people themselves, all of whom were over 17.

Thus, through a combination of the circumstances of birth parents and the gatekeeping of adoptive parents and adopted people, birth parents in 20 of the 26 families were not included in the sample. There were two instances of my not being able to meet with birth parents despite the assistance of the adoptive parents and the agreement of the adopted people: one birth mother and father, when approached by the adoptive parents on my behalf, agreed to be interviewed as long as this could take place during one of their visits to the adoptive home. However, because their visiting pattern had become irregular, and was usually at short notice (and also the adoptive parents lived two hundred miles from London), it was not possible for me to be present during one of their visits. In the other case, the adoptive parents had offered to telephone their son's birth mother while I was with them. However, I discouraged them as they had not seen her for more than a year and possibly changed circumstances could have caused her to object to their telephoning her regarding a meeting with a researcher. I suggested instead that contact be made through the agency worker, but despite her stated willingness and several telephone calls to remind her, she did not get in touch with the birth mother.

The birth parents in four families whom I interviewed were approached in a variety of ways:

- by an adopted person;
- via a letter from me passed on by adoptive parents;
- by an adoptive mother; and
- through a letter forwarded by the agency through which the child had been placed.

While interviews with birth parents in these four families were very revealing, particularly when considered alongside those with the adoptive parents caring for their child, the considerable loss of birth parents from the sample was disappointing. The one triad achieved, an interview with an adopted person, her adoptive parents and her birth mother, indicated what a rich source of data such parallel interviews could yield. It was not possible to interview the adopted child of the birth parents in the remaining three families: two had severe learning difficulties and the adoptive parents of the third child did not think it appropriate for me to interview her.

The birth parents who were interviewed could not be seen as in any way representative of the total potential sample: two had chosen their child's adoptive parents (only four had done so in the total sample); only one placement concerned a potentially contested case (whereas birth parents of 16 of the 32 children in the total sample were thought likely to oppose an adoption application); two of their adopted children had severe learning difficulties (there had been five in the sample of 32 children); and all the adoptive parents of the four children and young people had described contact in very positive terms, both in 1987 and in 1991. All the birth parents were white, although the birth father who was interviewed on his own, having been divorced, was the parent of a child of African/Irish heritage.

Once it became clear that so few birth parents would be interviewed, I did consider whether to extend the sample by recruiting to the study other birth parents who had maintained contact with their child after adoption. However, I was aware of other studies under way and completed in relation to the perspectives of birth parents and contact,[17,18] and so did not believe there would be any value in interviewing additional birth parents, the significant feature of the present study being the link with other parties in the triangle.

An unexpected additional dimension to the interviews with birth parents was that a birth mother and father asked me to meet their other two children, one younger and one older than their adopted child.

Interviewing the birth parents

An in-depth interview seemed likely to be the most effective method to discover the perspectives of birth parents. I had recognised beforehand that a group interview would not be feasible but additionally learned on meeting the birth parents that four of the five were not drawn to the idea of meeting other birth parents in a group setting.

Many items in the semi-structured schedule were designed to parallel those in the adoptive parents' schedule in order to understand the birth parents' perspectives on a range of issues. Questions regarding the impact of contact on agreement to adoption and on coping with loss derived from the literature on openness, the observations made by adoptive parents in the Stage 1 interviews, and from some insights gained from a meeting in 1987 with a birth mother. She had advertised in 1984 in the PPIAS newsletter for an adoptive family for her daughter, Charlotte, who would be willing to maintain contact. The decision to place Charlotte, then aged five, for adoption had been taken because the severity of her disabilities was such that the birth parents believed that neither Charlotte nor her brothers could receive sufficient attention within the birth family. They had requested an open adoption to enable them to be involved in the choice of adoptive family and to retain some contact afterwards. The birth mother had described to me the gains for the whole family as a result of such a placement being achieved.

- Their participation in the adoption process reduced some of their feelings of guilt – they would otherwise have felt they had abandoned her;
- the information received through contact about the progress subsequently made by Charlotte (and that of her brothers who remained at home) convinced the birth parents of the appropriateness of their decision to place her for adoption;
- the brothers were aware of their sister's whereabouts and were reassured about her welfare – a "clean break" could have been traumatic for them as well as for Charlotte and her birth parents;
- in the longer term, the love of her brothers for Charlotte could provide her with support after her birth parents and adoptive parents were dead.

The birth mother explained that continuing contact had helped those relatives and friends who had initially been condemning of the adoption decision to become reconciled to it. She acknowledged that there were painful aspects for herself and the birth father in seeing Charlotte but felt that continuing contact was a way of dealing with the pain rather than burying it.

It was not anticipated that questions would be put to respondents exactly as formulated, because of the likelihood that birth parents would deal with some points in the course of "telling their story" and the importance of ensuring that concepts and meanings were clearly understood. Many of the schedule questions were open-ended and there was scope for birth parents to introduce additional areas. I was particularly interested to learn how far the hopes of birth parents for the future (in relation to contact) coincided with those of the adoptive parents and young people.

I met the birth parents in three families in their home and the fourth in her studio. All the interviews lasted two hours or more. Although I had met none of the birth parents previously, they were all very open in sharing their experience and in expressing emotion – the three women wept and in all the interviews the atmosphere was highly charged. During two meetings I was near to tears myself and in all four interviews felt very moved by the degree of birth parents' love and commitment towards their adopted child, the pain involved in placing her or him for adoption and in the circumstances leading up to that, and by the warmth and appreciation expressed towards the adoptive families. And the interviews with the two siblings of an adopted child were particularly haunting.

In only one interview was the schedule used throughout. Birth parents in the other three families began to talk in great detail as soon as I arrived. Two women, who said they felt able to talk only to their partner (not the child's father) about their daughter, seemed to be releasing years of pent-up feelings, having felt silenced by the stigma of adoption and thus unable to seek support from friends.

The birth parents recognised that they were exceptional in having been permitted to maintain contact after adoption and their positive feelings about the experience appeared to be their main reason for having agreed to meet me; they hoped the study might help other parents to have the same opportunity and were happy for me to take notes. I gave assurances regarding confidentiality, not only in relation to the dissemination of the findings but also with regard to sharing information with the adoptive parents and, in one case, with the adopted person. One of the birth mothers had placed an earlier-born child for adoption on the closed model. The small number of birth parents involved has implications for the sharing of findings, since each of the birth parent respondents would be easily recognisable to agency workers and to adoptive parents.

The birth parents were from varied backgrounds in terms of occupation and education but I was not aware of this affecting their response to the interview. The two men were emotional and expressed strongly-held views but did not weep: I cannot judge whether my being a woman influenced their expression of feelings. After the interview, birth parents in three families said they had found it helpful, although in some respects painful, to have talked about their experience of adoption.

Despite the loss of sample in respect of all three groups of respondents in the second stage, largely because of a combination of ethical and practical considerations, the data collected did yield useful information. However, the account of the interviews is to some extent impressionistic and the findings cannot be generalised to other adoptive placements, or proposed adoptive placements. This limitation derives not only from the small size of samples and their unrepresentativeness, but also from the unreliability of the interview method – the effects of gender, class, race and culture and of my own attitudes and assumptions on contact.

II THE PARTICIPANTS

The adoptive parents

Adoptive parents in 22 families were interviewed in 1987, all but three of them living in the South of England or East Anglia. The sample comprised 20 married couples and two single women, one of whom had been widowed after the placement of her children, and one who had been divorced prior to adopting. One adoptive couple described theirs as a black family. They had a "mixed race marriage", with one partner "Black West Indian" and the other white. They had adopted four black children, one of whom was in touch with a birth parent and so included in the present study. Adoptive parents in the other 21 families were white. One or both adoptive parents in at least 18 of the families held managerial or professional posts and in most, but not all cases, the adoptive parents' economic and social status appeared to be more advantaged than that of their children's birth parents.

Between them, the adoptive parents had adopted 32 children whose birth parents had had some form of contact after adoption. Adoptive parents in 17 families had embarked on adoption as a response to their childlessness, a higher proportion than had been anticipated among a group of "open" adopters. In three families, parents who had given up hope of a pregnancy had had a child born to them after they had adopted. There were several large families: adoptive parents in ten families had four or more children, indicating an enjoyment of caring for children which was apparent during interviews. Adoptive parents in ten families had adopted more than one child who was eligible for inclusion in the study – most were siblings by birth but in three families there were unrelated children, each having contact with birth parents. In nine families, adoptive parents had experience of both "open" and closed adoption, which enabled them to make some comparisons of the effects of different models.

The two single women and the "mixed race couple" were among the adoptive parents in 18 families who participated in the further interviews in 1991. Despite the recession, no significant differences were described in the adoptive parents' economic circumstances. Two families had moved, one to larger accommodation and the other because of a change in employment. Fifteen adoptive families were living in East Anglia or the South of England, two in the North West and one in the North.

There were 27 children in this group of 18 adoptive families who had had some contact with birth parents. Two children not included in the 1987 sample had since then established contact with their birth parent and thus there were adoptive parents in four families who had adopted two or more unrelated children who had had contact. Since the previous interview in 1987, another adoptive child had joined three families and one couple had had two more children born to them.

The adopted children and young people

The profile compiled in respect of the 32 children in the 1987 sample comprised factual and subjective information – such as whether a child was described by a social worker and/or an adoptive parent as having had "emotional problems" at placement.

At the time of the first interview with their adoptive parents, the age of the children had ranged from two to 20 years, with a median age of 12. Seven were aged 16 or more, but only one young person was then living independently. Nineteen were male and 13 female. More than two-thirds of the children had been living with their adoptive families for at least four years, with the longest placed child having joined his family 12 years previously.

Ten were black children from a range of ethnic and cultural backgrounds. They were not in all cases described as "black" by their adoptive parents and only four of the six children who were interviewed for this study referred to themselves in this way. This group of children had one or both parents who were African, African-Caribbean, Indian or Sri Lankan. Twenty-two children were white. An African-Caribbean boy had been placed with the one black family in the study. Nine black children had been placed with white adoptive parents. Most of the children placed transracially had joined their adoptive families several years earlier, before agencies generally had begun to embark on policies and practice to recruit adopters of the same cultural and ethnic background. The adoptive parents in the six families who had adopted transracially varied considerably in the significance they attached to their child's background.

Given the assumption in the literature that adoption with some form of contact is likely to be most relevant for children who leave the care of their birth family at an older age, it was an unexpected finding of the study that only one child had been aged ten years or more on entering care. More than half the children (17) had left the care of their parents at the age of three years or under. However, only two of the 32 children could be regarded as not having had special needs at placement, due to a disability or health problem, their pre-placement history and/or their age at placement.

"Handicaps" and "problems at placement" were terms used in the Rowe/Thoburn study[19] questionnaire to identify what special needs might have contributed to a child being referred to a voluntary agency for placement and to being vulnerable to placement breakdown. "Handicaps" included Down's Syndrome, a mental handicap (learning difficulties severe enough to require special education), a disabling physical impairment and serious ill-health. "Problems at placement" included having had damaging experiences before entering care or prior to placement and the effects of those.

There were six children with disabilities: four had Down's Syndrome and one child had severe learning difficulties (cause unknown) and also a progressive disabling condition. The sixth child had severely restricted mobility and used a powered wheelchair.

Grouped within the "problems at placement" category were adverse circumstances or factors which had contributed to a child being described as having emotional problems and in some instances behaviour difficulties also. Not surprisingly, older children were more likely to have had negative experiences and consequently emotional problems and behaviour difficulties, whereas none of the five children placed before the age of twelve months was affected in this way. However, one little boy placed at 14 months had experienced multiple moves and several disrupted placements and was described by his adoptive parents and the social worker as confused and disturbed when placed. Nine years later the adoptive parents reported that he still occasionally showed signs of insecurity, finding changes, such as a recent move of home, unsettling.

It must be noted that some "problems" could not be objectively evaluated and adoptive parents and social workers will have used different criteria in their assessment. Two factors related to the child's pre-placement history:

- multiple moves/changes of caretaker, and
- at least one disrupted "permanent" placement.

Four, however, were open to interpretation:

- child "institutionalised"
- a history of deprivation or abuse
- behaviour difficulties
- emotional problems.

The tables that follow show how many children were described as having had one or more of these problems at placement. It can be seen from

Table 1 that only one of the 27 children over 12 months at placement (a boy who left the care of his birth relatives at the age of ten and joined his adoptive family three years later) was not described as having had "emotional problems" at placement.

Table 1

Number of children affected by each problem in relation to age at placement

Problem factors	0–12ms	1–5yrs	6–10yrs	11–14yrs	Total
Multiple moves	–	3	9	2	14
Institutionalised	–	1	3	4	8
Deprivation/abuse	–	5	12	2	19
Disrupted placement	–	1	3	2	6
Behavioural difficulties	–	3	9	2	14
Emotional problems	–	7	15	4	26
Total in age group	**5**	**7**	**15**	**5**	**32**

Table 2

Children affected by "problem factors" in relation to age at placement

Problem factors	0–12ms	1–5yrs	6–10yrs	11–14yrs	Total
None	5	–	–	–	5
One	–	–	–	–	–
Two	–	2	4	–	6
Three	–	1	2	2	5
Four	–	4	6	2	12
Five	–	–	3	–	3
Six	–	–	–	1	1
Total in age group	**5**	**7**	**15**	**5**	**32**

Table 2 indicates that more than one-third of the children (12) were assessed as being affected by four of the "problem" factors and three by five factors. Children placed at the age of eight to ten years seemed the most vulnerable group. Allowing for some inconsistency in the assessment of "problem factors", it nonetheless seems that many of the children had joined their adoptive families with a number of difficulties which could potentially affect their adjustment to their new family.

The complexity of the circumstances of some of the children, including their birth parents' initial opposition to the plan for adoption, resulted in lengthy periods between placement and adoption: fewer than half of the children were adopted within two years of placement, and between four and seven years had elapsed before adoption orders were granted in respect of ten of the children. Not surprisingly, half of the children were aged ten years or more when adopted.

At the time of the further interviews with their adoptive parents in 1991, the 27 adopted people in the 18 families ranged in age from six to 20 years. The median age was sixteen-and-a-half years, and so many of the adoptive parents were able to comment on the impact of contact on their child during and after adolescence, a particularly significant period for adopted children. Seventeen were male. Eleven of the children and young people were black. Nine black children placed transracially and the black child placed with the black family had remained in the sample. One of the children who had been added to the sample in 1991 had one Indian and one English parent.

The adopted children and young people had been placed for periods ranging from four to 16 years and in all but two instances had been a member of the adoptive family for seven years or more. The two children placed as infants who had not been regarded as having had special needs at placement had remained in the sample and were now aged 17 and eight respectively. The remaining 25 adopted children, including the two added to the sample, had all been described as having had special needs at placement.

Six adopted young people were no longer living in their adoptive family home at the time of the further interview: four, all adult, had independent accommodation; one had chosen to leave his adoptive home (at the age of 14) to live with his birth mother; and a young woman of 17 was being accommodated by the local authority at the request of her adoptive parents. According to their adoptive parents, the great majority of the children and young people who had experienced adverse early circumstances had largely overcome these and were functioning well: a boy who had been attending a special school was now well settled in the local secondary school; a young woman who had been unsettled as a young teenager had progressed well in the same job since leaving school; and a young man was coping well in the role of step-parent.

The birth parents

Agency representatives and/or adoptive parents had been asked in 1987 to provide some information about the birth families of the children in the sample, particularly what had been known about the circumstances leading to adoption and the birth parents' attitude to adoption. The amount of information obtained varied from case to case. There were potentially 24 sets of birth parents involved with the 32 children (of whom 14 were sibling pairs placed together and two were a brother and sister placed separately).

At the time of their entry to care, 24 children had been living with their birth mother only, their birth father having left the household or having never lived as a member of the family. Four children had been the subject of care proceedings because their mother had chosen to continue to live with a step-father who had abused them. One child, who had severe disabilities, had been living with his widowed father whose grief following his wife's sudden death had added to his difficulties in managing his son's care. Five children, also with disabilities, had been members of families in which their birth parents were married and living together at the time of the adoption. The remaining two children had been removed at birth from their parents because both had been diagnosed as having psychiatric and emotional difficulties. This couple had maintained contact with their children and were still together in 1991 when their younger child was nine years old.

Some of the birth parents were described as having had to contend with many emotional, health and financial problems. A number of adoptive parents were sensitive to these pressures (compounded in some cases by racism), and an adoptive mother commented: 'Would I have coped any better in her (the birth mother's) circumstances?' Birth parents of about 20 of the children were thought to be dependent on benefits while others were in paid employment, some in a managerial or professional capacity.

The birth parents of six children had requested adoption because, for a range of reasons, including the child's disability, they had felt unable to provide the care they wanted for their son or daughter. In two cases, birth parents whose children had disabilities had agreed to adoption with some reluctance, their first choice having been foster care.

The plan for adoption in respect of the remaining 24 children had been made after they had left their parents' care. Two children, whose mother was suffering from depression, were placed for adoption while accommodated on a voluntary basis (Section 2, Child Care Act 1980). However, 22 children were in some form of "compulsory" care: six were wards of court, 15 were subject of a care order and one of a parental rights resolution (Section 3, Child Care Act 1980). Reasons given for compulsory care included birth parents' mental illness, alcoholism, drug use, inadequacy or marital discord (17 children); or neglect, abuse and/or poor parenting (five children). Research has highlighted the greater difficulty in achieving a co-operative relationship between birth relatives and local authority social workers when compulsory measures are used, and this was indeed reflected in the present study.

The birth parents of 56 per cent of the children were not expected at the time of placement to give agreement to an adoption application (although this was not an issue at the outset for adoptive parents in three families whose children had been placed initially on a fostering basis). The parents of 16 of the children were expected to contest an application while the parents of two of the children were thought likely to withhold agreement (but not contest). Thus a higher proportion of contested cases was expected than in the total Rowe/Thoburn sample,[19] in which 31 per cent were thought likely to be contested. In the event, the birth parent of one child had opposed a freeing order and another had withheld agreement to the adoption application but had not actively opposed it. The extent to which contact had been a factor enabling some birth parents to give agreement is discussed in Chapter 4.

As a result of the smaller sample of adoptive parents interviewed in 1991, the number of sets of birth parents potentially in contact with their children was reduced from 24 to 22. Relatively few changes in circumstances since 1987 were reported by the adoptive parents or by the birth parents who were interviewed. However, two sets of birth parents had by now divorced and the widowed father, who was resident abroad, was believed to have died. The majority of this group of 22 sets of birth parents, had been expected initially to oppose an adoption application. It had been anticipated that birth parents of 17 children would not agree to an adoption application while in ten cases their agreement was expected. In the event, parental agreement had been given in all but one case, in which the birth mother withheld her agreement but did not oppose the application. Thus despite the sample loss between the two sets of interviews with the adoptive parents, most of the formerly contentious cases remained.

III THE PATTERN OF CONTACT

As "continued contact with parents" was defined in each case either by an agency social worker or by the adoptive parents, there was great variation in the nature and extent of the contact which was occurring at the time of the first interview with adoptive parents in 1987. Furthermore, there had been some changes in the pattern of contact, particularly as two-thirds of the children had been living with their adoptive parents for four years or more.

Contact prior to adoption

All the adoptive parents in the study had met one or both birth parents of their adopted children at least once, either before or during the introductory period (14 families), or after placement and before adoption.

Twenty-three children had had face-to-face contact with birth parents after placement. This had continued until adoption for all but two of them. They were in touch by letter – in one case following termination by the local authority of face-to-face contact and in the other through the choice of the adopted person herself. Adoptive parents in six of the seven families in which children had not had face-to-face contact had stayed in touch through an exchange of news, by letter or telephone, directly or via the agency.

It was perhaps not surprising that all the children placed at eleven years or older were having face-to-face contact with birth parents after adoption. Less expected, was that this was also the case for seven children placed at five years or younger. The frequency of face-to-face contact among the 21 children and young people who were having face-to-face contact at the time of their adoption ranged from once a fortnight to once or twice a year.

Contact after adoption

One of the children had not been adopted at the time of the 1987 interview, although a date had been set. He was having regular face-to-face contact with his birth mother and brothers. Of the other 31 children, 26 had had face-to-face contact after adoption with birth parents, 21 on an ongoing basis and five on one occasion only.

All but one of the 21 children who had had several meetings with birth parents had been in contact throughout the placement. Five children had not had face-to-face contact with their birth parents after adoption: two teenage girls had received letters from their birth mother, and the adoptive parents of the three other children had had contact with the birth parents which did not include them.

Only nine of the children (including two sibling pairs) had had contact with both their birth father and their birth mother. Two children had had contact only with their birth father: in one instance the mother had died and in the other the birth mother had rejected the child because of his disability. The remaining 21 children had had contact only with their birth mother. All but seven of the children, through their birth parents, had contact with other family members, including brothers and sisters and grandparents.

Although courts had the power when the adoption orders in respect of the 32 children were made to attach a condition of access, none had done so. All the contact arrangements had been through a voluntary agreement, in some instances set up after the adoption order had been made. The fact that contact had not been "imposed" by a court order was important to some of the adoptive parents, who felt that the voluntary arrangement gave them flexibility. However, adoptive parents in two families who had offered to maintain contact either before or during the court proceedings, subsequently found this restrictive.

The extent of contact at the time of the 1987 interview

Only two adoptive families were having no contact of any sort with birth parents at the time of the interview, and in one case contact (a meeting to be arranged by the agency) was pending.

Adoptive parents in six families, who had adopted seven children, were maintaining contact by means of letters, telephone calls, gifts, photographs and cards. In five families, contact was maintained directly between the birth parents and the adoptive parents while in the sixth case correspondence was forwarded by the voluntary adoption agency.

Adoptive parents in 14 families had adopted 21 children who were having face-to-face contact with one or both birth parents. In three families adoptive parents had each adopted unrelated children and so were having contact with two sets of birth parents. There was wide variation in the frequency of face-to-face contact at the time of the interview.

The most frequent contact was fortnightly. The less frequent contact arrangements (once or twice a year) included meetings on neutral territory supervised by a social worker. Table 3 indicates the frequency of face-to-face contact which was occurring in 1987. Three families* have been counted twice because their unrelated adopted children were having different levels of contact.

Table 3
Frequency of face-to-face contact in 1987

Contacts per year	No. of children	No. of families
One or two	9	8
Three or four	4	3
Five or more	8	6
Total	**21**	**17***

Changes in contact between 1987 and 1991

Adoptive parents in the two families who were not in contact with birth parents in 1987 were not reinterviewed. Contact in the other two families in which adoptive parents were not reinterviewed had been limited.

There follows a description of the changes in contact which had occurred between 1987 and 1991 in 17 of the families in which the adoptive parents were reinterviewed. The issue of contact was different in the eighteenth family because the adopted person had returned to live with his birth mother four years previously. Previous and current contact in relation to the two young people who had not been eligible for the 1987 study has not been included. The information below therefore relates to 24 adopted children and young people in 17 families.

The form of contact

Table 4 highlights the changes in contact which had occurred. Unrelated adopted children in two families were having different forms of contact: hence two families (asterisked) have been counted twice.

Table 4

Comparison of the form of contact between adopted people and their birth parents in 1987 and 1991

Form of Contact	Families (1987)	Children (1987)	Families (1991)	Children (1991)
No current contact	–	–	5	5
Face-to-face	12	19	10	15
Other	5	5	4	4
Total	**17**	**24**	**19***	**24**

Contact in ten cases was with a birth mother only; in one case only with a birth father; and in eight instances with both birth parents. Since the interviews in 1987, two adopted young people had been encouraged by their respective adoptive parents to re-establish contact with their birth father when he was terminally ill and in each case had met him before he died. One young person had ended contact with the birth mother but renewed contact with the birth father. Of the four black children with one black and one white parent, three were in contact only with their white parent. In those instances in which face-to-face contact was maintained, birth parents and adoptive parents mostly lived within a one-hour journey of each other.

Reasons for the lack of contact

There had been some contact by or with birth parents since the 1987 interview in all but one of the five instances in which no contact was occurring in 1991. In three instances in which contact had ceased, the adoptive parents were unable to get in touch with the birth parents as their whereabouts were unknown. In two cases, the initiative not to continue contact rested with the young people themselves. The young man and young woman who had not had contact with their birth mother for two years or more were both of African-Caribbean descent but their situations were quite dissimilar.

A young man aged 17 of African-Caribbean descent, adopted by the only black family in the sample, described having had contact with his birth mother and other maternal relatives from the time he joined his adoptive family at the age of 12 months. The initiative for meetings had usually rested with his adoptive parents rather than with his birth mother. During the previous two years, he had been occupied with exams and leisure activities, and his adoptive parents had been particularly busy, and somehow contact had lapsed. He expressed confidence that he or his adoptive parents could pick up the phone to arrange contact whenever they wished. He regarded ongoing contact over the years as having given him a good picture of his birth family.

I did not interview, although I met, the young African-Caribbean woman who was then aged 19. Her adoptive parents were white. They had, over many years, arranged meetings with her birth mother about two to three times a year. The last contact had been three years earlier when the whole adoptive family had attended a party at the birth mother's home. She had indicated to her daughter that she would like her in future to visit on her own and stay for the weekend. She was said by her adoptive parents to have felt uncomfortable with this suggestion and they had written to explain this when they had forwarded a copy of the video they had taken at the party. The young woman had asked them not to initiate further contact and her birth mother had not been in touch since.

The adoptive parents in this family had adopted two other children of

African-Caribbean descent who were spending occasional week-ends with their birth parents so it seems unlikely that it was they who had felt uncomfortable with the birth mother's request and conveyed this to their daughter. Without first-hand information it is not clear why the young woman had not sought further contact.

Negotiating contact

The most striking difference between 1987 and 1991 was the extent to which adopted young people were in control of contact and decisions about whether or not to maintain contact. In 1987 there were only two young people, then both aged 16 years, who had responsibility for negotiating contact. In 1991, 13 of the 24 adopted people were responsible for negotiating the nature and frequency of contact.

The young people in control of contact included five of the eight adopted people whose adoptive parents had described difficulties or tensions in relation to contact in 1987. Contact was dependent on birth parents in the three instances in which their whereabouts were unknown and in the fourth, the birth mother's emotional and psychiatric difficulties prevented her son seeing her as frequently as he would have liked.

Changes in the extent of face-to-face contact

Fourteen young people were in contact in 1991 with the same birth parent as in 1987 (the fifteenth adopted person was having face-to-face contact with the other parent). In those situations in which the young people (all aged 12 years or more) had responsibility for negotiating contact, this was mostly more frequent in 1991 than in 1987. Also within this group were the five young people who had begun to stay in the home of their birth parent for a weekend (and in two cases sometimes for longer). One adopted person was having different levels of contact with his birth parents who were separated. Where contact had decreased since 1987, this was within the control of the birth parent alone or of the birth parents and adoptive parents jointly. So the picture which emerged was that where young people had chosen to continue contact, and were in control, they were generally having more frequent meetings with their birth parents than in 1987.

Contact with brothers and sisters

Of the 24 children whose level of contact between 1987 and 1991 is being considered, five had no brothers or sisters living elsewhere. Four who were no longer in contact with their birth parents were as a result no longer having contact with their brothers and sisters in 1991. Fifteen children and young people were having continued contact with their brothers and sisters. Twelve of them were having some contact with brothers and sisters who were living with birth parents – as they had in 1987. A further three young people, all adult, were having separate contact with siblings and with birth parents.

As will be described later, contact with brothers and sisters was particularly important for most of the adopted people.

The two stages of the study were undertaken with a view to deriving insights and suggesting guidelines which could be of value to practitioners, particularly by illustrating issues through the analysis of case studies. While cautious in advocating that the study findings can be applied to other placements, I believe that the two stages, taken together, do go some way to fulfilling this objective. Bloor and McKeganey argue that addressing qualitative research findings to practitioners, rather than to policy makers and administrators, can be an effective way of achieving changes in practice.[20] It has been largely as a result of the creative and innovative ways in which practitioners in foster care and adoption have sought to achieve greater openness, as well as the increasingly heard voice of participants, that the legislation which is pending at the time of writing is likely to endorse greater openness in adoption.

References

1. Fratter J, Rowe J, Sapsford D, and Thoburn J, *Permanent Family Placement*, BAAF, 1991.

2. Fratter J, *Perspectives on Adoption with Contact: Implications for policy and practice*, Cranfield University, PhD Thesis, 1994.

3. See 1 above.

4. Small J, 'Ethnic and racial identity in adoption within the United

Kingdom', *Adoption & Fostering*, 15:4, BAAF, 1991.

5. Redgrave K, *Child's Play*, The Boys' and Girls' Welfare Society, Manchester Free Press, 1987.

6. Finch R, and Jaques P, 'Use of the geneogram with adoptive families', *Adoption & Fostering*, 9:3, BAAF, 1985.

7. Rose E, 'Art therapy – a brief guide', *Adoption & Fostering*, 12:1, BAAF, 1988.

8. Striker S, and Kimmel E, *The Anti-Colouring Book*, Hippo Books, 1981.

9. Morrall M, and Ryburn M, *Adoption in the 1980s* (video and teaching notes). Shipley's Vision and Sound, Christchurch, New Zealand.

10. Silber K, and Dorner P M, *Children of Open Adoption and their Families*, Corona Publishing Company, 1990, USA.

11. Triseliotis J, 'Identity and security in adoption and long-term fostering', *Adoption & Fostering*, 7:1, BAAF, 1983.

12. See 8 above.

13. Smith D W, and Sherwen L N, *Mothers and their Adopted Children: The bonding process*, Tiresias Press, 1988, USA.

14. Thoburn J, *Success and Failure in Permanent Family Placement*, Avebury Gower, 1990.

15. Fahlberg V, 'What is attachment?', *Adoption & Fostering*, 103, BAAF, 1981.

16. Rich J, *Interviewing Children and Adolescents*, Macmillan, 1974.

17. Wells S, 'Post-traumatic stress disorder in birth mothers', *Adoption & Fostering*, 17:2, 1993.

18. Bouchier P, Lambert L, and Triseliotis J, *Parting with a Child for Adoption: The mother's perspective*, BAAF, 1991.

19. See 1 above.

20. Bloor M, and McKeganey N, 'Ethnography addressing the practitioner', in Gubrium J F, and Silverman D (eds), *The Politics of Field Research: Sociology beyond enlightenment*, Sage, 1989.

3 The experience of contact
Adopted children and young people

This chapter describes how contact and its effects were perceived by the 15 adopted children and young people who were interviewed. Also reported are the views of the adults (adoptive and birth parents) as to how contact had affected the children and was experienced by them.

I THE SUB-GROUPS OF THE 15 CHILDREN AND YOUNG PEOPLE WHO WERE INTERVIEWED AND 11 WHO WERE NOT INTERVIEWED

The 15 young people who were interviewed ranged in age from nine to 20 years. Nine were male and six were black, of whom five were placed transracially. The exclusion of children with learning difficulties from this group meant there was a higher proportion than in the sample of 26 of children who had been in compulsory care (11) and of children in respect of whom a contested application to adopt had been anticipated at placement (ten). At the time of interview, ten children and young people were having face-to-face contact, three were having other forms of contact and two were not in contact with their birth parents.

In general, the children and young people seemed to be quite comfortable in talking about their experience of adoption with contact, and some were particularly articulate.

The youngest child of those not interviewed was aged six and the oldest 20. Four were female. Six children had been subject of compulsory proceedings prior to adoption. Four children had been placed for adoption primarily because they had learning difficulties. The five black children had all been placed transracially.

The views and experiences of the adoptive parents of Craig, whose placement had disrupted in 1987, shortly after the first interview with his adoptive parents are not included in this chapter. (Their account is given in Appendix I.)

Before moving on to report the observations of the children and young people who were interviewed, I shall briefly describe the circumstances of six adopted people whose experiences and comments were particularly revealing in order to illuminate some key issues. The informants were mainly the young people themselves but some additional background information has been derived from social workers and/or adoptive parents. (A brief summary of the circumstances of the six young people described below can be found as Appendix II.)

Antoinette

Antoinette was 20 at the time of the interview, living in a shared house within easy travelling distance of her adoptive parents. She was employed as a dental nurse and very much enjoyed her work. Antoinette was apparently coping well with the practical and social aspects of living independently.

Eleanor, Antoinette's birth mother, was a white Scottish woman and her birth father was of African-Caribbean descent. They had never lived together and from the time of Antoinette's birth, Eleanor had had sole responsibility for her, her parents and other relatives having rejected her for having given birth to a black child. Antoinette's father had never seen her. Antoinette's birth mother had a longstanding history of psychiatric illness. After several short-term placements with foster carers, Antoinette was made subject of a care order when aged four and placed on a permanent basis at the age of six with Frank and Lorna, a white couple who had three older children, all adopted.

For three years or so, Eleanor visited Antoinette at the then foster home every two weeks. According to Frank and Lorna, she was becoming increasingly unpredictable and so they asked if a social worker could come towards the end of her visits to give her some emotional support – she found it hard to leave. Because resources were said to make this impracticable, the pattern of contact was changed: less frequent meetings in the social work office. When

Antoinette was about ten years old, Eleanor was abusive to the supervising social worker on several occasions and face-to-face contact was terminated. Four years later, after eight years as a foster child, Antoinette was adopted with Eleanor's agreement.

Frank and Lorna encouraged Antoinette to write to her birth mother and they also wrote and sent news and photographs. When interviewed in 1987, Frank and Lorna expressed considerable sympathy for Eleanor, who was by then resident in a long-stay psychiatric unit, many hundreds of miles away. They felt Antoinette was not very keen to write to her birth mother but encouraged her to do so as 'she's all that Eleanor has'. The other children in the family had been adopted on the closed model and Frank and Lorna felt that they and Antoinette were at an advantage in their having adopted with continuing contact. This had remained their view in 1991. They were continuing to correspond with Eleanor.

Janine and Andrew

Janine and Andrew were 18 and 17 respectively at the time of the interview and still living with their adoptive parents. Janine had done well at school academically and had worked with the same company since leaving school. Andrew, by contrast, had underachieved at school, having been expelled at the age of 14 because of educational difficulties and behaviour problems. He had then attended a school for children who were deemed "maladjusted". Having left school, he had had an erratic work record, not staying with any employer for long. Both young people led an active social life and were described as popular in their neighbourhood, although Andrew's relationships were said to be more volatile.

Paula and John, the children's birth parents, who were both white, had separated when Janine and Andrew were six and five years old respectively and both had met new partners. Because of stress and anxiety, Paula requested a year later that Janine and Andrew be admitted to care on a voluntary basis (Section 2 of the Child Care Act 1980). The children had several short-term placement disruptions in foster and residential care and within ten months of admission to care had been placed for adoption with Alex and Naomi. This was done by a voluntary agency on behalf of a local authority whose permanency policy required children to be placed for adoption if not returned home within six months. Although the children had remained in care on a voluntary basis ("accommodated" in current terminology), neither Paula nor John felt able to care for the children themselves – indeed Paula was still receiving medication for her anxiety and depression.

Prior to their placement for adoption, Janine and Andrew had been having frequent contact with their younger brother, Adam, who had remained at home with Paula, and with both their parents, who were now divorced. In recognition of the importance of contact to all the children, the voluntary agency had sought adoptive parents who would maintain contact between Janine and Andrew and their birth parents. Alex and Naomi gave an undertaking in writing to John and to Paula, prior to the adoption hearing, to arrange meetings three times a year. Paula made it clear to the agency that she would not have given agreement to the adoption had continuing contact not been promised.

When Alex and Naomi were first interviewed in 1987, Janine and Andrew were aged 14 and 13 and Naomi was seeking legal advice as to whether contact could be terminated. She felt that she and her husband had been used as "guinea pigs" and that contact was contributing to Andrew's challenging behaviour and emotional problems both at home and school. Contact had been taking place in a social work office with a social worker present, although the most recent meeting had been in a McDonald's restaurant ("playing at Happy Families"). Naomi described a rivalrous relationship between herself and Paula, although she got on well with John, and Alex had no relationship problems with either Paula or John. However, despite having described herself as angry about having had to maintain contact, Naomi did wonder whether it would have been fair to have terminated contact: 'I suppose that's a totally selfish view. If I'm honest, it's better not to leave the children being cut off, feeling abandoned.' Naomi said that contact created no difficulties for Janine.

Alex and Naomi were among the adoptive parents in six families who had expressed reservations about adoption with contact in 1987, and were one of the two families assessed as "less open" in attitude. However, by 1991, they were feeling more positively about contact.

Paul and Nicola

Paul and Nicola were aged 15 and 13 respectively at the time of the interview. Both children were of African-Caribbean descent and had the same birth mother but a different birth father. They presented as confident, outgoing young people who were doing well at school, participating in numerous out-of-school activities and having many friends.

The children had been removed from the care of their birth mother, Corine, who had been caring for them on her own, on a Place of Safety order when aged four and two. They had been found alone in their home after Paul had alerted a neighbour and were subsequently made subject of a care order (Children and Young Persons Act 1969). After a number of moves in local authority care, they were placed for adoption, aged six and four, with a white couple, Jan and Malcolm, who had already adopted an older girl, Maxine, also of African-Caribbean descent. Jan and Malcolm were selected as the adoptive family for Paul and Nicola because they were maintaining face-to-face contact with Maxine's birth mother and grandparents and it was anticipated that contact would continue after adoption between Paul and Nicola and Corine. Days before the adoption hearing, when Paul was nine, his birth father, Darren, heard of the arrangement and considered applying to care for Paul himself. However, after meeting Paul and Jan and Malcolm, Darren was willing for the adoption to go ahead and the adoptive parents undertook to maintain contact with him as well.

When interviewed in 1987, Jan and Malcolm expressed very positive views about adoption with contact, particularly in relation to that with the birth relatives of Paul and Nicola. Contact with the birth families of the three children had taken the form of visits on a family to family basis, either in the adoptive home or, more frequently, in the home of birth relatives. By 1991, Maxine was no longer visiting her birth relatives but Paul and Nicola had begun to visit independently of their adoptive parents, as well as with them. Paul had stayed for weekends with his birth father and Nicola with their birth mother. Jan and Malcolm were still feeling positively about contact with the relatives of Paul and Nicola but described some unease associated with Maxine's last contact with her birth mother three years earlier.

Hayley

Hayley was 20 at the time of the interview, living in a house near her adoptive parents with her husband Mark and baby son, Aaron. She had a supportive relationship with both her adoptive parents and her in-laws, who were willing babysitters for their first grandchild. Hayley was enjoying being at home full-time to care for Aaron. Prior to his birth Hayley had worked in a travel agency for three years.

Hayley's early life had been unsettled. Her parents, Mary and Mike, both of whom were white, separated when Hayley was 15 months and her older sister, Laura, was three-and-a-half. The girls were placed with foster carers for a month when their half-brother, Craig, was born. Six months later, when Hayley was three, all the children were placed together in a children's home because they had sustained injuries at the hands of their mother's partner, a man in his early fifties. Hayley was the most seriously hurt, both her arms having been broken, and the children were made subject of a care order through wardship jurisdiction. They returned to live with their mother when their step-father was convicted of injuring them and imprisoned, but placed back in the children's home when he left prison a few months later and resumed his relationship with their mother.

The three children remained together in the children's home for almost seven years. Mary's contact was spasmodic and their return home was ruled out by the presence of their step-father. When Hayley was ten, she and her sister Laura, then 12, were placed together with

Barbara and Ken with a view to adoption. Craig, who was eight, was placed with a different adoptive family (also included in the 1987 sample). While Hayley was pleased to be living in a family, Laura apparently could not adjust and after six months ran away, asking that she be allowed to live with her step-father and Mary. Within weeks, however, Mary requested her removal, and Laura lived in a series of children's homes and hostels until she set up home with her boyfriend in a town some fifty miles away from Mary's home.

The delays inherent in wardship, together with Mary's uncertainty as to whether to give agreement to adoption, meant that the applications to adopt by the respective adoptive parents of Hayley and Craig were not heard for almost five years. Meanwhile, there had been supervised access meetings twice a year with Mary and Laura, attended by both adoptive families. In court, Mary eventually gave agreement to the adoption of both children, the judge having approved an offer made by the adoptive families to attend access meetings twice a year. The two adoptive families made separate arrangements to meet each other more frequently – about once every six weeks.

When interviewed in 1987, Barbara and Ken were among the group of adoptive parents in six families who had expressed doubts about the benefits of adoption with contact for Hayley. In 1991, they felt that subsequent events had confirmed their reservations, as Hayley had decided, once she was 16, not to attend any more access meetings. (Craig's placement had disrupted in 1987, as described in Appendix I.)

II ATTITUDES TO CONTACT

Feelings about contact with birth parents (and in some cases with other relatives) were an important area to explore with the adopted children and young people. It was possible to learn about any discrepancies between their descriptions of their feelings about contact and their adoptive parents' perceptions. With one exception, the adoptive parents were broadly in touch with their children's feelings about contact. This situation is not described in detail because of the undertaking given regarding confidentiality.

All but one described contact with their birth parents in largely positive terms, although contact had now ended or was limited for six young people. However, only Antoinette had not had at least one meeting with one or both birth parents since her adoption – she had been exchanging letters with her birth mother, Eleanor, for ten years.

Antoinette

Antoinette described contact as very important to her. Frank and Lorna, her adoptive parents, knew that Antoinette had maintained letter contact with Eleanor, as she sometimes shared bits of information with them. They had assumed in 1991 that the frequency of correspondence was about the same as when she had lived with them – two or three times a year. However, Antoinette said she was writing to Eleanor much more often now she was living separately, explaining: 'I feel freer'. She wrote 'long letters, pouring out my feelings'. Eleanor "needed" her letters, as she had no other relatives in touch, while Antoinette needed to know how her birth mother was: 'I could not cope if the letters stopped. I love to write. I tell her things – not the average boring letters.'

Antoinette was very open in describing herself as a black person. She did not suggest that her transracial adoption had been a factor contributing to her need to maintain contact with her birth mother, although through correspondence she was learning more about her father's ethnic and cultural background.

Janine and Andrew

Janine and Andrew had different feelings about contact with their birth mother, Paula. Both confirmed the account given by their adoptive parents, Alex and Naomi, in 1987, of difficulties and tensions around contact during the early years of the placement. Like them, they felt in 1991 that these had largely been resolved – due to an improvement in the relationship between Paula and Naomi. Also, they now negotiated contact themselves and visited Paula or stayed with her independently of their adoptive parents (although with their agreement). Janine, who had been described by Alex and Naomi as having made a good attachment to them early on in the placement, said she had been to visit Paula four or five times during the previous nine months, sometimes staying for a few days. On the other hand Andrew, who had been described as having found adjustment to the adoptive home much harder, and who had appeared to have been much more unsettled by contact in the past (he had run away to his birth mother on four occasions when he was 14), appeared at the time of the interview to be less interested in visiting Paula than his sister. He said he had not been to see her for several months, although he had telephoned. Both spoke of their enjoyment in seeing their younger brother, Adam.

Neither Janine nor Andrew had had face-to-face contact for about two years with their paternal relatives (with whom, in 1987, their adoptive parents had described positive contact). There appeared to be some jealousy of their birth father's younger children and they had had an argument with their grandparents. Andrew's and Janine's account of their feelings about contact with various birth relatives confirmed their adoptive parents' perceptions.

Paul and Nicola

The pattern of contact for Paul and Nicola had changed since 1987 in that both now stayed (separately) with their birth mother, Corine, and Paul also stayed with his birth father, Darren. Paul described his feelings about contact with great thoughtfulness: visiting his birth parents on his own was "more difficult" than when contact was on a family to family basis. He usually felt uneasy before visiting but wanted to continue this form of contact nonetheless, and hoped to get to know his birth parents better. Paul found it easier to talk to his birth father; when he visited his birth mother he always took a friend, also adopted but without contact: 'I'm nervous. I don't know what to talk about. We're both nervous. Nicola handles contact with Corine much better than I do.'

Nicola confirmed this. She described Corine as "nervous and shy" except with friends and relatives – 'She's OK with me'. Because of this, Nicola was aware that Corine preferred the children to visit her (with or without their adoptive parents) rather than see them in their adoptive home.

Their adoptive parents, Jan and Malcolm, were very sensitive to, and supportive of, Paul's and Nicola's feelings about contact. While the children referred to themselves and their birth relatives as "black" in a matter of fact way, Jan and Malcolm drew attention to this as an extra positive dimension in maintaining contact.

Maxine

Jan and Malcolm had adopted Maxine, then 19, as well as Paul and Nicola. Maxine was not interviewed. She was also of African-Caribbean descent. There had been ongoing meetings, family to family, until, as described earlier, Maxine's birth mother had suggested that in future her daughter should visit without her adoptive family and stay for the weekend. There had been no contact since. Jan and Malcolm felt their daughter was of an age to initiate contact if she wished (with their help if needed).

Jan and Malcolm wondered whether cultural factors may have had some relevance to Maxine's decision not to initiate contact with her birth mother following the weekend invitation. Maxine had lived with white carers almost all her life – although not placed for adoption until she was eight, she had spent very little time with her birth mother while young. Jan thought Maxine may have felt unable to respond to her birth mother's expectations. She speculated that her birth mother may have hoped Maxine might return to live with her once adult, as might be more usual with an informal adoption in the Caribbean.

Two of the young people interviewed were not having contact with their birth mother, although face-to-face contact had been occurring in 1987.

As described above, a young man aged 17 had not seen his birth mother for two years. He described the contact over the years as 'pretty good' and thought he might ring his birth mother once he had finished his exams. His attitude was quite casual, seemingly based on feeling confident that he could make contact when it suited him, with or without the involvement of the adoptive family. The fact that he was a young man of African-Caribbean descent placed with a black family who described having cultural attitudes towards contact which were similar to his birth mother's may have contributed to this relaxed attitude.

Hayley's adoptive parents had accurately described her rejection of contact with her birth mother, Mary, and her reasons for this. Hayley had ended contact with Mary as soon as she reached 16, almost four years earlier. Hayley recalled that she and her brother and sister had had to go back to a children's home when Mary had chosen to resume her relationship with their step-father once he had completed his prison sentence: 'I feel bitter. I don't want to know her. Mary chose a man instead of her kids. I couldn't do that. If Mark (her husband and father of her child) hit the baby, he'd have to go. I can't ever forgive her, though the others (Laura and Craig) have.' Hayley thought Mary's motives in having wanted contact were not for her children's sake but for her own.

Taking into account past as well as current contact, there were four young people whose contact had been quite limited, both in nature and extent.

One of these, a young man of Anglo/Indian descent, then aged 17, had not been having any contact with birth relatives in 1987. Since then, largely at the instigation of his adoptive parents, he had begun when he was 16 to establish contact with his birth mother, who was white. She had been delighted by the contact ('over the moon', was how he described her reaction), and had hoped to meet her son. He, on the other hand, had been pleased to receive family photographs and 'fill in the gaps', but was not wanting at that stage to go beyond letter contact. He did not regret having written to his birth mother (although, as he put it and his adoptive mother acknowledged, 'Mum pushed me into it – she said I might regret it later if I didn't'). However, he explained that his birth mother, and the brother and sister he had now learned about, were 'not part of my life. I am part of this family. These are my real parents.'

Adoptive parents' observations about the feelings regarding contact of the eleven adopted children who were not interviewed, were broadly similar to those made in 1987. They believed that six of those who were having ongoing contact with birth parents (five face-to-face) regarded this positively. The birth father and siblings of one child visited regularly but it was not thought that he was able to attach any special significance to this because he had severe learning difficulties. Two adopted people were no longer having contact, and their birth parents' whereabouts were not known. However, as both had learning difficulties and contact had previously been very limited, it was thought they were unaware of the absence of contact.

There had been two other changes in the pattern of contact since 1987. As described above, Maxine had not had contact with her birth mother for three years. And a young woman aged 17, Melanie, whose circumstances will be more fully discussed in Chapter 5, from the perspective of her adoptive parents, had ended visits to her birth mother. However, there had been telephone contact. Melanie was being accommodated by the local authority in 1991 and her adoptive parents described her attitude to contact as 'ambivalent'.

Through contact with their birth parents, 14 of the 26 young people were enabled to have contact with other members of their extended family, in addition to that with brothers and sisters. According to the young people themselves and their adoptive parents, contact with brothers and sisters was particularly important for most of them. Five of the 26 adopted children and young people had no brothers or sisters living elsewhere. Of the remainder, 17 had at some stage had face-to-face contact with siblings through their contact with their birth parents. At the time of the interview, 13 were having such contact, four independently of their contact with birth parents. In one instance, adoptive parents did not encourage sibling contact. Only two of these young people were likely to have been able to maintain contact with their brothers and sisters had parental contact been terminated at placement.

In view of the value attached to contact with siblings by the young people, it would seem that this is an aspect of the practice of terminating parental contact which has received too little attention. Clearly the opportunity to maintain contact with brothers and sisters, or the denial of it, has far-reaching effects on an adopted child's relationships during childhood and beyond.

III INVOLVEMENT IN DECISIONS REGARDING ADOPTION AND CONTACT

The 15 adopted children and young people were asked to try to recall what involvement they had had in decisions regarding adoption – in particular, whether they thought they had been clear about what adoption meant, and how important for them at that time continuing contact with their birth parents had seemed.

Four had little or no recollection of discussion on these points (three had been very young when adopted). Most thought they had been well-informed about adoption. A typical comment was: 'We always discuss things like that in our family.' Janine and Andrew recalled having been told when they left their birth mother that they were going to have a holiday for six months. There followed several moves before their placement with Alex and Naomi. Janine remembered that subsequently adoption was explained and they had gone to court. Andrew had a less clear recollection.

Contact with birth parents had not been envisaged at the time when four had been adopted, but had been ongoing in respect of the other eleven children. Nicola and another child adopted at the age of six had assumed contact would continue.

Paul

Paul had been nine when adopted. Six years later he did not have a clear recollection of the discussions which had taken place, although he knew that both his birth parents had wanted to know from him that he wished to be adopted. Like his sister, he was aware of the arrangements for ongoing contact, so was not faced with having to weigh up the importance of contact in relation to adoption: 'I can't really remember my feelings at that time. Looking back, I'm pleased I was adopted. But I can't remember.' Paul added that he knew his adoptive parents had encouraged contact: 'I'm glad it's continued.' Paul's adoptive parents' perception in 1987 was that he had been "desperate" to be adopted and that this would have taken priority at that time over contact.

Antoinette

Antoinette was one of three young people who stated that their agreeing to adoption depended on knowing contact would be continued: 'I would not have agreed to adoption if I had not been promised that I could still write. I would really have questioned.' As Antoinette had been fostered for eight years prior to adoption at 14 years of age, she was well placed to comment on the difference made by adoption. At that time, she had wanted to be adopted but with hindsight she wondered whether it had been the right thing: 'It was difficult at the time. My mum meant the world to me, but there was no possibility of going to live with her. So if I couldn't be with her, I wanted to be adopted. I'd spent most of my life with my adoptive parents. That was my home.' Antoinette thought the advantage of fostering prior to adoption was that it 'gives the child more time to adjust to what's happened'.

Antoinette was aware that if circumstances had been different (her adoptive parents had been unable to afford to adopt without an allowance), she might have been adopted sooner and contact with her birth mother ended: 'I would have accepted it I suppose. I would have been too young to protest. But I would be angry now.' A disadvantage of adoption, which Antoinette had not envisaged at the time, and only understood looking back, was that adoption changed, she thought, her adoptive parents' emotional expectations of her. She commented: 'But adoption can't change things emotionally, only legally.' Antoinette had found it hard after so many years to refer to Frank and Lorna as "mum and dad".

The other two young people for whom continuing contact had been necessary for their agreement to adoption were unrelated by birth but had been adopted by the same adoptive parents. Rachel's views will be described in Chapter 4, together with those of her birth mother who was also interviewed.

Colin

Rachel's adoptive brother had been placed at the age of nine direct from the care of his birth mother. A ward of court, his previous prospective adoption placement had proved to be so unsatisfactory that he had been removed. He had then lived with his birth mother for a period, on the understanding that he would be placed in an adoptive or foster home if this did not work out. His birth mother had met his adoptive parents prior to introductions. He knew she liked them and that contact would continue.

Aged 13 at the time of the interview, he explained what he understood to be the difference between fostering and adoption: 'Fostering means not really being part of the family. Adoption means being a full member of the family. I really belong. Adoptive parents can talk and decide things but foster parents can't.' By contrast with Antoinette's experience, the adoptive parents of this young man had not expected him to start calling them "mum and dad" after the adoption.

Hayley

Hayley felt strongly that her views regarding contact after adoption were not considered (or even sought). Although placed at the age of ten, she had not been adopted until she was 15. For her, contact had been 'a good idea for the first few years (after placement), till I was 12 or 13. Then I should have been able to make my own decisions.' Hayley's perception was that contact was continued after adoption because 'Mary made it a condition of the adoption agreement'. If the judge had asked her, Hayley would have said she wanted to maintain contact with her brother and sister, but not with her birth mother. The judge had not asked her.

Hayley could recall telling the official solicitor how much she had wanted to be adopted: 'After seven years in a children's home I wanted to put roots down. I wanted to be part of the family – I have a fantastic nan and grandad.' Hayley contrasted her enthusiasm for adoption quite early on in the placement with Laura's attitude: 'I was thrilled when they (her prospective adoptive parents) said you can call us

> mum and dad. But Laura never did. She ran away because she'd never wanted adoption. She still says Mary's the world's best mum – even though she's let her down so many times.'

> Hayley's adoptive parents were the only ones to have said in 1987 that, with hindsight, they thought it might have been better if there had been a "clean break" (a severing of contact with her birth mother) at the time of placement. Looking back, Hayley was not sure she would have accepted this at that time.

It was difficult to get a clear picture of the extent to which young people were consulted about decisions regarding adoption and contact: how much information had they had about alternatives and how relevant was this in relation to their age and understanding? Most seemed satisfied that the decision which had been reached had been right for them. A few expressed the view that children should be consulted on these issues: Janine thought that children could be asked their views from the age of four, and added that she thought 99 per cent would want to continue contact with their birth relatives.

IV PERCEPTION OF THE ATTITUDES AND RELATIONSHIP OF BIRTH AND ADOPTIVE PARENTS

Given the impact of the attitudes of adults on children and young people (in reconstituted and foster families as well as in adoptive families) it was relevant to discover what the adopted people who were interviewed perceived to be the attitudes of their parents to contact and their relationship with each other. In addition, young people were asked about their birth parents' feelings about adoption.

The birth parents of all 15 young people had given their agreement to adoption but at the outset, birth parents of ten children had been expected to oppose adoption or withhold agreement. However, by the time the application had been lodged (sometimes as long as five years after placement) all but two birth parents had given agreement – after, in two instances, birth parents had talked to their children to confirm that they did indeed wish to be adopted and were not being put under pressure by their adoptive parents. One boy said: 'She was a bit upset. But she knew I was well looked after. I told her I wanted to be adopted so she agreed.' The two children whose birth parents gave agreement only after the application had been lodged were Paul and Hayley.

Jan and Malcolm, the adoptive parents of Paul and Nicola, had applied to adopt them some three years after placement. During this time, contact with their birth mother, Corine, had been maintained (through meetings either in her home or that of the adoptive parents) and she was willing to give agreement to adoption. However, Paul and Nicola, as well as their adoptive parents, were aware that adoption was something she had never liked to talk about. When asked about the possibility of Corine being interviewed, Nicola commented: 'She never refers to the adoption – I think she's a bit ashamed.'

Paul's birth father, Darren, had been separated from Corine for many years and only learned of the adoption application a few days before the hearing. A meeting was arranged for Paul and his birth father: 'I know Darren tried to stop the adoption. He wanted to look after me himself. But he agreed to the adoption when he realised how happy I was here. But he did ask to see me.'

Jan and Malcolm were quite willing to come to a voluntary agreement for contact with both Corine and Darren. One factor contributing to their openness of attitude was that as transracial adopters they felt that they and their children would benefit from contact. Both Paul and Nicola described their adoptive parents as supportive of contact and conveyed the impression of a relaxed and warm relationship between their two sets of parents.

In Hayley's case, her birth mother's agreement to adoption appears to have been less than wholehearted. The adoption application by Craig's adoptive parents was heard at the same time in the High Court.

Reflecting on the anxiety which attended the hearings, Hayley expressed considerable anger that her mother had delayed giving her agreement to the adoption 'until the last minute'. She explained: 'Mary had never liked the plan for adoption. She was wanting to get us back. She said no to the adoption. That really hurt, after she'd left us in a children's home for seven years. She even let us down in the court. She didn't turn up so the case had to be adjourned. She was being spiteful. She wanted her own way.'

In the event, Mary gave her agreement but requested that the arrangement for supervised access meetings twice a year be continued on a voluntary basis. The judge approved these arrangements, making it clear that Hayley could reach her own decision once she reached 16 (18 months later). Hayley expressed cynicism about Mary's request for contact: 'She was not really interested in us – just trying to get us back.' When asked about the importance of her birth mother's agreement, Hayley commented that it had seemed important at the time, but 'looking back, it wasn't really. Being adopted was more important.'

Hayley described how upsetting her adoptive parents had found the supervised access meetings. Hayley commented that her adoptive mother, Barbara, had 'never liked the meetings'. However, as Hayley had not had contact with her birth mother for almost four years, there had also been no contact since 1987 between Barbara and Mary. Hayley was aware that her adoptive parents were not encouraging of much contact between her and her brother and sister, believing that they might unsettle her. And that they were pleased she had chosen not to have contact with her birth mother once she reached 16.

Hayley conveyed more vividly than Barbara and Ken had done when interviewed in 1987 and 1991 the atmosphere at supervised access meetings (at which Craig and his adoptive parents were also present). Speaking of Barbara and Mary, Hayley said: 'They were at each other's throats. I felt good about that – they were fighting over me. They cared enough to want me. After years in a children's home, I was pleased someone liked me. But later I realised Mary just wanted her own way.'

Barbara and Ken had described Mary's hostility to the adoption plan and her attempts to undermine the placement but they had appeared to have a tolerant approach and did not convey the mutual antagonism which Hayley recalled. Ken had commented in 1987: 'You can never judge by someone's actions. Mary seems a bit lazy, a bit casual. But we may be wrong. She may have been a good mother until Hayley's father left her.' In 1991, Ken said: 'We've tried never to criticise Mary.' It is not clear whether Ken and Barbara were playing down, when interviewed, their negative feelings about Mary; whether they had perhaps not been able to be honest with themselves about the strength of these feelings; or whether Hayley had a need to highlight the differences between her parents, having rejected her birth mother and identified with her adoptive parents.

In addition to Paul and Nicola, who knew that adoption had been a painful process for their birth mother (and, in Paul's case, for his birth father), and the two adopted people whose birth mothers had been reluctant to give agreement without hearing at first hand that this was what their children wanted, Antoinette spoke movingly of what giving agreement to adoption had meant for her birth mother: 'It took a long time to get her agreement. I was all she had. The adoption hurt her so much. It was heart-breaking for her.' It seemed that Antoinette had not been so aware of her birth mother's feelings at the time, but had learned more of them recently through her more frequent and open correspondence.

Antoinette spoke with particular appreciation of her adoptive mother, Lorna, whom she described as 'very open. She used to encourage me to write to mum when I was younger and I was always putting it off. She's interested in news of my mum.'

Janine and Andrew were also aware (although they may not have been at the time of the adoption) that although their birth parents had given agreement to adoption, their birth mother, Paula, had found the adoption distressing. Their perception when interviewed (possibly based on discussions with Paula more recently, as well as having observed her distress at the supervised access meetings) was that Paula had been 'forced into it (giving agreement)'. Janine added quite firmly: 'It should always be a parent's decision to give up a child.'

Janine and Andrew were also very aware that in the past their adoptive mother, Naomi, had experienced the meetings on neutral territory as very difficult. Janine remembered that she would be 'very upset by meetings. Dad used to try to sort things out.' Their adoptive father, Alex, had tended to be present less frequently at meetings because of work commitments and had, according to his own and the children's account, a relaxed relationship with the birth relatives.

There had been a marked difference in the way in which contact was managed between the interviews in 1987 and 1991. When I had first met Naomi, she was seeking legal advice as to whether contact could be discontinued. She and Alex had written to the children's birth parents, Paula and John, before the adoption application had been made, assuring them that they would be happy to continue contact after adoption. Naomi had recognised that Janine and Andrew wanted to see their birth parents and their brother, Adam, but felt that contact was disturbing and unsettling to Andrew and she resented Paula's "tears" at meetings – in part, she was able to acknowledge, because of her jealousy that she had not given birth to the children herself.

Subsequently, Alex had offered to take Janine and Andrew to visit Paula in her home as an alternative to the strained meetings in the social work office or in McDonald's. Twice, when the adoptive parents had felt in need of a break, they had asked Paula to have the children to stay for the weekend! From this had evolved the arrangement which obtained in 1991 whereby Janine and Andrew made contact themselves with Paula. Naomi found this quite acceptable and Janine conveyed no sense of her "disapproving" of contact as she had done in the first four to five years of the placement.

However, Janine and Andrew recalled Naomi's formerly hostile attitude. Andrew said: 'Mum hated Paula.' Naomi would probably not have been surprised by this observation! When interviewed in 1991, Janine and Andrew described Naomi and Paula as 'getting on OK'. They thought that Alex had always got on well with both Paula and John (whom they had not seen for two years but who had previously attended the supervised access meetings).

The adoptive parents of Hayley and of Janine and Andrew were more financially secure than their children's birth parents and also enjoyed higher occupational and social status. It is not clear whether this contributed to the antagonistic relationship described by the young people. In 1987, Naomi had described Paula as being affected by "class jealousy". She explained that the adoption panel which had recommended the placement had expressed concern about the great differences in the circumstances of the prospective adopters and the children's birth family, but said Janine had taken to her adoptive home "like a duck to water".

Differences in socio-economic status, where applicable, did not appear adversely to have affected the relationship of birth parents and adoptive parents in other families. It was noticeable that the hostility described by the young people related primarily to the relationship between the adoptive and birth mothers – indeed Janine and Andrew, and Naomi and Alex, said there were no difficulties in the relationship between Alex and Paula.

While in one instance, in which contact was very limited, differences in race and culture between the adoptive parents and the birth parents may have inhibited the development of contact, such differences in respect of Paul's and Nicola's two families did not appear to be a barrier.

To summarise, although their birth parents had given agreement to their being adopted, eight young people were aware when interviewed (but possibly not at the time of the adoption) that they had done so with reluctance and/or with some distress. Seven thought agreement would have been withheld without a plan for contact or that giving agreement would have been even harder.

At the time of the interview, 14 of the 15 young people felt that their adoptive parents were currently supportive of adoption with contact. Included among this group were four people who had been placed at three years or younger and whose adoptive parents had negotiated face-to-face contact from the outset. However, one young person was having contact with a birth relative of which it was anticipated the adoptive parents would disapprove.

Contact had been too limited for five young people to form an opinion about the relationship between their adoptive and birth parents – contact had either been by letter or had comprised only one or two meetings. However, seven young people seemed confident of a good relationship between the two sets of parents.

V ADOPTED PEOPLE'S RELATIONSHIPS WITH BIRTH PARENTS AND OTHER RELATIVES

The way in which the 15 children and young people referred to their birth parents or, as they were sometimes described, first parents, had been clarified at the outset of each interview. Ten referred to their birth parents by their first names and three by their first name prefixed by "mum" or "dad". Two of the three young people who spoke of their birth mother as "mum", called their adoptive parents by their first name (although when talking about them they would say 'my mum and dad'). The young man who had grown up in a black family spoke of his birth mother as 'auntie', and a young man of 16 who had met his birth parents only once since placement at the age of three referred to them as 'Mr and Mrs L'. None found the question of how to refer to people difficult or confusing.

Three young people, one of them being Antoinette, spoke of their birth mother as "mum". They had retained a strong sense of loyalty/attachment to her: it was they who would not have agreed to adoption without both continuing contact and their birth mother's agreement. The terms used by the other young people seemed to derive from a combination of the degree of contact and the way their adoptive parents spoke of birth parents. For example, Janine spoke of her birth mother as "my mum Paula" but of her birth father, whom she had not seen for two years, by his first name. Their adoptive parents, in conversation with them, referred to both birth parents by their first name. Hayley called her birth mother by her first name. The young man who referred to his birth parents by their family name was using the terms employed by the two sets of parents on the one occasion when they met – limited contact and sensitivity to cultural differences were probably inhibiting factors.

For four young people, contact with their birth parents had been too limited for the link with them to be seen as a relationship with an emotional content. Hayley was hostile and rejecting towards her birth mother, described above. The remaining ten young people described or appeared to have experienced some warm and positive aspects of the relationship with at least one birth parent. One young man described his birth mother as 'like a friend of the family'. Antoinette spoke of a sense of closeness even though there had been only letter contact for ten years: 'There is a strong bond.'

Paul, who had for a year or so been having contact which included staying for week-ends with both his birth parents (who were separated) described the complexities of the relationship: 'My relationship – I'd describe Corine and Darren as being like friends, not relatives. They're like strangers that I've got to know. People think it's good that I know my first parents and it is – but it's more difficult than people think. Just because I was born to them, it doesn't mean automatically that I get along with them easily. It needs adjustment on both sides. I don't feel as if I'd known them all my life, although of course I have known them since

I was born. I find it hard to talk to Corine – I'm nervous. We're both nervous. That's why I took my friend Damian with me who's also adopted – it made it easier. I don't know what to talk about. I find it easier to talk to Darren.'

By contrast, his sister Nicola described their birth mother and other members of the family of origin as "like relatives", and had a much more straightforward view of contact: 'I get on OK with Corine. It's OK when I'm staying there and it's OK when I get back home.' Both Paul and Nicola appeared to be comfortable with their identity as black people and it was not clear whether or how much their being transracially adopted had affected the development of their relationship with their birth parents and other relatives.

Janine and Andrew were rather dismissive of their birth father, although in the past, by their own and their adoptive parents' account, contact had been quite amiable (at the time of the interview they had not seen him for two years). While both spoke with some warmth about their birth mother, Andrew seemed to be more ambivalent, in that he was making less effort to visit than Janine, but said: 'She'd take us back if she had the chance.' To which Janine, who visited approximately every six to eight weeks and usually stayed overnight, responded, with some amusement: 'Only if you paid rent!'

It seemed from these and other comments that Janine had positive feelings towards her birth mother, but also acknowledged some of her difficulties, whereas Andrew was more overtly uncritical but sought less contact. In 1987, their adoptive mother had described Andrew as looking on Paula, his birth mother, as a "fairy godmother". However, when during a particularly stressful period subsequently Andrew had run away to Paula's, she had made it clear he could not stay there. Alex and Naomi wondered whether Andrew had seen this as another rejection and was as a result more tentative about contact than Janine and possibly quite angry with Paula.

There were eight young people who described or appeared to enjoy a good relationship with their brothers and sisters (which included a degree of reciprocity) and a ninth person had done so in the past. Among this group were Janine and Andrew, whose younger brother, Adam, had remained in the care of their birth mother. Looking back to the first few years of the placement, when they had been meeting their birth parents on neutral territory, Andrew commented: 'Adam was all over us. He used to ask when we were coming home.' Both admitted Adam sometimes "got on our nerves", but overall they were pleased to have had continued contact.

Five young people, including Janine and Andrew, had, while still in the care of their birth parents, lived with siblings who had remained "at home". Recognising that such permanent separation would have affected these sibling relationships, it was relevant to learn what had been the reactions of the brothers and sisters who had not been adopted.

Hayley's brother and sister, who had spent seven years with her in residential care, had also been placed for adoption, but both had left their adoptive families, in Craig's case a year after the adoption order had been made. They were visiting their birth mother in 1991 whereas Hayley was refusing to have anything more to do with her. Hayley did not think this had proved to be a barrier: 'They understand that adoption's worked out well for me. They've wished me good luck.' Hayley believed that her sister now had a more realistic picture of their mother: in talking about her not having come to a family christening, Laura had said: 'You know what she's like. She probably went to the pub instead.'

Another young woman had spent several years in residential care as part of a sibling group. As the youngest, she had been placed for adoption, whereas her brother and sisters had been placed with foster carers when the children's home closed down. She described her brother as 'a bit jealous. He thinks adoption makes me special. The others are OK about it. They get on OK with my mum and dad.' This young woman was maintaining contact with all her siblings, who now lived separately from one another, and valued this. She described her relationship with all of them as "good".

From their own account it seemed that despite having been adopted, these five young people had been able to maintain a strong connection with their brothers and sisters.

Five young people also had face-to-face contact with other relatives and another had done in the past. Four had attended weddings and other celebrations with birth family members. A brother and sister had been a pageboy and bridesmaid at their mother's remarriage and Nicola had been a bridesmaid, alongside her birth mother, at an aunt's wedding. Such family events were described as happy occasions. One adopted person appeared to have more warmth in her relationship with her birth grandmother than her birth mother.

It was noticeable that despite differences in the lifestyle of the adoptive and birth families of most of the young people, these were rarely referred to, explicitly or implicitly, either in describing relationships or in other contexts, by the young people themselves. Some differences were attributable to class, race, educational attainments, economic power, health and disability, culture or priorities in child care. Hayley was the only young person who was critical of her birth mother's priorities: 'She chose a man instead of her kids.'

In eight instances there were quite considerable differences in the socio-economic status of the adoptive and birth family, with birth parents being on benefit, or not having a permanent home, or having been diagnosed as having psychiatric problems, or having other children accommodated by the local authority. Only four young people acknowledged this, but not as a factor which affected their relationship with their birth parents (except in a practical sense).

Three of the five young people who had been placed transracially had had contact with their black parents. In one instance, in which there had been only one meeting in twelve years, the differences in culture seemed to have affected the development of a relationship, in that the young man's birth mother barely spoke English (although he described his birth father as well educated and with a good command of English). The other two children, Paul and Nicola, had been having ongoing face-to-face contact with a number of birth relatives. Paul had found his birth father's wish to introduce him to many relatives and friends somewhat bewildering but he and Nicola seemed quite at ease at family events.

Overall, adoptive parents were much more likely to comment on differences in life-style than the adopted people.

Thus nine of the 15 young people interviewed described relationships with birth parents (and sometimes with other relatives) which were characterised by some warmth and satisfaction, currently or in the past. Contact had been helpful to four of the young people interviewed in giving them greater understanding about their family history but it had not been sufficiently extensive for any degree of attachment to be maintained or developed. Hayley was the only young person interviewed who expressed hostile feelings towards her birth mother.

VI IMPACT OF CONTACT ON SOCIAL/EMOTIONAL/ PSYCHOLOGICAL DEVELOPMENT

It is in the area of social, emotional and psychological development that some commentators have expressed most concern about the impact of contact on adopted people and on their relationships within the adoptive family. Four key areas central to an adopted child's adjustment were considered in this study:

- understanding of the circumstances of adoption;
- attachment to her or his adoptive parents and other relatives;
- sense of personal and social identity; and
- sense of permanence.

In addition, young people were asked to consider what difference not having contact might have made.

Understanding the circumstances of adoption

With very few exceptions, the adoptive parents interviewed in 1987 believed that some contact with birth parents after placement had helped the child to have a fuller, and in some cases more realistic, understanding of the circumstances which had led to adoption. In reinterviewing adoptive parents and some of the adopted children and young people, I considered how comfortable the adopted children were in discussing adoption; whether their factual understanding of their adoption was in accordance with the information available from their adoptive parents and from social work records; and issues of "blame" and "self-blame" – the child's handling of the "message of opposites" inherent in adoption.[1]

The willingness of the 15 adopted children and young people to be interviewed in itself implied a degree of ease in talking about adoption and this was confirmed by their openness (several being more talkative than I had been led to expect) and their comments regarding attitudes among friends and within the community. Three young people were less forthcoming, but seemed at ease with being adopted. All had non-related adoptive siblings. Eleven were very relaxed and quite talkative while Andrew was talkative but restless. The five black young people in this group who had been adopted transracially were clearly, in the eyes of the local community, not living with their birth parents, but it was two white adopted children who referred to some negative comments about adoption. One young woman said: 'People skit you because you're adopted.' A girl of nine quoted comments from other children at school such as 'Nobody wanted you' and 'Adopted means you were abandoned'. She described how she would put them right: 'No it doesn't! Mummy Shelley couldn't look after me. She still loves me and comes to see me. She wanted mum and dad to adopt me.'

Some of the young people were living in families in which adoptive parents were actively involved in the world of adoption (for example, as PPIAS co-ordinators, adoption panel members or participants in recruitment campaigns) and so adoption issues were often discussed. One boy described having had an adoption party both at church and at school – he had been 'embarrassed but pleased' when the head teacher had announced his adoption in assembly when he was ten years old! It seems likely that the openness with which adoption was discussed in these adoptive families and the information available to them contributed to the adopted children feeling able to acknowledge their adoptive status with apparent comfort.

All 15 adopted people had a good understanding of the circumstances surrounding their being adopted. Ten explicitly stated that having contact (whether ongoing or more limited) had enhanced their understanding, in varying degrees, of their adoption story. The importance to birth parents of knowing that their children had a good understanding is discussed in Chapter 4.

In explaining her feelings about adoption, Antoinette described a non-related adopted sister (placed as a baby) who had felt a very keen sense of rejection, having said: 'She (her birth mother) gave me up – I don't want to know.' As a teenager this feeling of abandonment had seriously affected her relationship with their adoptive parents. By contrast, Antoinette explained: 'I don't blame mum for agreeing to adoption. She felt she couldn't ever look after me – that she'd never get out of hospital.'

Antoinette's birth mother had written to say that she felt guilty that she had been unable to look after her but 'I did not reject you. I did not get rid of you.' Antoinette commented: 'I didn't feel rejected. There was always love there. She really struggled to keep me during the first few years.' This confidence that she was not rejected had enabled Antoinette to be open about being adopted: 'There's nothing bad about being adopted. I explain to people that I needed a family. At first I was looked after by Frank and Lorna and then they adopted me. I talk about it openly.'

In the 1987 interviews, some adoptive parents had described as an advantage of contact the opportunity it provided for the adopted children to gain greater awareness of the difficulties (whether related to health, social circumstances or problems in relationships) which had led to their parents relinquishing them or agreeing to their being adopted. This was certainly evident in the comments of some of the children and young people, who were able to describe a parent's limitations (where applicable) without being judgmental. However, in Hayley's case, contact had led her to develop a much more critical attitude than her brother and sister in the ten years since she had left the children's home: 'I was the only one of the three of us who could understand her. I saw through her at access meetings. The others thought the grass was greener. They believed her promises. Mary didn't really want us. Once she'd got her own way, got them (Laura and Craig) back, she didn't want them. She threw them out.'

Andrew, according to his adoptive parents, was coming to terms with knowing that he, but not Janine, had been subjected to ill-treatment by their mother's boyfriend and that their brother Adam had remained at home throughout. It would be hard to assess whether continuing contact had been beneficial to Andrew in reducing the sense of "blame" he was thought to have felt as the "scapegoated" child (to quote the adoptive parents). Andrew himself commented: 'We only had to go away because of him (mother's boyfriend). Paula would have taken us back otherwise.' Nonetheless, by his own and Janine's account, and that of his adoptive parents, Andrew seemed to have a more ambivalent and less comfortable relationship with Paula than Janine.

Adoptive parents in two families in 1987 had described how their adopted child (one of a sibling pair in each case) had felt at the time of placement that it was his "fault" he and his sibling had been removed from their parents' care. I was not able to reinterview the adoptive parents in one of these families in 1991 (they were involved in a family crisis that was not related to adoption or contact). The parents in the second family had adopted Paul and Nicola. They felt that contact had helped their son to understand that he had not been responsible for the care proceedings: the two children had been left alone at home by their birth mother when Paul was four and Nicola two, and Paul had gone to a neighbour for help. The adoptive parents' perception was that initially Paul thought his mother blamed him for the loss of her children into care and then through adoption. However, they thought that the face-to-face contact which had been maintained in the ten years since then had reassured Paul on this point.

Both Paul and Nicola said that their mother did not like talking about events leading up to their being adopted. Paul had on occasions felt the need for further information: 'Adoption has caused a few problems in school work – having to write in English about when I was a baby. I didn't know. I can't really ask Corine – she never talks about the past. Mum has had to write in for me to do separate work from the rest of the class.' Despite this recognition of some limits on open communication with his birth mother, Paul thought contact had helped him understand the circumstances of his adoption better and he compared his situation favourably with that of a friend, also adopted, who had very limited information and 'sometimes says he'd just like to see his first parents'.

The adoptive parents of seven of the children and young people not interviewed were asked to comment on whether contact had assisted their understanding of the circumstances leading to adoption. These areas were not thought applicable to the four children and young people with learning difficulties.

Included within this group of seven were four whose non-inclusion in the group of children who were interviewed may have indicated some lack of comfort in discussing adoption issues. Two had chosen not to be interviewed – although their sister placed with them had been – and the adoptive parents of a boy aged ten had thought he would rather not be approached. A young man living independently had initially offered to meet me and then cancelled the appointment. The adoptive parents of a nine-year-old girl thought she was quite comfortable about having been adopted 99.9 per cent of the time but on occasions was aware of "differentness".

Adoptive parents believed that six adopted children had gained in understanding through contact (in one case indirectly through the adoptive parents' greater knowledge). Adoptive parents did not describe any indicators of negative attitudes towards birth parents (although two children had been subject of a care order because of injuries), nor of adopted people appearing to blame themselves for the separation from their birth parents. However, Melanie, whose adoptive parents' account is reported in Chapter 5, was thought by them still to feel confused about some aspects of her adoption.

The adopted children's attachment to their adoptive family

It would not have been relevant in this study to consider whether the adopted children had formed an attachment of the degree and intensity which is described in the literature in relation to infants and young children. Only three children in this study, one of whom was interviewed, had been placed before the age of 12 months. In her evaluation of the placement of children with special needs, Thoburn[2] used the term attachment to mean 'a close, loving and lasting relationship, rather than in the precise sense of psychological literature' and attachment is considered in that sense in this study.

Eighteen of the 26 children had had many changes of caretaker in their early years, either through repeated separations from birth parents, moves while looked after by the local authority, or as a result of hospital or residential care. One of the six young people placed at ten years or older had had 22 changes of placement prior to her move to her adoptive family. A few children had been placed at an age when young people who had not experienced lack or disruption of attachment in their early years would be seeking greater independence and separation from parent figures.

Given the many barriers to the formation of close attachment experienced by the majority of the 26 children prior to placement, it is particularly difficult to assess how far contact, particularly continuing face-to-face contact, may have impeded attachment. Aspects of attachment considered included adopted children's sense of "real parents", whether they or their adoptive parents were aware of divided loyalties, and how (where relevant) the move to independence had been negotiated.

Twelve of the 15 young people interviewed were seen with their adoptive parents and generally a warm relationship was both described (explicitly or implicitly) and observed. Two young women said they felt closer to and confided more in their adoptive mother. Eleven of the 15 young people had brothers or sisters through adoption and eight were members of families with four or more children. They described their relationship with their siblings mainly in affectionate terms although as in any family, there were closer relationships with some than with others. Grandparents seemed significant figures for some adopted people, as were aunts and uncles and cousins. On the whole, the adoptive parents seemed satisfied with the extent of their children's attachment; clearly being realistic in their expectations was an important factor.

The term "real parents" (generally used by the community and media to mean birth parents) can be a source of confusion for adopted people, implying as it does, albeit unwittingly, some lack of legitimacy or shortcoming on the part of adoptive parents. Ten of the 15 adopted people interviewed made some observation on this point and eight were clear that their adoptive parents were their "real" parents.

This group of eight included three children who had had ongoing contact throughout the placement. A nine-year-old girl explained: '(Because they know I'm adopted) children say Mum's not my real mum – but I say she is.' Hayley illustrated that she regarded her adoptive parents as her real parents by pointing out that 'if anyone asks me how old my mother was when she had me, I say 32' (the age her adoptive mother was when she was born). Five young people, including two black children placed transracially, acknowledged the complexity of the situation. For example, Paul commented 'Real parents – I suppose that's really Corine and Darren. But in a way, the parents who brought me up are also my real parents.'

The remaining two young people, both adults, regarded their birth mother as their ' "real" mum' (neither had contact with their birth father). Antoinette explained: 'I do love my adoptive parents. But my birth mother is my real mum.'

Whether, in the view of the adopted people or their parents, contact had impeded the development of attachment, seemed to depend on a number of factors in combination, including:

- the age of the child at placement;
- the strength of the child's attachment to her or his birth parent prior to placement;
- the attitude of the birth parents to the placement;
- the attitude of the adoptive parents to contact; and
- the extent of contact.

Quite regular face-to-face contact (at least once every six weeks) was not thought to have affected the attachment of three children who had been placed at the age of four years, twelve months and three months respectively. These three children, when interviewed, said they could not remember ever having found contact confusing or unsettling. For example, the boy placed at twelve months had been living with his birth mother until that time. She had chosen the adoptive parents and had participated fully in the introductions. This sensitive handover appeared to have helped the little boy to transfer his attachment to his adoptive parents quite rapidly. Subsequent face-to-face contact until he was in his mid-teens had not led to any interference with his becoming attached.

It had been in relation to two children placed over the age of seven, Hayley and Andrew, that adoptive parents in 1987 had considered that contact had had some negative impact in the early stages on the child becoming attached to them.

Hayley's adoptive parents felt this even more strongly in 1991 than they had done four years earlier and Hayley in part shared this perception. Hayley recalled having wanted to maintain contact with her birth mother and brother and sister when first placed. However, she was aware that her adoptive mother, Barbara, 'had never liked the meetings and that affected my attitude'. Furthermore, Hayley described her birth mother, Mary, as having 'tried to unsettle me'. Barbara and Ken had asked for letters to be stopped when Mary had written a ' "nasty" letter', purporting to be from Laura, her older sister, which 'hurt my feelings'.

At the supervised access meetings, Mary used to say: 'I'm still your mum' and 'Don't let them hit you.' Hayley explained: 'The problem was,

I'd begin to be settling down and then have to go back to the past. I didn't want to go to see her. I wanted to look forward, not back.'

Barbara and Ken in 1987 had described difficulties before and after meetings and Hayley recalled: 'When I was older, Mum pointed out to me that I was always stroppy and bad-tempered and argumentative around access. I realised that was true.' Hayley would have liked to have ended contact with Mary (though not with Laura and Craig) when she was about 13. Hayley was clearly of the view that contact in her case had to some extent impeded her settling with her adoptive parents, although at the time of the interview, her attachment to her adoptive family was strong.

When interviewed in 1987, Alex and Naomi, the adoptive parents of Janine and Andrew, had described both children as wishing to see their birth parents and brother but Naomi had reservations about the effects of contact on Andrew. While Janine was thought to have made a firm attachment to her adoptive parents, Andrew was described as being unsettled by contact with his birth mother, Paula. This was manifested in his difficult relationship with Naomi (he was said to have told her she was 'not a proper mother') and problems in his behaviour and academic progress at school. Naomi described Andrew in 1987 as being on an 'emotional see-saw' after meetings (then taking place on neutral territory with a social worker). Naomi recalled that Paula had asked Andrew whether he wanted to live with his adoptive parents and whether he was happy there. Although Naomi wondered about the effects on the children if they were not able to see birth relatives, she had serious doubts about the wisdom of their maintaining contact with Paula: 'I hope we've done the right thing for the children.'

When reminded of this comment in 1991, Alex and Naomi were both of the view that contact had been beneficial, even though it had 'caused upset in the early years'. They now enjoyed a more co-operative relationship with Paula. She had made it clear to Andrew when he had run away three or four times that he could not stay with her – his home was now with Alex and Naomi. Furthermore, Naomi acknowledged that she had 'let go. I wanted the children all for me. They were mine.' The turning point in the relationship between the two families had come when Alex had taken over responsibility for facilitating contact – at Paula's home –

until the children were able to travel there independently ('the heat went out of the situation'). Alex and Naomi now realised that Andrew had been deeply adversely affected by events early in his life – they had learned only several years after the placement that psychiatric help had been recommended for him, but never followed up, when he was four. He still had limited ability to concentrate and to tolerate frustration. Andrew was said to have 'a low opinion of women', had not fulfilled his educational potential and had been unable to keep a job. However, Alex and Naomi no longer felt that contact was adversely affecting family relationships – they believed Andrew was quite attached to them and Alex said that plenty of their friends found their teenage sons troublesome. Possibly Andrew's emotional life was less complicated with the diminishing of the rivalry between Naomi and Paula.

When interviewed, neither Janine nor Andrew thought that contact had affected their settling with their adoptive family, although both recalled the distress which had attended meetings in a social work office and Andrew spoke of having run away to see Paula. Both Janine and Andrew spoke affectionately of their adoptive parents and had missed Naomi when she had recently been away in Ireland caring for a sick relative.

There were five adopted people for whom their birth parents' approval of their being adopted was important in allowing them to attach to their adoptive parents. None of their adoptive parents, either in 1987 or four years later, had regarded contact (in one instance by letter) as an obstacle to their becoming attached. These young people acknowledged that their adoptive parents had approved of and facilitated contact and this was particularly important for the three who had maintained a strong sense of loyalty to their birth mother. One young person described some difficulty in meeting the emotional expectations of her adoptive parents, although she did not think this was related to contact.

Three of the 15 young people had moved to independent accommodation (at the age of 17, 18 and 19 respectively). How an adopted person, with previous negative experiences of separation, "leaves" the adoptive home is often regarded as one measure of the successful accomplishment of the special tasks which adoptive status in the UK demands. All three had made this transition while maintaining an affectionate relationship with their adoptive parents and still receiving emotional and practical support. In each case, the move away from home had been achieved by mutual agreement and suggested that they had a sense of security, as adults, through the support of their adoptive family.

The adoptive parents of nine of the children who were not interviewed believed that contact had not in any way affected their child's attachment to them.

In the remaining two families, parents had each adopted an older child from residential care and they had been among the group of adopters in six families who in 1987 had described some difficulties or reservations about contact.

I had described the adoptive parents in one family as "less open" in attitude in 1987. Their son, who had one black and one white parent, then just 18, had left the adoptive home a few weeks earlier to live with his girl-friend's family. They felt he had not been as rewarding a member of their family emotionally as their older adopted children, all of whom had been placed as babies (and one of whom was of the same ethnic background as their youngest son). However, as he had met his birth mother only once or twice a year, the adoptive parents did not believe that contact had contributed to what they regarded as his limited attachment to members of the adoptive family. However, four years later they were much more positive about their relationship with their son and his with them. Although living and working in a town some sixty miles away, he regularly visited and there were 'always hugs and kisses'. Since leaving home, he had spent a brief period staying with his birth mother, and they did not think this has affected their relationship.

Adoptive parents in the second family had requested shortly before the second interview that their daughter be accommodated by the local authority because of her difficult behaviour. They still felt, as they had done four years earlier, that contact was "a side issue", especially as their daughter had chosen not to visit her birth mother for two years. Their perspective regarding Melanie's difficulties are described more fully in Chapter 5.

A sense of personal and social identity

In his studies in the early 1980s of white children adopted by white families, Triseliotis identified three key factors which contributed to the formation of a personal and social identity:

- feeling loved and wanted within a secure environment as a result of a warm and caring relationship within the adoptive family;
- having knowledge of personal and family history; and
- being perceived as a worthwhile person within the community (a factor which is likely to assume greater importance as children move through to adulthood and separation from the adoptive family, especially children from black and minority ethnic groups placed transracially).[3]

Triseliotis hypothesised that 'during childhood the quality of parenting may be the most important factor in building self-esteem and a positive self-concept'.[4] However, for the 22 children in the present study who had been placed after early adverse experiences, including repeated separations and, in some cases, neglect or abuse, this factor was linked with the other two key factors – for children may be unable to feel loved and wanted, however much they are loved by their adoptive parents, if they have not been helped to make sense of the implicit or explicit rejection by their birth parents and succeeding carers and have experienced community stigma, for whatever reason. These two factors are independent of the attitudes and skills of the adoptive parents. However, the development of a sense of a personal and social identity by black children placed transracially is likely to be significantly affected by how their adoptive parents handle issues of race and culture.

The 15 young people who were interviewed will be considered in three groups: the four who had had very limited contact with their birth parents; the three who, having been placed while three years old or younger, had had face-to-face contact over many years – for as long as they could remember; and the eight placed as older children who had had ongoing face-to-face contact until the time of interview (with the exception of Antoinette, who maintained contact through letters).

All four children whose contact had been limited had adoptive parents who had adopted several children, who were confident in their role, and who were open in attitude. There was a demonstrative and caring atmosphere in these households and the four young people seemed to be in no doubt that they were loved – although one young woman was described as lacking in confidence to some degree because of a progressive loss of hearing. These young people stated that contact had helped them understand more about who they looked like and why they had been "given up" – two very important questions for all of them. Two black children in this group, both still at school, had very little interest in their racial and cultural heritage.

The three adopted people who had been placed at a young age and who had had ongoing face-to-face contact with birth parents had been placed in very different circumstances: an African-Caribbean child voluntarily relinquished by his birth mother at 12 months and placed with a black family chosen by her; a white girl placed at three years with her younger brother following abuse by her mother's partner; and a white girl placed at two months with her brother, a year older, because of the psychiatric and other difficulties of both parents. The first two children had grown up with regular contact with a wide range of birth family members on their mother's side; they had attended family celebrations and knew several generations of relatives. However, they had only photographs of their birth father rather than personal contact. The third child, nine at the time of the interview, had been seeing both parents every six weeks in 1987, but they were visiting less frequently in 1991. Her adoptive parents believed that contact had been particularly important for her and her brother as they had gradually developed greater understanding of their parents' psychiatric difficulties, as well as having an awareness of who they looked like and information to help them deal with any questions about adoption. They commented: 'There'll be no skeletons in the cupboard'.

These three adopted people appeared to be very secure with their adoptive status, self-confident and aware of being much loved. Contact did not seem to have impeded their sense of belonging within their adoptive family. Their adoptive parents believed they had benefited from contact in relation to their developing a sense of identity. The young black man conveyed pride in his racial origins. Two of the children had siblings adopted without contact and one adoptive mother particularly felt quite acutely the lack of knowledge of heritage of one of her children.

The eight young people who had been placed at ages ranging from four to eleven years had had continuing face-to-face contact in the early years of placement: but in Hayley's case she had discontinued contact with her birth mother and Antoinette was now having letter contact.

All the children in this group had had adverse emotional experiences prior to placement. For at least two, self-blame, and a consequent difficulty in achieving a sense of self worth, had been diminished by contact (in the view of their adoptive parents). The eight young people in this group had an explanation for the circumstances leading to adoption which was more to do with their birth parents' difficulties than their own unlovableness or "bad" behaviour and contact seemed to have been helpful in this respect.

Most described feeling very much a part of their extended adoptive family. Hayley, explaining that she felt no stigma about being adopted, nor any need to keep it a secret, said: 'Mum's and dad's families always accepted me. They've never made a thing about me being adopted. I never mind telling people.' Hayley made sense of her heritage by acknowledging that she was like her birth mother only in her physical appearance and she identified with her adoptive parents (especially her adoptive mother) as the parents she "took after" (in values, lifestyle and ideas about child care). Hayley's confidence socially derived from her membership of her adoptive family. She regarded her adoptive mother rather than her birth mother as the grandmother of her baby, Aaron: 'I am never going to let Mary see him. She has let me down so many times. Aaron is not her grandson as far as I'm concerned.'

The adopted people within this group were able to draw on their knowledge of their birth family in constructing a sense of "who they were" to different degrees. Antoinette, while feeling loved by her adoptive parents (and stating that she loved them), was quite clear that her self-esteem and the confidence she obviously possessed derived primarily from her relationship with her birth mother, and that termination of contact when she was younger would have been detrimental: 'The security that I have now comes from my mum and from having contact with her.' Antoinette contrasted her situation with that of an adoptive sister who had limited knowledge of why she was placed for adoption and had had no contact of any sort: 'I do not have rocky foundations. I've always known my mother loved me.'

Antoinette was aware, both from what her adoptive parents had told her and from her birth mother's letters, that 'Mum tried to get back on her feet. But she had no family support. She was sad she couldn't look after me. She found it (agreement to adoption) a hard decision.' Antoinette had been told that her birth mother's "middle-class" family had refused to help her care for Antoinette because she had a black father. Despite lack of information about her African-Caribbean father during her childhood, and her upbringing in a predominantly white neighbourhood with white adoptive parents, Antoinette had a strong sense of pride in her ethnic origins. Her adoptive parents had positively sought to help her achieve this and, more recently, her mother had answered her questions about her birth father – who he was and what he looked like. Antoinette's confidence that she was loved and the information about her origins meant she felt no embarrassment about her adoptive status: 'I've got all the answers.'

Paul and Nicola were also black children placed transracially who had achieved a strong sense of their ethnic identity. In part, their adoptive parents' willingness to maintain face-to-face contact with their birth relatives was to assist the children gain more confidence about their heritage. Paul and Nicola had grown up with other adopted children in an atmosphere of openness and warmth. Furthermore, the adoptive parents believed that contact had reassured Paul that his birth mother did not blame him for the children's placement in care and subsequent adoption. Both Paul and Nicola were making good progress at school and were popular with their peers. In speaking of the ease with which she related to her birth mother and other relatives, Nicola said: 'Most of my friends are black' (quite significant in an area in which very few black families lived).

During the seven years of the placement, Paul's and Nicola's contact had been maintained in the form of visits by the adoptive family to the birth parents' home and vice-versa. Videos had been taken on some of these occasions and Nicola was keen to show me one. While their strongest attachment was to their adoptive family, Paul explained how he drew on his knowledge of his birth relatives: 'When I do a family tree I include all my brothers and sisters – adopted and half.' Nicola was able to identify some of her interests, as well as her physical appearance, as being derived from her birth relatives. She explained: 'I like cooking – I take after an uncle . . . I know I look like Corine. Some people think we're sisters, but I'm taller than Corine.' Nicola added that, through contact, 'I have more family – that's a good thing.'

The remaining four adopted young people from this group of eight were similarly able to draw on first-hand knowledge of a range of birth relatives in order to identify whom they were like, in appearance and sometimes personality and interests. Three were clearly confident about being loved by their adoptive parents and reassured by the evidence of their birth parents' continuing interest in them, although one would have liked more frequent contact. The fourth, Andrew, as previously described, had needed to test out his adoptive parents' commitment to him through difficult, and at times rejecting, behaviour, although this appeared to have lessened in the year or so before I met him and Janine. Possibly he had been helped by his perception that his birth mother and adoptive mother were now able to demonstrate approval of one another. Andrew did not convey the same sense of feeling comfortable with himself and his adoptive status as the other 14 young people who were interviewed.

Of the 11 children and young people who were *not* interviewed, four had been placed when aged two-and-a-half years or under. As would be anticipated, the adoptive parents of the children placed when young, believed that they would feel confident about being loved and wanted within the adoptive family. Furthermore, contact was thought to have been helpful in enabling three of the children to have a good understanding about their personal and family history. The fourth child, who had moderate learning difficulties, was only six at the time of the second interview. His adoptive parents described him as not having an understanding of the implications of adoption. The adoptive parents hoped that their first-hand knowledge of his birth parents would help him in the future if he needed further information (his birth parents had not been in touch since their marriage broke up). This boy had been placed transracially. His age and developmental delay had so far protected him from exposure to any negative community attitudes on account of his ethnic background (or his learning difficulties).

The adoptive parents of these four children believed that they had a good sense of self-esteem. All were said to be progressing well at school and had good peer relationships.

Of the seven young people placed as older children, two had learning difficulties of a degree which was thought to prevent their having any awareness of the concept of adoption. They were black children placed transracially and certainly one, and possibly both, had such limited understanding that issues of race and culture were not thought by their adoptive parents to be relevant. The black parents of both children had visited in the past. A third young person had moderate learning difficulties and was described by both his adoptive parents and his birth parents as happy in his adoptive home. Ongoing face-to-face contact was thought to have helped him understand that he used to live with his birth parents and to provide continuity.

The four other older-placed children were aged 17 years or more at the time of the 1991 interview with their adoptive parents.

Maxine was the older adopted sister of Paul and Nicola. Like them, Maxine was of African-Caribbean descent. In 1987, when Maxine was 15, Jan and Malcolm were concerned that on a number of occasions Maxine had said she did not like being black (although she had been having face-to-face contact with her birth mother and other relatives and Jan and Malcolm had a positive attitude to their daughter's ethnic and cultural background). By 1991, the adoptive parents described an increase in her self-confidence, particularly in relation to her black identity: I was shown a video recording of a television programme in which Maxine described herself as 'black on the inside as well as the outside'. Her adoptive parents acknowledged that Maxine was still wary in developing relationships – a legacy, they thought, of the insecurity of her early years.

Two adopted people who had been placed at the age of 13 were living independently at the time of the interview. They were thought by their adoptive parents to feel confident about their relationship with their adoptive families, maintaining regular and affectionate contact. Both had a good knowledge of their family history, having had face-to-face contact with paternal as well as maternal relatives. As young adults, they appeared to be functioning well in the wider community; one young man, who was white, had a reputation as a hard worker and was a caring stepfather; the other also had a good work record. His adoptive parents appeared to attach little significance to his having one black and one white parent and it was not known whether his sense of ethnic identity was important for him.

Of all the children in the study, Melanie, the young woman living in local authority accommodation, seemed to have gained least from contact in terms of her sense of self-esteem and self-worth. Although her adoptive parents appeared to be very committed to her, they described her as 'feeling herself to be a failure' and not seeing herself as a worthwhile person. Her limited trust in adults and her anti-authority attitude resulted in her provoking further rejection – confirming her poor self-image. While her adoptive parents valued her contact with her birth mother as the only thread running through her personal history, the young woman herself appeared to have some angry feelings towards her birth mother. Melanie's placement is described in more detail in Chapter 5.

Melanie's poor self-image and sense of identity were exceptional, according to the perception of the adoptive parents and the young people who were interviewed. In most cases, contact (of whatever degree) was thought to have contributed to the development of self worth and a sense of identity based on knowledge or information about their family of origin, together with their feeling valued within the adoptive family.

A sense of permanence

One of the key objectives of permanency planning is to ensure that a young person separated from her/his family of origin does not embark on adult life lacking a secure base and a "family for life".[5] Given the widely-held conviction when the children in this study were placed for adoption that contact with birth relatives needed to be severed in order to ensure permanence, it was particularly important to discover whether contact had impeded the child's sense of permanence.

When they were interviewed, all the 15 young people conveyed or articulated a sense of confidence about being secure members of their adoptive family and those who were already teenagers or indeed adult were envisaging the adoptive home as their base in the future. The three young people already living independently demonstrated this through the close and affectionate contact they maintained. Eight of the remaining twelve young people were aged 15 years or more. Four were having on-going face-to-face contact with birth parents while four had very limited contact, but both these groups regarded their adoptive family as their base for the future.

Paul described having been confused and temporarily upset a few months earlier when, during a visit, his birth father Darren had asked him whether he would like to live with him. Paul had told Jan and Malcolm that he did not know how to handle this. When Jan had telephoned Darren, he had explained that he was not seeking to undermine the adoptive placement but felt it was important that Paul knew he cared for him. Darren was sorry his remark had led to distress and Paul felt the matter had been resolved satisfactorily. However, Paul wondered whether Darren might envisage his moving to live with him when he was 18 which, at that stage, he did not anticipate: 'Darren may say he wants me to live with him when I'm 18 – I'll have to explain I'm not ready for that.'

The four younger adopted people, ranging in age at the time of the interview from nine to 13 years seemed well established in their adoptive homes and to feel secure.

A seemingly important factor in relation to the nine young people having ongoing contact was that by the time of the interview, they all felt they had their birth parents' approval or at least acceptance of their being part of the adoptive family (although, as described previously, there had been tensions and difficulties regarding contact for at least three of the young people at an earlier stage).

The adoptive parents of the eleven young people not interviewed did not consider in 1991 that contact had undermined their child's sense of permanence. One young man had gone to live with a maternal uncle for a period as an older teenager but had returned to the adoptive home prior to moving on to live independently. Peter's situation is described in Chapter 5.

What if there had been no contact?

Seven of the 15 adopted people made comments on what differences there might have been if they had not had contact with birth parents.

Three were aware that without contact they would have had less information about their family background and who they looked like. Others thought there would have been a gap. A young man of 17 who had had face-to-face contact from the time of placement until he was 15 said: 'I'd have been annoyed. It's been pretty good to see her. If not, I'd have thought, why not? I'd have wondered why . . . I know all about her.' And Paul thought that in addition he would have had anxieties about seeking information: 'I would have been curious – but I would have been nervous about finding them (his birth parents). I would have been worried about what I would have found out.' The view of Janine and Andrew was that contact was an entitlement and that had this been denied, they would have 'needed to find out' and 'gone looking, whatever the law says'.

Hayley's perception was that although contact with her birth mother had been a negative experience overall, without contact, she might not have gained a realistic picture of her: 'I might have thought the grass was greener. I knew where I stood. I knew who was the better mother. I wasn't left wondering.'

Finally, Antoinette felt that contact had been essential to her emotional well-being: 'I could not have coped without the letters. I would still be angry if contact had been stopped.'

VII CONCLUSION

These young people's comments illustrated the range of functions contact can fulfil: increasing a young person's knowledge and understanding about her/his personal and family history; lessening anxiety about the circumstances of birth parents and the need to search them out; reducing the potential for fantasy about birth parents; and contributing to an adopted child's self-esteem. Hill identified 'a challenge for adoption in the 1990s. How can we best reconcile greater *openness* (original emphasis) with children's and adopters' needs for security, belonging and positive social status, in other words – permanence?'[6] From the interviews with this group of adopted people and adoptive parents, I gained the impression that the majority of children and young people had largely accomplished successfully the extra developmental tasks of adoption and that in most instances contact, whether limited or more extensive, had contributed to this.

For about half of the young people interviewed, contact was a significant part of their lives. Seven had ongoing face-to-face contact while Antoinette was frequently in touch with her birth mother by letter. Three young people said they would not have agreed to adoption without the promise that contact would continue. They had maintained a sense of loyalty to their birth mother while becoming attached to their adoptive parents. For most of them, contact included meetings with other birth relatives in addition to birth parents, and some managed to negotiate arrangements with quite a complex network of family members, including two children of African-Caribbean descent who had been placed transracially. Contact with brothers and sisters was particularly valued.

At the time of the interview, contact was of limited significance for the remaining seven young people: either contact was no longer taking place or it was very infrequent. However, they and the other eight young people all identified ways in which contact had been helpful to them. Even Hayley, who had ended contact with negative feelings towards her birth mother, felt that meetings had helped her sort out to which family she wished to belong. Quite limited, as well as more extensive contact, had contributed to the development of a sense of identity and greater understanding of the circumstances leading to adoption. However, a number of children nonetheless had gaps in their knowledge, mostly regarding their birth father and his family, since the majority had contact only with maternal relatives. Face-to-face contact had been particularly helpful for a few of the children who had been placed transracially, but two black children placed with a white family attached little significance to their ethnic origin.

Adopted children were perceptive about the attitudes of their parents. Most young people felt that their adoptive parents had been encouraging of contact and had welcomed this. However, Hayley, Andrew and Janine had been vividly aware of some resentment in the earlier stages of the placement on the part of their adoptive parents. Hayley knew her adoptive parents were pleased she had chosen to end contact with her birth mother. By contrast, Janine and Andrew welcomed the fact that they were now free to negotiate contact with their adoptive parents' agreement.

Eight of the young people were aware of feelings of distress or shame regarding adoption on the part of their birth parents, either in the past or currently. Only Hayley was critical of her birth mother for expressing her opposition to adoption, since she believed her feelings were selfishly motivated. The other young people appeared to understand their birth parents' feelings and in some instances to regard this as a measure of their concern for their child. Where young people were aware of a good relationship between their two sets of parents, they described this with satisfaction.

Whatever the degree of contact, all the adopted children and young people expressed or conveyed that contact had been beneficial in some way. The observations and suggestions made by the young people regarding social work input and contact after adoption are recorded in Appendix III.

References

1. Brinich P, 'Adoption, ambivalence and mourning: clinical and theoretical inter-relationships', *Adoption & Fostering*, 14:1, BAAF, 1990.

2. Thoburn J, *Success and Failure in Permanent Family Placement*, Avebury Gower, 1990.

3. Triseliotis J, 'Identity and security in adoption and long-term fostering', *Adoption & Fostering*, 7:1, BAAF, 1983; 'Obtaining birth certificates', in Bean P (ed), *Adoption: Essays in social policy, law and sociology*, Tavistock, 1984.

4. Triseliotis J, 'Intercountry adoption', *Adoption & Fostering*, 15:4, BAAF, 1991.

5. See 3 above, 1983.

6. Hill M, 'Concepts of parenthood and their application to adoption', *Adoption & Fostering*, 15:4, BAAF, 1991.

4 The experience of contact
Birth parents

Birth parents in only four families were interviewed and as they had little in common apart from their loss of a child through adoption, their account of their experiences will be described separately. There follow some observations made by the young people and adoptive parents who felt able to offer comments on the effects of contact on other birth parents, and common themes which emerge are highlighted.

The first account concerns Beverley, who, as a single teenage mother, had decided that adoption would be in the best interests of her baby, Claire. Only one other child without disabilities in the study, in addition to Claire, had been "voluntarily" relinquished as a baby, so Beverley was not typical of the birth parents whose children comprised the study sample. Birth parents in the second and third families had each maintained contact with their son who had been adopted as a result of his having disabilities: Eve and Gerald had agreed to the placement for adoption of Stephen, who had Down's Syndrome, when he was nine. At their suggestion, I also interviewed their other son and daughter. Ian's son, Jamie, had joined his adoptive family at the age of seven. The cause of Jamie's disabilities was unknown. Stephen and Jamie were two of the six children in the study who had been placed for adoption, with their birth parents' agreement, as a direct or indirect result of their disability. Cathy, the birth parent in the fourth family, had, in common with birth parents of more than half of the children in the original group of 32, been asked to agree to the adoption of her daughter Rachel who was in care through compulsory means. A contested adoption had originally been envisaged in Rachel's case.

(A brief summary of each birth family is given in Appendix II.)

One of the birth mothers interviewed had previously relinquished a child who had been placed with adoptive parents soon after she was born. The birth mother had been given no information about the adoptive parents, nor about her daughter once she had been placed. She had not divulged this to the agency or the adoptive parents of the child included in the study. Therefore, although her experience of both "closed" and "open" adoption was very relevant to this present study, only brief and non-identifying references are made to the birth mother's account, in order to safeguard her confidential disclosure.

I BEVERLEY

Beverley had given birth to Claire, a white child, a year or so after leaving school. Claire's birth father had been Beverley's first boyfriend. They had been "going out together" for just over two years when Claire was conceived. The relationship ended before Beverley realised she was pregnant and she did not subsequently inform Claire's father (for what she felt were good reasons). Nor did Beverley confide in her mother until shortly before Claire was born, because previous events within her family led her to believe that she would be under pressure to have an abortion.

When Claire was twelve days old, she was placed by a voluntary adoption agency with experienced pre-adoption foster carers, Helen and Chris, to give Beverley an opportunity to make a decision about Claire's future. During the next few weeks, Beverley, sometimes with her mother and an aunt, visited Claire several times (her father had not been told about his grandchild's existence on the insistence of Beverley's mother). Once Beverley had decided that adoption would be best for Claire, the agency introduced prospective adopters to Claire. Beverley asked to meet them and felt so strongly that they would not be right for Claire that she considered not going ahead with the adoption plan. (Helen, who had previously been involved in the placement of many babies for adoption, had had exactly the same reaction as Beverley, although she had not discussed this with her.) Beverley's objections led to delay and she then asked Helen and Chris whether they would consider adopting Claire.

At that time, Helen and Chris had two children born to them aged 13 and 12 and an adopted son, aged nine, who had spina bifida and who had been placed with them four years earlier. They had never had an opportunity to meet his birth parents and had virtually no information about them. Chris and Helen had not intended to extend their family on a permanent basis. However, Helen explained that she and Beverley 'had established a good relationship right from the start' and, after much thought, she and Chris asked the adoption agency to consider them as adoptive parents for Claire.

The agency case committee (as it was in 1983) initially refused their request, apparently on the grounds that babies should be placed with childless couples. However, Beverley refused to accept this decision, and having heard of the strength of her feelings when they reconsidered, the case committee members approved the placement. Subsequently, according to Helen, the guardian *ad litem* who was preparing the report for court advised the adopters to move, declaring they were "mad" to adopt a child whose birth mother knew their identity and whereabouts (which highlights the strength of the view which then prevailed about the necessity for a "clean break").

Until Claire was about two, Beverley used to visit her daughter regularly. However, she observed her becoming more "clingy" to Helen and thought Claire seemed worried and puzzled sometimes – 'maybe she saw some resemblance'. At that time, Beverley was still living at home and her mother discouraged her from visiting, saying it would confuse Claire. So to avoid any risk of unsettling Claire, Beverley discussed with Helen and Chris her wish to discontinue visiting but to send birthday and Christmas presents. This arrangement was still continuing in 1991, when Claire was eight. Helen and Chris would send photos and news of Claire to Beverley and she would ring and speak to Helen, and often also to Claire, to discuss what present might be suitable.

Helen spoke to Beverley about the possibility of my interviewing her, as none of the social workers who had known Beverley was by then still working in the agency and Helen felt quite confident about broaching the subject. Helen told me that Beverley 'didn't need persuading – she values the continuing contact and feels strongly about it'.

I met Beverley in the studio where she worked as an interior decorator. She had been living for nearly five years with a divorced man whose ex-wife had care and control of their daughter, a little older than Claire. He maintained regular contact with her and he and Beverley had in common that he too had 'lost a child'. Beverley had had no other children: 'I gave a promise to Claire in the hospital that I would not have another child unless I was in ideal circumstances and I could be at home full time'. The interview lasted for more than two hours; Beverley wept on two occasions but said she had found it helpful to talk about Claire.

How the adoption process was experienced

'There could never be anything in the rest of my life as difficult as parting with Claire.' This was Beverley's first comment when asked about placing Claire for adoption. Beverley added that she had felt 'totally worthless – I felt I was being punished and chastised'. She felt she had been given no real choice as to the adoption decision: her mother was "pressurising" her and in the absence of any support and acknowledgment from her extended family, she recognised she could not offer Claire the security she wanted for her. Beverley had felt angry and hurt by her mother's attitude and "tormented" by the pain of realising that she would have to let Claire go. Moreover, 'the pain of parting with Claire was doubled by the fight I had to get to meet the prospective adopters. I shouldn't have had to fight. I shouldn't have had to go berserk. I said to the social worker: "I must know where she's going and who is going to adopt her".' (Beverley had been the first birth parent allowed by that agency to meet the prospective adopters prior to the placement.)

Beverley had been "very distressed" by the choice of adopters made by the agency. Firstly, they and the child they had already adopted were completely different from Claire in appearance and Beverley did not want Claire in the future to stand out as an adopted child and 'perhaps be an object of pity'. Beverley believed that some children within her extended family who had been adopted transracially had been subjected to additional pressures because their adoptive status was so public. Secondly, she feared that the prospective adoptive mother would seek to deny that Claire was an adopted child: 'I resented their attempts to make her their child. She said that Claire wrinkled up her nose just as their adopted child had done as a baby. I was unsure about their motivation. I saw them as vultures who were wanting to steal away my child.'

Beverley found the agency social worker very unsupportive and unsympathetic regarding her conviction that the selected adopters were 'not right' for Claire: 'I felt desperately sad. I was made to feel as if I was "mentally defective" (as they used to say) for getting pregnant, when it was just that I was the one who got caught.' Beverley's aunt had been able to arrange for her to meet up privately with another social worker whom she knew through her church. This Beverley had found very helpful as she felt her feelings had been understood and acknowledged for the first time.

Being able to choose adoptive parents for Claire had helped Beverley enormously: 'I felt I was able to be a responsible parent in choosing what I still regard as an ideal family for Claire. This has lessened the pain.' Furthermore, the offer made by Chris and Helen of continuing contact made it easier for Beverley to give her agreement to adoption: 'I might have delayed signing if I'd thought I could never see Claire again, although I realised I could not offer Claire what Chris and Helen could.' Beverley explained that the with the possibility of continuing contact 'it was as if God had offered me a consolation prize. I felt such relief and joy.'

The burden of secrecy which had compounded Beverley's anxiety and distress during pregnancy had to a great extent continued until the time of the interview, in that her mother had forbidden her to tell her father and very few relatives knew. However, Claire's grandmother had continued to send small gifts to Helen and Chris for Claire. Helen felt it must be desperately sad for a grandmother to be unable to acknowledge her grandchild publicly, whereas Beverley felt her mother could have helped avoid the need for adoption if she had been more supportive, and so was critical towards her.

Beverley's relationship with Chris and Helen and with Claire

Both Beverley and Helen had described the development of a good relationship early on and this had continued. In 1987, Helen had described 'a good understanding between the two of us', although then, as in 1991, she said there was not the same closeness between Beverley and Chris. This Helen attributed largely to the fact that in the early days, Beverley had almost always visited when Chris was at work (sometimes abroad). However, she acknowledged Chris was less relaxed about contact than she was, wondering whether Beverley found it easier to relate to her as another woman. For her part, Beverley thought Chris was 'wary' of her and she did not converse with him as she could with Helen when she telephoned. At one time, Beverley had felt that the now adult children of Chris and Helen had also been somewhat anxious about her involvement ('Maybe they thought I would abduct Claire') but she no longer felt this.

Helen's openness of attitude appeared to contribute significantly to the comfort of the relationship between Beverley and herself. She had said in 1987: 'If you love a child, and you have had children yourself, you can appreciate how natural it is for a mother to want news of her child's progress.' Four years later, Helen described a 'friendly relationship with mutual trust', adding that Beverley would sometimes confide in her if given the opportunity. Helen felt it was Beverley's attitude and consistency which has made contact so 'easy': 'She keeps in touch because she genuinely cares, not out of duty. She has always kept her side of the bargain – she has never tried to interfere and has always been reliable.'

Beverley described how reassured she felt to know that Helen acknowledged her as Claire's birth mother and did not attempt to exclude her: 'Helen is super! I regard her as a relative – a blood relative through Claire.' Beverley was pleased that Helen had kept all the cards and letters she had ever sent and would highlight similarities in taste or interests between Claire and herself (Helen had quoted a recent telephone conversation with Beverley regarding what Claire might like for her birthday, in which she had told Beverley: 'If you like it, it will be perfect for Claire.')

Reciprocally, Beverley drew attention to expressions or interests of Claire which she knew had been derived from the adoptive family. Thus, far from there being rivalry between the two women, each of them acknowledged the other's special place in Claire's life. Beverley felt that their background and level of education had been similar and she was pleased that Chris and Helen were 'good, Christian parents'. She did not anticipate that she would ever feel unhappy about their way of handling Claire: 'Their attitude to people is one of love and forgiveness – they are not judgmental.'

Beverley described the part she played in Claire's life as like 'a caring relative or friend'. At the time Beverley and I met, Helen and Chris had not explained to Claire that the person called Beverley to whom she sometimes spoke on the phone was her birth mother. When I had interviewed Helen, about three months before my meeting with Beverley, Helen told me that in response to a question from a friend as to who Beverley was, Claire had said: 'She's my very special friend but I've never met her.' Although she anticipated that Claire would soon be told or would realise who her birth mother was, Beverley did not anticipate that her relationship or her role with Claire would change, unless the initiative for this came from Claire and/or her adoptive parents.

The difference made by contact

Beverley spoke very movingly of the extent to which contact had helped her to become reconciled to the loss of Claire through adoption: 'Contact has been my lifeline. Without the security of knowing how she is, I would have become anti-social and anti-authority. I would still have feelings of anger, but with nowhere to direct it.' Without regular news of Claire, Beverley felt she would not have been able to grieve: 'To have never known would have been the worst, like her being dead, but not dead. I couldn't go through the rest of my life wondering. I think of her every day.' Beverley had recently learned that her sister-in-law was pregnant (the baby would be her first niece or nephew), and she felt she would cope without the feelings of jealousy and anger which might have surfaced had she 'lost Claire altogether'.

Contact had also given Beverley reassurance: 'I know whether she's dead or alive. I would have worried about whether she was being abused, whether she was happy. I would have had no way of knowing. I know Helen has been the mum I couldn't be and that she and Chris have never regretted adopting Claire.' Beverley also spoke of 'sharing in the joy of all her milestones. I know when she cut her first tooth, what her first words were. I get comfort from knowing all these things.' In addition, Beverley felt she could make a positive contribution to Claire's well-being, by providing information when Helen and Chris requested this – recently, she had forwarded to the adoptive parents a photograph of herself for each year from birth to sixteen years.

Although contact had been limited (in comparison with some other placements in the study), Beverley felt it would ultimately enhance Claire's understanding about the reasons for her adoption and it was also reassuring to Beverley to know what information was being given to

Claire about her and the circumstances of adoption: 'I know that Claire is being brought up to understand that she was loved. I'm pleased that Claire will realise I still care about her.' Beverley was relieved that Claire had been brought up from an early age to know of her adoption and understood from Helen that 'she feels special to have two mothers'. In the absence of information as to what and how Claire had been told of her adoption, Beverley would have worried as to whether Claire might have been given a negative or judgmental picture of her.

Helen had been aware of Beverley's concerns as to what Claire might think of her in the future. Her view was that contact would have helped to explain the paradox that Beverley had placed Claire for adoption although she loved her. Helen was keeping Beverley up to date with any comments made by Claire and what had been said to her regarding adoption. I had met Beverley a few days before Claire's birthday, and when I had subsequently telephoned Helen (to let her know the meeting had taken place), she told me that as usual, Claire had received 'a lovely present from Beverley, beautifully wrapped'. A day later, Helen had found a doodle in one of Claire's notebooks: 'I have two mummies – Helen and Beverley.' Helen was confident that Claire would ask further questions when she felt ready.

Beverley did not anticipate any divided loyalties on Claire's part as a result of contact because she would want to convey to Claire how happy she had been with the adoptive placement and she felt so confident about being able to work together with Helen in the future.

Current feelings about having placed Claire for adoption

'One doesn't ever get over it but I'm feeling OK now – I'm no longer feeling like a bad girl.' Nonetheless, Beverley had talked to very few people about having placed her child for adoption, as she had experienced some negative reactions and felt there was still condemnation of parents who placed their child for adoption. In an "adoption story" in a women's magazine, for example, the adoptive parents and the adopted person were always more sympathetically regarded: if the question of reunions were being discussed, birth parents would be criticised if they were anxious about being traced and also if they were longing to be traced – they were seen as selfish and undeserving in either event.

Beverley felt that she had made an emotional commitment to Claire that she would always acknowledge her and help her in any way she could in the future. She could not have become established in a long-term relationship with a man who would not accept this, as she did not wish to make any decisions that could be detrimental to Claire in the long term. Beverley's current partner understood this and would, she felt, support her in the future if Claire ever wanted to meet her. She kept photographs of Claire in their bedroom – she could not have them on display elsewhere because she did not wish to explain to visitors who the little girl was.

Beverley described how hurt and bitter she had felt some years earlier when a man who had spoken of marrying her had said he could not possibly do so when he learned about Claire – he had his professional reputation to consider. And yet he had been living, unmarried, with a woman for over a year prior to his meeting Beverley! Ironically, she felt she would have been condemned less if she had had an abortion, although she felt adoption was much the more caring option. Beverley found it hard when people commented or teased her about not having had any children yet.

Within her family, only her mother, an aunt and her brother knew about Claire. Beverley still felt upset about her mother's lack of support at the time of Claire's birth. Looking back, she could acknowledge that her mother probably thought adoption would be in the best interests of Claire and Beverley – she wasn't simply being punitive, although Beverley had felt she was being punished, then and subsequently. Beverley believed her mother's discouraging of contact had derived from her fear that Beverley might be tempted to abduct Claire or that contact would perpetuate her distress. Now, she had become more willing to listen to news about Claire.

With the stigma and the secrecy she had experienced, Beverley imagined that she would still have been feeling distressed and bereft had she not had contact and the opportunity to talk about Claire several times a year with Helen. She recalled that when she was considering adoption, she was told she would have forgotten all about Claire in five years time: 'That was absolute rubbish!'

Overall feelings about adoption with contact and hopes for the future

'If I look back, I would not have wanted to do anything differently – other than wishing I had enough support from my family to care for Claire myself.' Beverley could envisage no disadvantages to Claire as a result of her having maintained contact and would continue to be guided by Helen in the future as to what contact would be helpful for Claire. Beverley was appreciative of the fact that Claire had been accepted by the families and the community of Helen and Chris, and not regarded 'as a poor little unloved girl who had to be adopted' (Beverley had heard a nurse describe Claire in this way when she was in the maternity ward). In summing up why her relationship with Chris and Helen had been so positive, Beverley said: 'They see Claire as a gift. They are grateful to me for having chosen them to be her adoptive parents and I am grateful to them for being such wonderful parents to Claire. And I treasure all the cards and photographs I have received – and the piece of Christening lace.'

In thinking of the future, Helen had felt Claire would gain from having an understanding of Beverley's current circumstances and an assurance that face-to-face contact would always be welcome. She added: 'I can see Claire and Beverley coming together in a natural way when Claire is older and probably they will become good friends. I can see Beverley there at Claire's wedding (if Claire wanted her there, and I expect she will) and I'll be thrilled for Claire.' Beverley hoped that contact would continue – 'as long as it's OK with Chris and Helen and causes no problems for Claire'. She had considered the possibility of Claire wanting to meet her in the future and commented: 'If Claire wants to come to see me in the future, I would welcome her. If she never comes, I would accept that.'

II EVE AND GERALD

Eve and Gerald, a white couple, were the parents of three children. At the time of my interview with them in 1991, Louise was aged 19, Stephen, who had been adopted, was aged 14, and Joshua was ten years old. I spoke with Eve and Gerald, then with Louise and Joshua (without their parents being present).

Stephen had been born with Down's Syndrome and some related health problems. This had been immediately apparent to Eve, a nurse, but had been denied by the paediatrician for almost a week (he later said he preferred to delay informing parents of the diagnosis until they had bonded with their child so as to minimise rejection). This denial had added to the distress of Eve and Gerald and delayed their adjustment to Stephen's potential disability. In addition, within weeks of Stephen's birth, Eve was found to have lupus; she was virtually bedridden for many months and then made a gradual recovery. A neighbour assisted Gerald in the care of Louise (as a solicitor he was able to work partly from home) but Stephen was placed with local authority foster carers because he needed special care. Contact was maintained. When Stephen was two-and-a-half, Eve and Gerald brought him home – by this time he was in good health.

Both extended families were living hundreds of miles away, and Eve and Gerald said they had very little in the way of practical and child care help from the local authority, even after Joshua was born. They found it hard to get babysitters and by the time Stephen was seven, Eve and Gerald requested that he be placed in residential care nearby – he had become very demanding emotionally and had behaviour difficulties. Eve and Gerald felt the strain on family members was adversely affecting Eve's health and the development of Louise and Joshua. Stephen seemed to settle well in the residential unit (having been received into care under Section 2, Child Care Act 1980), and Eve and Gerald were pleased with the arrangement, having their son home to stay regularly at weekends and during holidays. When it became clear that they did not envisage being able to resume full-time care of Stephen in the foreseeable future, the local authority informed them of their policy to place for adoption all children who were not returning to the care of their parents within two years.

Eve and Gerald felt they had no option but to agree to this plan, although they stated that this would be conditional upon their being able to maintain contact with Stephen, who was then eight. A year later, Stephen was placed with Doreen and William, a white couple who were experienced adoptive parents and who had been approved by a voluntary agency. There had been no plan for face-to-face contact when

Stephen was adopted, but subsequently, Doreen and William had invited Stephen's family to visit. Thereafter, Eve and Gerald, with their other children, had visited twice-yearly, and this was continuing at the time of the 1991 interviews.

Contact with Eve and Gerald was made on my behalf by the voluntary agency which had placed Stephen and I visited the family at their home. In their response to my letter, Eve wrote: 'We are willing to be interviewed as we think it has been important for us to be able to keep contact with Stephen for the rest of our lives.' Describing his being adopted and their feelings about Stephen was an emotional experience for all four family members. The observations of the parents and of the children are recorded separately.

How the adoption process was experienced

Following the local authority decision to place Stephen for adoption, Eve and Gerald had very little contact from Stephen's social worker, although they maintained regular contact with their son and attended reviews during the twelve months or so while an adoptive placement was sought. On the one occasion when Eve attended a review on her own, she was informed that the family could have Stephen home for a long week-end, as usual, for his birthday, three weeks later, but that introductions to prospective adoptive would begin a week after that and there would be no further contact.

Eve cried when she described her feelings on coming away from the meeting: confusion, anger, distress and helplessness. She felt the social worker should have made a point of preparing her and Gerald for the fact that an adoptive family had been selected and to ensure that both were present at the review. Subsequently, they were shown a video of the prospective adoptive family and met Doreen and William at the residential unit during the introductions. Gerald commented that they would have liked more participation in the planning and they were not clear whether, had they had any reservations on meeting the prospective adopters, these would have been taken into account.

It had been particularly distressing to learn, after the placement had been made, that their social worker had never informed the voluntary agency social worker of their wish to maintain contact with Stephen. Eve described the senior social worker as negative regarding the possibility of contact and the social worker as 'ineffectual': 'It would have helped if she could only have understood why we wanted to keep in touch with Stephen and looked at our track record – we had always maintained contact in a responsible way.' They were told that their request for news of Stephen was 'unfair' to the adoptive parents. Eve and Gerald recalled how distressed Louise had been when she realised she might never see Stephen again.

When it came to signing the agreement to adoption, Eve and Gerald felt they were in a dilemma: they did not want to disrupt Stephen's placement with William and Doreen but were desperately upset at the prospect of losing touch with him for ever. The adoption hearing was adjourned twice while Eve and Gerald sought legal advice and discussed their reservations with the guardian *ad litem*. They wondered whether they could hire a private detective to find out where Stephen was and whether he was progressing well. Eventually, the voluntary agency social worker had discussion with William and Doreen and they agreed to maintain contact by letter. On that basis, Gerald and Eve signed the adoption papers. Although subsequently, they had been able to see Stephen twice a year, Gerald described the pain of parting with a child for adoption as being 'worse than a bereavement – like a continual bereavement'.

Eve's and Gerald's relationship with Doreen and William and with Stephen

Although Eve's and Gerald's first meeting with Doreen and William had occurred in distressing circumstances for them – in that they expected never to see Stephen again – they recalled having liked them and having immediately felt confident that Stephen would do well in their care. Because they had realised by then that Doreen and William had not known of their request to stay in touch, they did not hold negative feelings towards them about contact being ended.

Doreen and William had found the pre-placement meeting helpful in that they had gained an understanding of the birth parents' difficulties and had liked them. They felt the local authority's decision regarding adoption had been 'rather drastic'. As a result, when following the adoption Gerald and Eve had written to the adoption agency seeking news of

Stephen, Doreen and William had suggested they visit. Both sets of parents felt the relationship had developed well thereafter.

Gerald had wondered if Doreen had felt anxious initially, as they noticed that if William was out she always invited her adult daughter to be there. Doreen had (in 1987) acknowledged feeling apprehensive before Eve, Gerald and the children had visited for the first time, not because she did not trust them but because she thought they were "upper class" and might be disappointed with her home. However, this had not proved to be a problem and in 1991, Doreen and William described Eve and Gerald as 'exceptional people. We got on well from the start . . . It's no hardship to have them. They make themselves at home and always bring presents for all the children, not just for Stephen. They're just like friends.'

Eve acknowledged the considerable differences between the two families in terms of occupational background and accommodation, but felt these were not important: 'We value what William and Doreen can offer Stephen. We have all become more relaxed over the years. There's such a friendly atmosphere – it's just like visiting our extended family.' Eve and Gerald felt there was no tension or rivalry between the two families. They felt quite confident about the adoptive parents' handling of Stephen and had 'never felt the need to interfere' – they would do so only if they were gravely concerned about Stephen's welfare.

When asked about their role in Stephen's life and his relationship with them, Gerald felt that 'like a godparent' was the most apt description: 'We are concerned about his welfare and although we don't participate in the day-to-day decisions, we would be there if anything happened.' Eve said that Stephen was always pleased to see them. Doreen had told them that Stephen got excited when he knew they were coming and called them mummy and daddy (this is how Doreen and William referred to them – they had initially signed cards, etc, using their first names). William recalled having wondered at the outset whether Stephen might wish to leave with his birth family when they visited, but this had never happened: 'Stephen remembered them when they came the first time and he realises they're special, that they're his, but he treats them like other visitors. Visits don't unsettle him.'

The difference made by contact

Eve and Gerald felt that they and their other two children had been helped enormously by their ongoing contact with Stephen. They had the reassurance of seeing him progress and this had helped them to feel more reconciled to his having to be adopted: 'We have been exceptionally lucky. We have the best of both worlds. We know Stephen is happy and well cared for while we are freed from the stress and worry of his day-to-day care.' In addition, Eve and Gerald felt that contact had been helpful to them and to Louise and Joshua in their adjustment to the loss of a family member. Gerald explained: 'Contact enables grieving to be accomplished. Visiting gives us opportunities to talk together about Stephen, to share our sadness and keep the matter open.'

The main benefit Eve and Gerald saw for Stephen, in view of his limited understanding about the complexities of adoption, was continuity. He had had many changes of carer prior to his placement for adoption and they felt it was important that they did not appear to have abandoned him. Also, they valued the preservation of the relationship between Stephen and his sister and brother – not just for his sake but also for theirs.

Current feelings

Eve and Gerald said that the adoption of Stephen was a continuing source of pain for family members – particularly for Eve and for Joshua. But contact had removed some of their feelings of guilt by reassuring them that they had been "justified" in relinquishing his care to another family, and they felt the pain involved in contact was healthier than the pain of not knowing. Eve's father had disapproved of Stephen's placement for adoption, but was pleased that contact had been maintained and forwarded presents for his birthday and at Christmas. Some of their friends had been embarrassed about Stephen's adoption and seemed to prefer that they did not talk about it. On the other hand, others would enquire about his progress, particularly those who were practising Christians and two or three who were social workers.

Eve commented: 'Having Stephen has changed me.' She felt she had become less judgmental on a range of issues – previously she had probably shared to some extent 'the stereotyped view that "bad" parents reject a child for adoption while "good" parents accept'. Both Eve and Gerald felt there was a stigma associated with parting with a child for adoption, and that they were to some degree affected by this, even though they now believed this had been right for Stephen. Eve still became upset when talking about Stephen but would always acknowledge him. For example if asked how many children she had, she would always reply: 'I have two sons and a daughter. Stephen has been adopted.' Gerald, however, said it would depend on the circumstances as to whether he mentioned Stephen or not.

Overall feelings about adoption and contact

Neither Eve nor Gerald could think of any negative aspects of having maintained contact, for themselves or for any of their children, and they hoped there were no disadvantages for Doreen and William. They commented: 'Stephen will always be a part of our lives' and they were confident that Louise and Joshua would always be concerned for Stephen. While recognising the love and care offered by Doreen and William and their extended families, they felt their continuing interest was valuable because 'we belong to him'. For them, contact evoked pain as well as providing reassurance but Eve added: 'Pain is part of accepting the situation.'

As to the future, they hoped to be able to maintain the current level of contact and to give any support they could to the adoptive family. They had considered inviting all the members of the adoptive family to stay with them for a holiday but had not done so in case revisiting his former home proved unsettling to Stephen. They thought they might do so in a year or so, when they hoped to have moved. They had no expectation that Stephen would ever leave his adoptive home and return to live with them (although, unfortunately, an adoptive parent who was a friend of Doreen's and who disapproved of continuing contact had suggested to her that they might 'claim Stephen back' when he reached 18).

Overall, Gerald and Eve felt adoption with contact had worked out particularly well for their family. And it was because they thought that local authority social workers, in deciding to terminate contact, had failed to consider the needs of their three children, that they particularly wanted me to interview Louise and Joshua.

Louise and Joshua

Louise had been 13 and Joshua five when Stephen had been placed for adoption. However, he had already been living in a residential setting for nearly two years. Joshua and Stephen were described by both their parents and by Louise as having been close companions when Stephen had lived at home full time, as his developmental delay diminished the significance of the age gap between the boys. Joshua had maintained this attachment despite the separation (which had been lessened by the weekends and holidays Stephen had spent at home).

Doreen and William had recalled in 1987 that when Eve, Gerald and the children had visited Stephen for the first time after the adoption, he had been particularly pleased to see Joshua, who had cried when it was time to go and had said he did not want to leave Stephen. Louise was thoughtful and self-possessed during the interview. Joshua was serious in his attitude and very near to tears on occasions. Both had a very open attitude and I gained the impression that Stephen was often spoken of within the family.

The impact of Stephen's adoption

Louise stated that her parents had involved her in discussions about Stephen being adopted. She remembered 'tensions and arguments and a lot of pain around the whole thing causing stress. Mum and dad were edgy.' Her parents had made it clear all along that they wanted contact and Louise had not realised at the time that this might not have been possible. She had been used to Stephen not being around much and did not remember 'being really upset at the time of his adoption'. Louise said she had 'no reservations about Stephen being adopted'. She did not feel embarrassed about people knowing she had a "mentally handicapped" brother who had been adopted, although it would depend on the context as to whether she included him when asked about her family.

Joshua remembered knowing that Stephen was to live with Doreen and William, but he did not understand at the time what adoption meant. However he recalled that 'mum and dad were hyped up about the adoption'. He had assumed they would continue to see Stephen, as had happened in the residential unit, and it was only recently that he had realised contact usually ended with adoption. When he was eight or nine, Joshua had begun to 'think it strange that I had a brother who was not near me. And how different my life would be if Stephen had been living at home.' Joshua was much more definite than his sister about including Stephen if asked about brothers and sisters: 'I always say one brother and one sister. Stephen is still my brother. We still have a lot to do with Stephen. We often talk about him.'

Contact

When asked to describe how she felt about contact, Louise said she had only missed one visit to Stephen, when she could not get out of another commitment. However, 'part of me doesn't want to visit. There's so much pain involved – mainly for mum and Joshua, less so for dad and me. I feel it's our duty to go – we owe it to ourselves. Afterwards, I'm always glad we've gone.' If contact had not been allowed, Louise thought she would have worried about Stephen and would have been angry. She was uncertain as to the effects of contact on Stephen: 'I'm not sure whether Stephen needs to see us as much as we need to see him. He gets excited and I believe he looks forward to our visit, but maybe it's just an interruption to his routine.'

Joshua described his feelings about contact vividly: 'I always have the same feeling when I leave. Is he going to be OK while I'm not there? I feel upset for a few minutes after we leave. It's quite worrying, leaving him. When I get back, I re-live leaving him. But I know he's happy and content. I know he's in good hands. He seems natural there. I'd rather go than not go at all.' Joshua found it hard to imagine what it would have been like if he had not seen Stephen once he had been placed for adoption – he supposed he would have got used to not having a brother. He did not think he would have felt angry but 'it would have been distressing to lose all contact. I think a mixture of upset and frustration. I would have been very worried about Stephen. If I wasn't allowed to see him, I'd worry about him more.'

Like Louise, Joshua was not sure about the effect of contact on Stephen. He believed that 'because he's mentally handicapped, Stephen looks on Doreen and William as his mum and dad and us as close people.' He was pleased that Stephen referred to Louise and himself as his sister and brother, even though their relationship was 'more like cousins'. He added: 'We're not just visitors – we make more fuss of Stephen'.

The future

Louise saw herself as continuing to visit with other family members, rather than independently and added that 'perhaps I'm being protective of myself'. In the longer term, Louise thought she would definitely want to help financially and to visit, without being 'too heavily involved, although if the chips were down, I couldn't say no to looking after him myself. When Stephen moves into adult accommodation, I would certainly want to keep close tabs on him.' Joshua commented: 'This sounds awful. I probably wouldn't think about him as much as I do now. But I would not put Stephen out of my life. I would have to go and see him.'

By way of final comment, Louise said: 'Open adoption has been fantastic for us. Doreen is an amazing person and Stephen has been very happy there. If Stephen had just been taken away without contact, there would have been guilt. I'd feel we'd have let Stephen and ourselves down. Not visiting Stephen would have been denying the problem instead of dealing with it.' Joshua was briefer: 'I'm glad Stephen is not locked out of our lives. I feel I have a right to see him.'

In 1987, Doreen and William had identified Louise and Joshua as a potential source of support for Stephen in the future: 'He has gained a new family without having to lose his original one. When we and Eve and Gerald have died, he will still have his brother and sister to care about him.' The comments made by Louise and Joshua in the interview would seem to justify their confidence about this.

III IAN

I interviewed Ian at his home. He and his wife Anna, who had lived separately for almost three years, had three children – Jamie, then aged 12, Charlotte, aged nine and Sophie, six. By the time Jamie was four months old, it had become clear that he had profound learning difficulties. Later, physical disabilities became apparent also. At the time of the interview, Jamie was unable to sit without support and was thought not to recognise people with whom he came into daily contact, such as the physiotherapists. During his early years, in the absence of any diagnosis (possibly birth injury), Jamie's potential was uncertain. Ian gave up his job as a statistician in order to spend more time with Jamie, while Anna continued her full-time work as a solicitor. Anna was an African woman from Kenya and the family's main source of practical and emotional support when the three children were young was Anna's aunt, who was living nearby. The relatives of Ian, a white man from Dublin, were too far away to be consistently involved. Caring for Jamie proved very stressful for the family and from the age of five, he was attending a residential school from Monday to Friday.

Ian and Anna had got to know Carol and Rob, who eventually adopted Jamie, because at one time, before they moved, they had attended the same Catholic church. Carol and Rob had already adopted a child with severe disabilities and Carol had at one stage mentioned that they would be willing to care for Jamie if the family reached the point at which they could no longer cope. When Jamie was six, the paediatric consultant caring for him told Anna and Ian that his disabilities were so profound that he would not be adversely affected emotionally by being cared for outside the family and that such an arrangement would benefit Charlotte and Sophie. Eventually, after the local authority had first advertised for alternative adoptive parents, Jamie was placed with Carol and Rob, a white couple, when he was seven. All arrangements for contact were negotiated directly between the two families.

Initially, Jamie spent one weekend in six with Ian and Anna in order to give Carol and Rob some respite. In addition, Ian and Anna visited at least once a month and this had been the pattern of contact when I met Carol and Rob in 1987. The two families attended celebrations together – for example, Jamie's four parents had been present when Jamie had made his first Holy Communion at a special service. Subsequently, with the ending of their marriage, weekend stays had ended and Ian's visits became more frequent while Anna's contact lessened considerably. Following the return of her aunt to Kenya in 1990, Anna had not visited at all, but telephoned to enquire about Jamie's progress. Ian continued to visit at least once a month, sometimes more, bringing Charlotte and Sophie with him (the girls were living full time with their mother but visited their father fortnightly).

Carol and Rob had forwarded a letter on my behalf to Ian about the possibility of an interview (they did not feel they could contact Anna because they had not seen her for over 18 months and felt her ending of face-to-face contact derived from her distress about Jamie's disabilities). In agreeing to meet me, Ian wrote: 'The circumstances of our adoption are unusual in the UK but not among the (tribal group to which Anna belonged). The norm in that society remains the extended family.'

Like the other birth parents whom I met, Ian described painful experiences and at times this was evidently distressing. However, unlike them, it had not been the process of adoption which had been painful but rather the severity of Jamie's disabilities and the impact on family relationships of caring for him. The ending of his marriage and Anna's limited contact with Jamie subsequently seemed to have been particularly hurtful.

The process of adoption

When Ian and Anna were considering adoption for Jamie, they received considerable emotional support from his paediatric consultant, who reassured them that Jamie 'would not miss us'. This had helped Ian to 'let go any feelings of guilt'. His and Anna's preference would have been for foster care rather than adoption (in keeping with the practice within Anna's culture), but they could understand why Carol and Rob wished to adopt rather than foster Jamie and respected this. The only alternative for Jamie's care was a specialist children's home more than a hundred miles away, and in the circumstances 'adoption was a positive choice'. Because Carol and Rob had offered to care for Jamie in the past, Ian viewed adoption without any sense of shame or stigma – it seemed like an extended family arrangement. Rather than feeling that to request alternative care for Jamie was an admission of "failure", Ian described adoption as 'a release – we were exhausted by caring for Jamie'.

Having requested placement within an alternative family for Jamie, Ian and Anna felt they had no choice but to go along with the local authority plan to advertise for adoptive parents. However, they were clear that they would have wanted to be involved in the choice of any adoptive family and to have offered the adopters ongoing support and help: 'I could not imagine this would not be accepted.' Ian and Anna would not have agreed to Jamie's placement with adoptive parents who would not have welcomed contact. In the event, the local authority agreed to place Jamie (who had been received into care under Section 2 of the Child Care Act 1980) with Carol and Rob via the voluntary agency which had placed their older child with them.

Ian's relationship with Carol and Rob and with Jamie

When interviewed in 1987, Carol and Rob had spoken of Ian and Anna as friends. They described them as 'very good parents, who want the best for Jamie' and described their relationship as one of 'trust and confidence'. Carol and Rob acknowledged several differences between the two families in terms of race, culture and educational background, but they and Anna shared a strong religious faith and there was mutual respect. By 1991, their contact with Anna was limited to telephone and written contact but their friendship with Ian was described as having strengthened over the years. During the previous summer, he had stayed with his daughters in a cottage near where the adoptive family were holidaying.

It was clear that Ian felt as warmly towards the adoptive family. He spoke of 'mutual liking and acceptance' and described how much Sophie enjoyed visiting and playing with children in the family who were of similar age – indeed he sometimes arranged for her to spend a Saturday there. Ian felt that Sophie and Charlotte and the daughter born to Carol and Rob were in some ways sisters, since they were all sisters to Jamie. Over time, Ian's friendship with Carol and Rob had deepened and he felt there was no rivalry or tension between them. While Ian wanted to offer any support he could, he accepted that adoption had 'curtailed' his parental responsibility and he would not interfere. He had complete confidence in the care provided within the family (this was important to Carol and Rob, as Jamie's physical health had shown some deterioration and they were relieved to know that neither parent blamed them in any way). With regard to differences of race and culture, Ian said this was a 'difficult' area on which to comment. However, because of Jamie's very limited understanding, Ian did not feel there had been any adverse effects from his being placed in a white family.

It was acknowledged by Ian that he was not a significant person in Jamie's life: indeed, he knew there was doubt as to whether Jamie recognised him. According to Carol, this had been so from the time Jamie was placed with them, although she had wondered in 1987 whether Jamie knew Anna's voice. Ian regarded his role with Jamie as being like a member of the extended family, interested in his progress and welfare and he had been named by Carol and Rob as testamentary guardian.

The difference made by contact

Ian commented that a major benefit for him of contact after Jamie's adoption had been 'delight at seeing him alive'. In his experience, contact entailed 'a mixture of pain, satisfaction and delight. It would be sad to deny birth parents this.' He thought that without contact, the pain associated with a situation like Jamie's would still be evoked, perhaps by a television programme, but that would be more likely to be 'unmixed pain'. Moreover, contact enabled him to play a continuing role in Jamie's life, even though his son was not aware of this, through being supportive to Carol and Rob: 'I know Jamie and care about him. I understand the problems of caring for him. I am an interested audience.' Speaking generally, as well as about his own situation, Ian commented: 'Birth parents have the key to unlock the door to events in the child's early years.' Clearly there were fewer direct benefits to Jamie from Ian's commitment to contact but he hoped that he had helped Jamie by providing continuity.

Current feelings

At the time of the interview Ian was feeling that the pain of letting Jamie go was eased by his awareness of his son's needs and his confidence that these were being met within the adoptive family. He felt able to be completely open with people about Jamie and his circumstances and would always speak of having a son as well as two daughters (whereas he knew that Anna spoke only of the girls, unless with friends or relatives who already knew about Jamie). Because he had been 'educated in the Classics', he regarded adoption as having a 'long and respectable history and tradition' and felt that it was only in recent times that societies such as those in the UK had stigmatised adoption because of its associations with illegitimacy. Ian had not felt aware of criticism or condemnation by other people.

It was important to Ian that Charlotte and Sophie knew that although

Jamie was being cared for and had been adopted by another family, 'he is still part of us'. He acknowledged that Charlotte found visiting Jamie more difficult than Sophie, and that Anna was not entirely happy with his taking the girls with him. However, Carol and Rob were impressed with the way Ian had helped the girls to understand about Jamie and that they made cards and brought little presents for him.

Overall feelings

On balance, given that he could not have continued to look after Jamie within the family, Ian believed adoption had worked out well for his son and for himself and his daughters. Explaining why some time earlier he and Anna had decided not to pursue litigation to obtain compensation for Jamie's (probable) birth injury, he said: 'The outcome might have been a large sum of money. But that would have been "Fool's gold" compared with the real gold of the care offered by Carol and Rob – which money can't buy.'

With regard to contact, Ian felt that the pain which 'must be there' would be hard to manage or even be 'unstoppable' had he not been able to continue to visit Jamie. Drawing on his own experience, he felt that an adopted child could only gain from the continuing involvement of a 'concerned person: it's a birth parent's instinct to be protective and supportive and it must be a privilege for adoptive parents to be able to count on their involvement'.

IV CATHY

Cathy, a white woman of Scottish descent, had been brought up in a convent children's home from the age of three. Her father had placed her there following her mother's suicide and had then disappeared. Cathy could not remember him. She had no brothers or sisters, as far as she was aware, and the only relative she had known while growing up was a paternal aunt who had died when she was 17. Knowing 'nothing of the facts of life', she became pregnant at 18, while living in a hostel, and married the father of the baby she was expecting. Cathy had four children in rapid succession and having no experience of child care or of running a home, no support from relatives, and a husband who 'drank the dole money', she became overwhelmed with exhaustion, financial problems and a sense of inadequacy. She turned to the Social Services Department for help. The four children, then ranging in age from 15 months to five years, were received into care (Section 1, Children Act 1948) and placed together as the youngest in a family group home run by a voluntary organisation with a Christian focus.

Soon afterwards, Cathy left the marital home in order to separate from her husband. She found visiting her children very distressing: sometimes they would be clinging and cry when she left; sometimes it seemed as if they ignored her and could not care less whether she came or not. Cathy felt she could not possibly provide as well for the children materially as "the home" and that the staff discouraged her contact (this was confirmed by the social worker who had become involved with her many years later when the home was due to close). Furthermore, she found it impossible to obtain private or council accommodation large enough for her to take discharge of the children. In any event, this possible course of action was pre-empted by the council's assumption of parental rights and duties (via a Section 2 resolution) on the grounds that the children had been in care for more than three years. There appeared to have been no active attempt by the Social Services Department to restore the children to her care.

When the youngest child was ten and the oldest 15, the home was due to close. By this time, Cathy was visiting only three or four times a year. She was living in a one-bedroom flat with her second husband. It was planned that the two youngest children should be placed together for adoption and the oldest with foster carers. The question of Cathy resuming care of the children was apparently not considered at that stage by either Cathy or the social workers. Cathy was strongly opposed to adoption (although not to foster care). In the event, the youngest child, Rachel, then 11, was placed on her own with foster carers with a view to adoption, as her sister, 18 months older, had decided after the first introductory visit, that she would prefer to stay in the children's home until it finally closed. Subsequently, she was placed with foster carers a year later with another sister, and the oldest sibling, the only boy, moved to a hostel.

Gareth and Jane, Rachel's prospective adoptive parents, had been willing to care for a child on a permanent basis while maintaining contact with members of the family of origin. They had met Rachel's three older siblings at the children's home during introductions. After she had been placed, Rachel's contact with her sisters and brother and with Cathy took place at the children's home. Their birth father had not been in touch with them for several years and his whereabouts were unknown. Gareth and Jane were not introduced to Cathy.

A year or so after placement, Rachel said she would like to be adopted. Cathy was opposed to this, but said she would give agreement if she were satisfied that Rachel was not being "pressurised" by Gareth and Jane. At around this time, Cathy and her husband moved to a house nearer the adoptive home and this made Gareth and Jane anxious – unnecessarily, as they later realised. There followed a meeting between Rachel and Cathy at the children's home at which Rachel became very upset. In order to reassure Cathy, and to provide a more relaxed atmosphere for Rachel, Gareth and Jane invited her to visit their home. When she was 13, Rachel was adopted with Cathy's agreement.

At the time of the 1987 interview, Rachel was visiting her mother quite regularly, sometimes as often as once a week (the journey took about ten minutes by bike). Often she would be dropped off by Gareth and collected later. Rachel's sisters and brother were also made welcome in the adoptive home. Four years later, when Rachel was 19, the pattern of contact was much the same, although Rachel had no need of lifts, having an old car of her own!

It was through Rachel that my interview with Cathy was negotiated. I met Cathy's husband only briefly as I was leaving. Cathy told me she had welcomed the opportunity to talk over her experience of adoption. She was tearful on several occasions as she described how she had been deprived of bringing up any of her children. Her contact with her older children was currently less than she would have liked, and much less than with Rachel, although she had been the only one to have been adopted. All were living independently and one daughter had married. Ironically, at the time we met, Cathy had a very responsible job as a carer in a small residential unit for young people with severe learning difficulties and she commented that she wished she could have had the opportunity to spend as much time with her own children when they were growing up.

The process of adoption

Cathy prefaced her comments about adoption by recalling the many years of sadness and distress she had experienced as a result of having her children in care from an early age. She had been very aware of stigma and condemnation and had learned not to confide in anyone. Thus she had already been feeling inadequate and powerless when she was asked about the possibility of Rachel being adopted. Cathy described this as traumatic. Her opposition to Rachel being adopted was in part because she felt it would be wrong to cut her off from her brothers and sisters and she was worried as to whether she fully understood the implications of adoption. Not having met Gareth and Jane, she was suspicious and resentful: were they 'pushing Rachel into it?' Cathy described herself as 'not wanting to let go' and feared that Gareth and Jane were 'taking Rachel off me'. At this time, Cathy received emotional support from her husband, who pointed out that Rachel would not thank her for standing in her way, and from the adoption social worker. Having met Gareth and Jane, she felt appreciative of the care they were giving Rachel. Although she would have preferred Rachel to have remained as a foster child, she did not want to cause Rachel and her adoptive parents distress by contesting the application. However, she would not have been able to give agreement had she not been assured by Gareth and Jane that they would have no objection to Rachel keeping in touch with her and with her sisters and brother. This was also true for Rachel who told me that if contact would end with adoption, 'That would have upset me. I wouldn't have got adopted.' Cathy was particularly pleased that Rachel had chosen to keep her family name as a middle name.

Cathy's relationship with Gareth and Jane and with Rachel

Looking back, Cathy thought it would have been helpful if she had met Gareth and Jane much earlier, for their sake as well as hers. She had the impression that they had an expectation of what she would be like as a parent of children in care. When she visited the adoptive home, by invitation, for the first time, she thought from Jane's expression when she opened the door that 'she had been expecting a tramp'. Cathy described the relationship between her and Gareth and Jane as 'strained at first', but gradually tensions lessened, particularly after the adoption. Gareth and Jane also wished they could have met Cathy sooner (they had met the birth mother of the second child they adopted before introductions had begun). Jane referred to 'mutual suspicion' before they met and acknowledged that she (but not Gareth) had felt 'threatened' by her uncertainty about Cathy. She realised how difficult the first visit had been for Cathy: 'It was very brave of her to visit on her own.' Subsequently trust had developed and they had involved her more, for example, by inviting her to Rachel's confirmation. In 1987 and again in 1991, Gareth and Jane had described Cathy as 'supportive, not undermining'.

Cathy was more diffident when asked to describe her current relationship with Gareth and Jane. She felt they were all working well together for Rachel's sake, but found it easier to relate to Gareth. Although she felt sure that Jane was supportive of Rachel's relationship with her, she found her 'less forthcoming' than Gareth and wondered 'whether Jane liked her'. Although she appreciated being invited for special occasions to the adoptive home, Cathy did not much like going there: 'I feel like an intruder.' However, Rachel seemed unaware of any tensions and told me, with evident satisfaction: 'My mum likes Gareth and Jane and they like her.'

Cathy felt closer to Rachel than to any of her other children. She appreciated Rachel's sensitivity to her feelings, for example, although she referred to Gareth's parents as grandad and grandma, she always spoke of Gareth and Jane by their first names and not as mum and dad. Cathy saw herself as 'still Rachel's mum even though she's got another mum and dad'. However, she did not anticipate that Rachel would ever want to come and live with her and thought her role was that of a non-parental relative. As an illustration of this, she described a humiliating experience when she had attended the wedding of her oldest daughter a few months previously. Her son-in-law had asked her to stand aside when the photographs were being taken and to sit at the back after the registrar had called her forward as the mother of the bride. However, in recognition of her different status in relation to Rachel, she said: 'I'd take a back seat at her wedding. Her adoptive parents should be the ones to be there with her – they've cared for her all these years.'

By coincidence, in the interview with me, Rachel had also referred to seating arrangements should she get married. Explaining why she had kept her original family name and added her adoptive parents' name, she said: 'I want them all there in the front row at my wedding – my adoptive parents and (my adoptive brother), my mum and my brother and sisters. It would sound stupid if my brother and sisters were there and I did not have the same name.' Asked what difference adoption had made to her relationship with Cathy, Rachel commented: 'I still think of her as my real mum. I see her a lot more than I did in the children's home. I go much more often than my brother and sisters, which is funny, as I'm the one who's been adopted.'

It was evident that Cathy had worked very hard at supporting Gareth and Jane as the parents with the authority to set limits and exercise discipline. Rachel had told me that in the past she had been quite manipulative, telling Gareth and Jane that she would 'run to my real mum' and also complaining on occasions to Cathy that her adoptive parents had punished her too severely. Gareth had felt quite confident that Cathy would not allow herself to be manipulated: 'We know and Rachel knows that she'd send her straight back if she ran to her.' However, Cathy had sometimes felt her loyalties divided: was she 'betraying' Rachel by not interfering? She had gradually come to appreciate that Rachel had not been an easy young person to manage and that the adoptive parents' approach, which she had initially thought too strict, had been good for her (her husband had pointed out that she was wanting to compensate the children for all the years they had been away, and she had not been strict enough with the others if they had come to stay for a few days, with the result that they had got out of hand). Cathy said she had only once queried with Gareth his handling of a problem, and when he had explained, she had seen his point of view. Thus although it was sometimes difficult for her, she 'would never take Rachel's part' against the adoptive parents: 'Rachel may have a moan, but she knows I'll support Gareth and Jane.' Overall, she felt this had worked: 'Rachel's turned out to be more thoughtful and more hardworking than any of the others.' And it had not resulted in resentment on Rachel's part: 'I think she looks forward to coming – she calls in most weeks, even if it's only for five minutes.'

The difference made by contact

Unusually, as described above, Rachel's contact with Cathy had increased after her adoption. This, together with the greater self-confidence Cathy had achieved through her work as a carer, had gone some way to lessen the 'shame' she felt about her 'failure' as a mother. Cathy had the reassurance of knowing of Rachel's progress; she was particularly pleased that with her adoptive parents' help, she had worked steadily since leaving school and was highly regarded by her employers. Furthermore, while recognising the limited role she could play in Rachel's life, she hoped Rachel knew that she was 'there for her'.

In considering the impact of contact on Rachel, what Cathy felt to be most important was that she knew of Cathy's continuing concern and, particularly, that she had an accurate understanding of the circumstances leading to her admission to care and the reasons for Cathy's agreeing to adoption. Cathy believed that sometimes adopted people were given negative information about their birth parents and led to believe that they had been rejected. Contact had given Cathy the opportunity to explain something of her difficulties when the children were small and to assure Rachel that by giving agreement to adoption, she was not 'throwing her out' (indeed when I spoke with Rachel I was impressed by her level of understanding on these points, and Cathy would have been reassured to hear that Rachel felt pleased, rather than rejected, by Cathy's agreement to the adoption).

It was acknowledged by Cathy that Gareth's and Jane's encouragement of contact between Rachel and her birth relatives had been crucial; she had been particularly impressed by the fact that when she had learned that her first husband was terminally ill, Gareth had taken Rachel to see her father in hospital – their first meeting for fourteen years. Furthermore, Cathy knew that her other children were made to feel welcome when they visited the adoptive home. Because of the co-operation between the adoptive parents and herself, Cathy did not believe Rachel experienced divided loyalties. My discussion with Rachel seemed to confirm this: the good relationship, as she experienced it, between Cathy and Gareth and Jane, had contributed to her feeling relaxed about maintaining contact.

Current feelings

As far as Rachel's adoption was concerned, Cathy had 'no regrets'.

However she felt a continuing sense of loss and sadness that she had been unable to 'be a proper mother' to her children, particularly as it seemed to her that the oldest children were growing further away from her, emotionally and physically. Cathy did not believe they had such a good understanding as Rachel about the circumstances which had led to their reception into care and that their resentment showed itself in their contacting her only when they wanted material help. Furthermore, having no close relatives, Cathy felt isolated and could not share her sadness with friends or colleagues because of her strong sense of stigma. However, Cathy's husband was supportive.

Overall

'I now realise that Rachel's adoption was for the best – she's happy.' Cathy could think only of advantages, for everyone concerned, in contact after adoption, and hoped Rachel would continue to see her on a regular basis. Cathy had told Rachel to think of her as 'another mum' – someone she could always turn to (although Cathy recognised, and valued for Rachel's sake, the strong attachment she felt for her adoptive mother). Contact had provided many benefits for Cathy: the reassurance of knowing that Rachel was happy and understood her perspective; the opportunity to offer support if this were ever needed in the future; and therefore, the sense that she had not entirely 'failed as a mother'.

V ADOPTIVE PARENTS' AND YOUNG PEOPLE'S PERCEPTIONS OF THE EXPERIENCE OF CONTACT FOR BIRTH PARENTS

A number of common themes run through the first-hand accounts of the birth parents in four families described above. There now follows a summary of the observations made by adoptive parents in 1987 and in 1991, and by some of the adopted young people who were interviewed, about the effects of contact on birth parents.

The birth parents who were interviewed spoke of the pain associated with adoption, although in Ian's case it was Jamie's disability and the impact of this which had caused the most acute distress.

Adoptive parents in 22 families who had been interviewed in 1987 were caring for children who, between them, had 24 sets of birth parents.

Excluding the birth parents in four families who have spoken for themselves, adoptive parents were aware that birth parents in 16 families had experienced distress in relation to their child's adoption. This was not necessarily linked with whether a contested adoption was envisaged – as Beverley's account had highlighted. However, in 12 instances, the fact that birth parents intended to oppose an adoption application or withhold agreement was sufficient to indicate to adoptive parents that birth parents were finding the prospect of losing their child through adoption upsetting. In four families, birth parents were not expected to oppose an application, but there were two instances of one birth parent rejecting a child with disabilities whereas the other probably wished to care for the child; one birth mother would only sign the agreement form once her son had told her himself that he wished to be adopted; and the birth mother of Janine and Andrew, as described in Chapter 3, showed evident distress at contact meetings.

Adoptive parents in four families had been less aware of birth parents being distressed on account of the adoption. In two instances this concerned children with disabilities – one birth mother appeared "flat" emotionally due to medication for a long-standing psychiatric illness, and another had identified adoption as a positive choice for her child and had been able to be involved in the choice of adoptive parents: she felt 'good about being involved'.

When asked about the apparent feelings of birth parents at the time of the first interview, adoptive parents in nine families felt unable to comment because contact was too limited. However, birth parents in seven families were thought to be less distressed than previously (as evidenced by their having given agreement to adoption and meeting the children and the adoptive parents without evident sadness or hostility). It was thought the assurance of continuing contact had been helpful to all these birth parents. In four instances, however, birth parents were still seen to be distressed about the adoption (which took the form of conveying hostility towards the adoptive parents or being obviously upset during meetings).

Adoptive parents believed that contact, whether limited or ongoing, had helped birth parents in twelve families to give agreement to adoption. In the one case in which a birth mother withheld agreement but did not contest the application, as she had originally planned, the adoptive mother described her 'tearfully saying she would not stand in her way' after her daughter had told her at a review that she wished to be adopted. And, as described by Beverley and by Eve and Gerald, there were birth parents in four families who had not been likely to contest the adoption but were apparently enabled to give agreement more readily when they knew contact would not be severed.

Janine and Andrew and three other adopted people who were interviewed – Antoinette and Paul and Nicola – indicated that their birth mothers continued to feel upset in relation to adoption. It would not have been possible to interview Antoinette's mother but when I asked Paul and Nicola about this, Nicola commented that Corine did not like to talk about the adoption: 'I think she's ashamed.'

When asked about the difference contact had made to them, the birth parents interviewed had highlighted particularly the reassurance of knowing that the adoption decision had been right for the child and that he or she was alive and well cared for; some restoration of self-esteem through being able to participate and make a positive contribution, in the adoption arrangements and/or subsequently; being enabled to grieve; helping brothers and sisters who remained at home to understand and deal with the loss; and believing that the child had an appreciation of the circumstances leading to adoption from their point of view.

In 1987, adoptive parents in 13 families had felt able to make some observations about the effect of contact on birth parents in sixteen families: all thought that birth parents had gained in some or all of the ways described by the birth parents interviewed. In two instances adoptive parents thought there might also have been negative aspects: a child's disability being more serious than the birth parents had perhaps anticipated and a birth mother possibly having unrealistic expectations of her daughter's involvement with her. However, it seemed likely that in some of the placements in which the adoptive parents did not feel able to comment (these included those in which there was a poor or hostile relationship between the birth and the adoptive parents), contact had not proved helpful.

Adoptive parents in seven families (in addition to those whose observations have been noted in relation to the birth parents interviewed) felt able to make comments about the impact of contact in 1991. Among this group were adoptive parents in one family who had been uncertain in 1987 but who had since learned from the birth mother how much she felt she had gained. Another adoptive mother believed that contact had increased the self-confidence of a birth mother whose children had been removed from her care when they were born.

The benefit of contact most often cited by the adopted people who were interviewed was that their birth parents knew they were 'getting on OK', as Paul put it. Anil, a young man with disabilities whose circumstances are described in Chapter 5 commented: 'I should think it would have put their minds at rest. It would have reassured them. One disadvantage was that I'd hurt my arm before they came so they didn't see me drive my car. But they know I'm still living.' Another advantage mentioned by Anil was that his brothers and sisters 'now understand about me'.

In the second interview, more adoptive parents referred to birth parents' concerns to know what their children understood about their adoption – perhaps because the children were getting older. Anil's birth mother had asked the adoptive mother whether Anil ever asked about his birth family and if he understood why they had requested adoption. Another birth mother had said to adoptive parents of her son: 'I hope he won't hate me.' This had provided an opportunity for the adoptive parents to reassure her by involving her in a discussion about the circumstances of adoption with their son. A third example concerned a birth mother's question as to whether her children would blame her for having agreed to their adoption. The adoptive mother had assured her that 'they'll thank you for having loved them enough to give agreement'.

With one exception, the adoptive parents interviewed in 1991 described birth parents as having adjusted to their changed role and not continuing to regard themselves as fulfilling parental responsibilities. As the birth parents who had been interviewed had done, adoptive parents most often described birth parents who had ongoing contact as relating like a member of the extended family: speaking of Paul's and Nicola's visits to their birth parents, Jan said that they 'have a wonderful time – it's like being with a favourite aunt and uncle'. However, both Hayley and her adoptive parents described Mary as having continued to see herself as Hayley's parent; comments such as 'I'm still your mum' had been experienced as undermining.

Few of the adoptive parents felt able to comment on birth parents' overall feelings about adoption, recognising the sensitivity of this. Even where there was a relationship described as 'friendship', adoptive parents in only two families (excluding those in the four families referred to in the account of birth parents) said that birth parents confided in them regarding their feelings about adoption issues. However, the majority of adoptive parents who felt positively about contact hoped that this had made the painful aspects of adoption easier for birth parents to bear.

VI SUMMARY

The opportunity to maintain contact with their child who had been adopted had been welcomed and was described as beneficial by the five birth parents who were interviewed. One birth mother was able to contrast her experience of adoption with contact with the "closed" adoption of the baby she had relinquished while a teenager. Whereas the child's adoption with contact provided reassurance, the birth mother had found the adoption of her first child devastating. She had often thought of trying to trace her – not to interfere, but perhaps to see her from a distance and satisfy herself that she was still alive. Her greatest fear was that her child would think she had not been loved, and feel too rejected to consider tracing her. This birth mother had no doubt that the more open models of adoption are of benefit to birth parents and also enhance the self-esteem of adopted children. She planned to register her details on the Contact Register as soon as it became operative (a few months after the interview).

Contact had enabled this small group of birth parents to feel more comfortable about giving agreement to adoption. The negative feelings associated with parting with a child which have been described in the literature in recent years had been experienced in varying degrees by the birth parents and were vividly recalled. However, contact had gone some way to alleviate these feelings. Birth parents' sense of loss and pain had been eased by the reassurance through meetings or through receiving information and photographs that adoption was meeting their child's needs. Some other family members, particularly brothers and sisters, also drew comfort from contact. Ian believed that the stigma commonly associated with adoption in the UK was culturally determined, but the other birth parents described feelings of worthlessness, failure and shame. For them, the experience of being accepted by birth parents and acknowledged as someone important in their child's life had enhanced their self-esteem and lessened these negative feelings.

A sense of powerlessness had affected all the birth parents at some stage during the adoption process, partly because they felt they lacked any real choice in relation to the adoption decision and partly because of the lack of receptiveness of the social workers to their wish for contact. However, being involved in the choice of adopters and/or believing they were making a valued contribution to their child's welfare after adoption had reduced their sense of helplessness. The suggestions made by birth parents about improvements to social work practice are recorded in Appendix III.

The openness of attitude of the adoptive parents, which included their encouraging contact, was especially valued. The good relationship with them which birth parents on the whole described seemed in part attributable to this openness and in part to the sensitivity and respect with which birth parents negotiated contact. They were concerned that their involvement should be beneficial to the child and not undermine the adoptive parents in any way – they likened their role to that of an extended family member or guardian. The benefits which birth parents hoped their children would gain, directly or indirectly, from contact, varied with the child's age and level of understanding. Cathy and Beverley believed that contact would enable their children not to feel they had been rejected and to have a good understanding of the pressures which had resulted in their being adopted.

Beverley, who did not have face-to-face contact, thought Claire would be spared stress and anxiety if she wanted to meet her birth mother in the future, through knowing Beverley's whereabouts and that she would be welcome to contact. Ian and Gerald and Eve were very relieved that contact had enabled Jamie and Stephen respectively to be visited by their siblings who had not been adopted. This had not only been beneficial to those brothers and sisters, but was also seen to provide a safety net in the future for Jamie and Stephen. The brother and sister of Stephen conveyed vividly their belief that they had a right to remain in contact with him, for their sake and his.

The interviews with adoptive parents in 1987 and 1991, and with 15 of the adopted children, suggested that many of the feelings described above had been shared by other birth parents. While some adoptive parents and young people gave examples of how contact had proved helpful to birth parents, particularly in lessening distress over time, it seemed that a few had continued to find adoption upsetting, even when contact appeared to be going well. Some birth parents were reported to have shared concerns as to what their children understood about the circumstances of adoption and whether they would be critical of them for having given agreement to adoption. In twelve instances, adoptive parents believed that contact had helped birth parents to give agreement to adoption and had thus prevented the adoption application being contested. Only one birth parent was described as not having, apparently, adjusted to having a non-parental role in her child's life. A number of the adopted young people believed contact had proved reassuring to their birth parents in that they knew their children were 'getting on OK'.

The experiences and observations summarised above clearly indicate that contact after adoption, in various forms, can prove helpful to birth parents who are adjusting to the loss of their child, while also enabling them to make a positive contribution to his or her future well-being.

5 The experience of contact
Adoptive parents

The material for this chapter derives mainly from the second interviews with adoptive parents in 17 families. However, reference is also made to the earlier interviews to highlight whether views and attitudes had changed in the intervening four years.

As outlined in Chapter 2, adoptive parents in 15 of the 18 families re-interviewed were feeling positively about adoption with contact in 1991. The adoptive parents in the three families who did not perceive contact as having had a positive impact on the placement overall had been among the group of adoptive parents in six families who, in 1987, had described reservations or negative aspects of contact.

The views of Hayley's adoptive parents who felt strongly that contact had not on balance been helpful to their daughter have been outlined in Chapter 3. The adoptive parents of Craig (Hayley's birth brother adopted separately) were uncertain whether contact had contributed to the disruption of the adoption placement. Craig had left the adoptive family towards the end of 1987 when he was aged 14. At the time of the second interview, Craig's adoptive parents were still struggling to make sense of the experience, as reported in Appendix I. Because the disruption had occurred so soon after the 1987 interview, the views of Craig's adoptive parents are referred to only briefly in this chapter. The experiences and perceptions of the adoptive parents in the third family, whose daughter Melanie was being accommodated by the local authority at their request when they were reinterviewed in 1991, are described below.

There follows an account in some detail of the experiences of adoptive parents in four families, to illustrate a range of situations and degree of contact: Melanie was placed as an older child and her birth mother was hostile to the plan for adoption; the birth parents of Michael and Sara (who joined their adoptive family while very young) were also opposed to adoption; Anil had been placed for adoption with his birth parents' agreement and he had met them once, nine years after placement; and Peter had been placed as a teenager with the agreement of significant birth relatives. The adoptive parents in these four families were white. Anil was of Indian descent and so had been placed transracially. The other four children were white. A brief reminder of the circumstances of these four adoptive families is given in Appendix II.

Because they would be so readily identifiable, I have chosen not to write in detail about the only black family in the study. They had been selected by their son's birth mother after she had approached a voluntary adoption agency (in the mid-1970s) requesting an adoptive placement for him with a black family but stipulating that she meet and approve the adoptive parents. The adoptive parents had maintained contact through visiting her and sharing family celebrations over many years. By 1991, when their son was 17, this contact had petered out, but could have been resumed either by him or his birth mother. I have also not indicated which comments and observations were made by the adoptive mothers who were single at the time of the adoption, again to avoid their being identified.

I FOUR ADOPTIVE FAMILIES

Sally and Alun, adoptive parents of Melanie

Sally and Alun had not considered becoming adoptive parents at the time when Melanie came to live with them. They had known Melanie and the other children resident in a local voluntary agency children's home as they were involved as a "social aunt and uncle". They had previously had involvement over many years with a brother and sister who were by then adult and they had been approved as foster carers.

One weekend, there was a crisis in the home because of staffing difficulties. As Melanie's behaviour was particularly disruptive, it was suggested that she be moved. Learning of this, Sally and Alun invited Melanie to stay for three or four days until the situation improved. Melanie was nine and was described at that time to Alun and Sally as 'unfosterable and ineducable'. She had been in and out of local authority care from the age of 18 months, finally becoming subject of a care order when she was three. Thus Sally's and Alun's original involvement was as emergency foster carers. They recalled that Melanie had behaved 'perfectly' for 24 hours, and had asked whether she could call them 'mum' and 'dad'. Then she had 'run riot, kicking and spitting'. However, Melanie did not wish to return to the home and it was agreed to extend the placement, with Sally and Alun believing they 'could not do any worse' than the children's home!

During this time, it was Alun (for practical reasons) who helped maintain the previous pattern of contact between Melanie and her birth mother, Anne, by taking her to visit once a fortnight. Melanie appeared to thrive in the family setting and after some months the placement was confirmed as a permanent fostering arrangement: Sally and Alun had 'become attached' to Melanie and hoped they would be able to cope. Melanie had had 22 previous placements. Over time, contact between Melanie and Anne became less frequent.

It had been explained to Sally and Alun early on that adoption would be out of the question because Anne was opposed to this. However, when she was eleven Melanie had asked to be adopted. Anne, on hearing from Melanie directly that she wished to be adopted, did not oppose the adoption application. However, she withheld agreement, not feeling she could, according to Alun and Sally, 'sign her daughter away'. When the adoption order was eventually granted early in 1987, Melanie was almost 13.

Sally and Alun had moved after the placement and prior to the adoption. At the time of the first interview, they were taking Melanie to visit her birth mother and brother twice a year (a journey of about 200 miles each way). At that stage, Sally and Alun were feeling it was important to maintain contact (although Melanie was said to have told the guardian *ad litem* that if continuing contact would be a bar to adoption, then she would be willing to give up contact). The adoptive parents had described tensions in the relationship between Sally and Anne in the early years, although by the time of the first interview, they felt these were largely in the past.

When reinterviewed in 1991, Sally and Alun reported that for three years they had been experiencing many difficulties with Melanie. In 1988, Melanie had been admitted to the adolescent psychiatric unit in the local hospital and then placed in a boarding school for children of above average intelligence with behavioural and emotional difficulties. Recently, Melanie had again been arrested for theft and was awaiting a court hearing – her third. Shortly before the interview, Sally and Alun had requested that Melanie be accommodated by the local authority as they felt unable to control and safeguard her (there had been some self-harming behaviour). She had told a probation officer that she had never wanted to be adopted, which Sally and Alun had found quite hurtful.

There had been no face-to-face contact with Anne for two years (at Melanie's request). However, there was contact by letter and telephone and Sally and Anne were in regular telephone contact as Anne wished to be kept informed about what was happening to Melanie.

Martin and Joy, adoptive parents of Michael and Sara

When they applied to a social services department adoption agency, Martin and Joy had no children born to them but had already had experience of caring for children through fostering older children. Although Martin's mother had been adopted through a third party arrangement and had grown up knowing her birth mother, Martin and Joy wanted a closed adoption – 'a clean break'.

When their social worker discussed the needs of Michael and Sara with them prior to placement, they were informed that both parents had been diagnosed as 'mentally ill' (indeed they had met while fellow patients at a day centre in a psychiatric hospital) and that a contested adoption was anticipated. Continuing contact had not been envisaged. When placed, Michael was 18 months old and Sara eleven weeks. Both children had been removed from their mother's care within a few days of their birth on a Place of Safety order (Children and Young Persons Act 1969) because of concerns arising from their birth parents' health and low intelligence. Michael and Sara were placed with Joy and Martin before care proceedings had been completed. Relatives of the birth mother, Shelley, were opposing the plan for a care order and placement for adoption but were not offering to care for the children themselves or support Shelley and Sam (the children's father) to do so. Shelley and Sam were not married.

During the protracted legal proceedings, the children were taken by a social worker fortnightly to visit their birth parents and other relatives in a social work office. Sara had moved to live with Martin and Joy from the pre-adoption foster home in which she had been placed from the maternity unit but Michael had had four previous short-term fostering placements. He especially began to find being taken away by the social worker very distressing and after a year or so, Joy suggested that Shelley and Sam visit the children in the adoptive home. Joy received encouragement from their adoption social worker, but Martin was very apprehensive and the children's social worker strongly advised against it, describing the birth parents as 'potentially dangerous'.

The adoption order was eventually granted, with Shelley's agreement, almost five years after placement. Shelley had been willing to give her written agreement, in the presence of the guardian *ad litem*, only in the adoptive home. This was her way of ensuring, according to Joy, that the court knew she was wanting Martin and Joy to be the adopters. However, the guardian was said to have commented to Joy that this was 'highly irregular' and to have asked Shelley whether she had received any payment to persuade her to give her agreement!

At the time of the first interview in 1987, Shelley and Sam were continuing to visit once every six to seven weeks. However, by 1991, when Michael and Sara were aged ten and nine years respectively, visits had become less frequent. Joy had spoken with Shelley and Sam about their meeting with me. Shelley was willing to do so, provided this took place in the adoptive home. However, Sam and Shelley visited only three times in 1991, at relatively short notice, and I was unable to arrange to see Shelley because of work commitments. Sara wanted to participate in the interview with Joy and Martin. However, Michael went off to play soon after my arrival and his parents did not think he would have been willing to be involved.

Sue and Dave, adoptive parents of Anil

Sue and Dave were very experienced in caring for children. Both were involved professionally in child care and they had four other children in the family in addition to Anil (one fostered, one born to them and two adopted). Anil had been born with a life-threatening and disabling medical condition and his parents were informed that he was unlikely to survive. His older brother had serious heart problems and, according to Sue and Dave, his birth parents were advised to focus their attention on him rather than on Anil. When it became clear that Anil would survive, adoption became the plan. Sue and Dave, who lived about a hundred miles from the hospital where Anil was being cared for, were selected as his adoptive parents following extensive advertising. Anil was placed with the family when he was almost three years old.

Sue forwarded information about Anil's progress to his birth parents (whom she had met during the introduction) but had no response. She later learned that they had spent several years abroad, having returned to their country of origin. When Anil was twelve, his birth parents, having returned to the UK, contacted the social services department which had arranged the adoption to enquire after Anil (in particular, whether he was still alive). After discussion with Anil, Sue and Dave invited them to visit. Following that, there had been some letter contact and Anil's birth parents had attempted to visit again, three years later, but the adoptive family had moved.

Anil as well as his adoptive parents were interviewed in 1991. By then Anil was 16, and attending a boarding school able to cater for his health needs. He was achieving well academically. Anil had a busy social life, being quite mobile in a powered wheelchair.

Ruth and James, adoptive parents of Peter

Peter was 20 when I interviewed Ruth and James for the second time. Initially, Peter had agreed to be interviewed also, but then cancelled the appointment and did not rearrange it.

Ruth and James were unusual among the sample of adoptive parents in having approached the voluntary adoption agency with a positive view about maintaining contact after adoption. Peter was then 13 and had been awaiting an adoptive placement for three years (the main obstacle to placement being, according to the agency worker, his wish to maintain contact with his grandmother, Lillian and his mother, Sheila). Peter had been a ward of court but it was not anticipated that his birth mother would oppose an eventual adoption application. He was the youngest by ten or more years of a large family and his mother had never fully recovered from the post-natal depression she had experienced after his birth. Peter's grandmother had been his main carer until she became too frail. From the outset, Peter was able to visit his birth relatives independently, and in 1987, three years after placement, was doing so about once every three weeks.

Peter's later teenage years were experienced by the adoptive parents as quite stressful at times. Apart from the usual issues of control and negotiation, Peter left the family, fairly suddenly, in 1987, to stay with an uncle. He scarcely maintained contact with Ruth and James but then five months later, asked to return as suddenly as he had left. Peter had then lived in his adoptive home for a further 18 months before setting up home with his girlfriend, with the blessing of Ruth and James, when he was 19. This appeared to be a stable arrangement and Peter had a good employment record. By 1991, Peter's grandmother had died but he was continuing to have contact with his birth mother and a range of other relatives.

II OPENNESS OF ATTITUDE OF ADOPTIVE PARENTS

Adoptive parents in 20 of the 22 adoptive families had been assessed in 1987 as open in attitude and in two as "less open". Openness of attitude had appeared to be necessary for adoptive parents to describe a positive experience of adoption with contact. Having reinterviewed adoptive parents in 18 families, I was aware of differences in attitude in adoptive parents in only three families, including in the two previously described as "less open".

One of these two families has been described in Chapter 3: Naomi, the adoptive mother of Janine and Andrew, had expressed resentment of contact in 1987. However, she said when reinterviewed that if denied contact, the children would always have wanted to know, and that Andrew had been helped to develop a somewhat more realistic picture of their mother. She and Alex, the adoptive father, conveyed much more recognition of the difficulties and feelings of Paula, the children's birth mother: 'Adoption happened too quickly for her' (the children had been placed for adoption within ten months of having left home). And Naomi acknowledged her greater awareness and acceptance that parenting by adoption was different from parenting by birth: 'In the early years, I wanted the children to myself. They were mine. Now I've learned to let go.'

In the second family described as less open in 1987, the adoptive parents had expressed unease about contact, although without identifying any specific difficulties arising from it. Their son's birth father was black and his mother white. They had refused to meet his birth mother, as he had requested, and clearly had not approved of his occasional visits to see his birth mother and siblings (accompanied by his social worker). It was not clear whether their son's ethnic origin had affected their attitude to contact. When first interviewed, they had told me that their son had moved out (at 18 and a few weeks) to stay at his girlfriend's house. Overall, they had described their experience of adopting him as a teenager as disappointing in comparison with that of their older children, adopted as babies (one of whom was similar to him in racial and cultural heritage).

However, when reinterviewed, the adoptive parents explained that they had asked their son to leave when he became 18: their older children had long since left home and they believed that their son's occasional late nights, unreliability and noisiness had contributed to the adoptive father's nervous debility. They now felt they had derived more from having him as a family member than they had realised four years earlier (and medical investigation had found that an industrial injury was the cause of the adoptive father's health problems).

The adoptive parents had now met their son's birth mother and were pleased that he had stayed with her for a few weeks in the recent past to help her recover from a burglary. They commented: 'He accommodates having two mums.' They had also encouraged their son to visit his father (whom they had met several years previously during the court proceedings) shortly before he died, and acknowledged that he was pleased to have a photograph of himself with his father taken in the hospital. Since leaving home at their request four years earlier, their son had stayed in regular contact with them and his adoptive siblings. The adoptive father added that he hoped he had positive feelings about his adoption: 'I hope in retrospect he will look back on six happy years.'

In the third family in which some change in attitude was noticeable, Ken and Barbara, Hayley's adoptive parents, seemed less open in attitude when reinterviewed. In 1987, they had said they had sought to be non-judgmental in their comments to Hayley about her birth mother, Mary, and to look for positives in her ('It's not up to us to judge – she may have been a good mother before her husband left her'). However, they felt justified in being more critical of Mary in 1991, as indeed was Hayley. Ken and Barbara did not feel that contact with her brother and sister had been helpful to Hayley. Their different, or differently-expressed views, and some comments made by Hayley, indicated less openness than had been conveyed four years previously.

Overall, I was as impressed in 1991 as I had been in 1987 by the generosity of attitude of many of the adoptive parents. Some shared in varying degrees the inclusiveness and generosity of the adoptive parent who commented: 'When you love your adopted children, this must extend to their parents as well.' There was also a wish to understand the birth parents' viewpoint: 'I can understand why she finds contact so painful . . . adoption must be like a knife to her heart.' This comment was made by an adoptive mother who had helped all her adopted children to maintain a degree of contact with a birth relative or someone important from the past.

Even where contact had proved to be an additional complicating factor for children who had difficulty in making an attachment, most adoptive parents had been able to acknowledge that continuing contact had been important at some stage for their child. Adoptive parents in three families, caring for children with disabilities, had seen contact, initiated by them after adoption, primarily as a means to reassure birth parents. However, they had subsequently felt that they and their child had gained from the contact, whether directly or indirectly.

In five families, adoptive parents stated that their Christian beliefs had contributed to their openness of attitude and willingness to maintain contact with birth parents: the adoptive parents in the "mixed race marriage" described their religious faith and the adoptive mother's upbringing in the Caribbean as important influences. As Christians, they had wanted to show love and compassion towards the birth mother of their son, who had 'given him life' and had made 'a loving decision' to part with him for adoption. Also, the adoptive mother had known 'adopted' children back home who grew up with full knowledge of their birth parents. They felt that in their son's case this was a happy and natural arrangement.

Other reasons explicitly given by adoptive parents as contributing to their willingness to consider maintaining contact included their awareness of their children's cultural and ethnic identity; some personal or professional experience which had enabled them to have insight into the extra dimensions of adoptive parenthood; and the impact of agency preparation or of an individual worker's attitudes.

It appeared that adoptive parents in at least 14 families had been influenced by agency values and by social worker practice, either in terms of becoming more open in attitude or in undertaking a placement with a level of contact which they would not previously have considered.

III THE RELATIONSHIP ESTABLISHED BY ADOPTIVE PARENTS WITH BIRTH PARENTS

It was clear from the 1987 interviews that adoptive parents' perception of their relationship with birth parents affected their overall feelings about adoption with contact. Adoptive parents who described a good relationship (although in some instances based on very limited contact), all expressed very or mainly positive feelings. When adoptive parents were reinterviewed, therefore, it was important to discover what changes there had been in adoptive parents' perceptions of the relationship between themselves and their children's birth parents and what factors seemed to make a difference. There had been contact, or there was potential contact, with 22 sets of birth parents (adoptive parents in three families had unrelated children from two families while adoptive parents in one family had three unrelated children).

Initial contact

The majority of adoptive parents in the families interviewed in 1987 had met one or both birth parents prior to placement and all had met at least one birth parent prior to adoption. Those who had met birth parents prior to placement had found this helpful, even when there were some negative aspects to the meeting (such as discovering, for example, that birth parents were much more strongly opposed to adoption than had previously been conveyed). Some, with hindsight, wished they had met birth parents sooner, and those with experience of having met the birth parents of non-related children at different stages in the process had a preference for an earlier meeting. Moreover, adoptive parents who had not had an opportunity to meet the birth parents of other children they had adopted, generally wished they could have done so.

Overall, memories about the initial meetings and views about their impact had remained unchanged. The adoptive parents in the two families whom I had assessed as "less open" in 1987 had indicated some difference, however, in that Naomi acknowledged some responsibility for the tension between herself and Paula, while the adoptive parents who had refused to meet their son's birth mother for many years, had finally done so in 1990. This and two other accounts of initial meetings illustrate the range of experiences.

The adoptive parents, who in 1987, had been resentful of their son's contact with his birth mother had always refused to meet her, despite their son's requests. He had been taken by a social worker to visit his birth mother until he had been old enough to go independently. This couple had been assessed as less open in attitude. The adoptive parents and birth mother eventually met seven years after the placement! Two years after their son had begun to live independently, he had telephoned them to say his birth mother was in the area and that he would like them to meet. They had invited her to tea and described her as 'much more pleasant' than they had expected. They commented in 1991 that they wished they had met her years earlier! They had met their son's father during the court proceedings. However, there had subsequently been no contact until their son had visited him in hospital (with his adoptive parents' encouragement) when he was terminally ill.

Ruth and James described how helpful they had found their initial meeting with Peter's birth mother, Sheila and his grandmother, Lillian during the introductions. Sheila had appeared rather "flat" as a result of her medication but Lillian had been friendly and relieved that adoptive parents had been found for Peter. Ruth and James had found it helpful to have greater understanding of the family's circumstances and to reassure Peter and the family of their good faith regarding future contact. Furthermore, 'it showed both ourselves and Peter's relatives that we were all trying to do the best we could for him, thereby dispelling a lot of possible fantasies on both sides'. Ruth and James believed that a pre-placement meeting was essential, particularly where ongoing contact was envisaged.

Martin and Joy were the only adoptive parents who, in 1987, had described a distressing initial meeting but who had subsequently been able to develop a warm relationship with their children's birth parents and who felt particularly positive about adoption with contact. Their first meeting had been to accompany the children, shortly after placement, to a meeting with the birth parents, Sam and Shelley, and several other birth relatives. Martin and Joy described how they had left the meeting feeling very upset and angry: 'The atmosphere was very tense – we didn't want to know about the birth parents and they had not accepted the removal of the children from their care. There was mutual hostility.' Following this, the children were taken by their social worker to visit their birth relatives on neutral territory and the two sets of parents only met at reviews, 'when it was all so tense'. This mutual hostility was only dissipated when the adoptive mother invited the birth parents to visit in the adoptive home – because the children were becoming distressed by the fortnightly visits which involved their being taken by their social worker to a meeting in a social work office (a journey of 30–40 minutes).

Reflecting on this experience, and the distress caused to the children, to Sam and Shelley and to themselves by these meetings, Martin commented: 'It might have helped if we could have had two or three meetings at the start with Shelley and Sam without the children or the social workers present.' Joy added: 'Perhaps as well, having been told about the mental illness background in both families, we would have been reassured to meet Shelley and Sam and see how harmless they are.'

Adoptive parents in 13 of the reinterviewed families had described a largely positive relationship with birth parents in 1987 (in three families, with two sets of birth parents). This group continued to describe the relationship in mainly positive terms, although in three cases there had been no recent contact and adoptive parents in two families were having very limited contact because their adult children now managed contact independently. Of the adoptive parents in four families who had described previous or current tensions or difficulties in their relationship with birth parents in 1987, those in three families were feeling more positively, while in the fourth family there had been no contact between Ken and Barbara and Mary, Hayley's birth mother, for almost four years.

There follows a summary of the description given by some of the adoptive parents in 1991 of their relationship with birth parents, with particular attention to how contact was being negotiated; the perceived impact of ethnic background, culture, lifestyle and gender; and to aspects of contact which are potentially threatening to adoptive parents (sharing, fear of birth parents abusing knowledge of the child's whereabouts and rivalry). The adoptive parents are considered in three groups: the adoptive parents in five families having no current contact with birth parents (although in two families adoptive parents were having contact with the birth parents of another child); adoptive parents in eight families whose relationship was limited by the nature and extent of contact; and the adoptive parents in six families with ongoing contact who described a particularly good relationship with birth parents.

Adoptive parents whose children were no longer having contact

Among the group no longer having contact were adoptive parents in two families who had previously initiated ongoing face-to-face contact. Both had adopted children of African-Caribbean descent.

The black adoptive mother had said in 1987 of their relationship with their son's birth mother: 'We have respect for each other. We are friends.' Four years later, she and her husband did not appear to feel that the relationship had been diminished by the lack of contact, pointing out that contact between themselves and their own extended family members was limited. They commented: 'There's been no contact for two years. But (our son) could telephone her if he wished and we would welcome this.' During both interviews, they referred to the shared ethnic and cultural background of the adoptive mother and the birth mother as having contributed to the development of a relaxed and warm friendship between the two families. Furthermore, they had never felt threatened by the birth mother's knowledge of their identity and whereabouts: 'All credit to (the birth mother). She has never interfered or pestered.'

The other adoptive parents were Malcolm and Jan, who had continued to be on good terms in 1991 with the birth parents of Paul and Nicola, but who had never felt as close to the birth mother of their elder daughter, Maxine. They described some sense of unease about their relationship with her, which, as described in Chapter 3, they thought might have derived in part from different cultural assumptions about the meaning of adoption. Jan described the difference in her relationship with the two birth mothers: 'I didn't feel as close to her as I do to Corine (the birth mother of Paul and Nicola). I like Corine a lot. Corine and I always greet each other with a kiss, but this didn't happen with (Maxine's birth mother).' Jan described the wedding of an aunt of Paul's and Nicola's at which Nicola and Corine had been bridesmaids as 'a wonderful occasion. We were completely accepted by all the relatives and looked after. We were treated like members of the family.' As transracial adopters, and very aware of the sensitivities around such placements, Jan and Malcolm were especially appreciative of their acceptance by Corine and her family (they had been almost the only white guests at the wedding).

Jan and Malcolm commented in 1991: 'We have never minded our children having another family' – as transracial adopters, they regarded contact as a bonus. Over the years, they had interpreted the continuing contact by their children's birth parents as an indication of their concern, not that they were 'trying to get the children back'. However, with hindsight, they wondered whether this had been the hope of Maxine's birth mother. They also felt that having less in common with her than with the birth relatives of Paul and Nicola would have contributed to a less friendly relationship. Because of their different experiences of contact with three birth parents, all African-Caribbean, Jan and Malcolm were inclined to attribute the less comfortable relationship they had with Maxine's birth mother to a number of factors, including ethnicity, culture, lifestyle and personalities, not solely to their being transracial adopters.

A "limited" relationship

The second group of adoptive parents (in eight families) described a limited relationship with birth parents when reinterviewed in 1991, because contact (theirs and their children's) was primarily by telephone or letter; or because the adopted young person now maintained contact without their adoptive parents' involvement; and in one instance because although there were meetings at the home of the birth grandparents three or four times a year, the birth mother tended to take a back seat and the closer relationship was between the maternal grandparents and the adoptive parents.

Compared with their description of their relationship with birth parents in 1987, the differences within this group were that in two instances a previously tense relationship was now more amicable and in a third instance the adoptive parents had met their son's birth mother and felt they were on good terms with her. While the adoptive parents in these families were involved in adoption with contact in very different circumstances, common factors included the adoptive parents' valuing of contact, however limited; negotiation being undertaken by the adoptive parents and/or young person; and respect for different lifestyles.

Key points made by adoptive parents in this group included their confidence that birth parents would not abuse knowledge of their child's whereabouts (this had been particularly true of Antoinette's birth mother who at one time had visited in the adoptive home); the inclusion of all family members by birth relatives (for example, when an adopted girl had been invited to be a bridesmaid at her birth mother's remarriage, her non-related sister had also been a bridesmaid); and no sense of being criticised/undermined by birth parents.

Different family backgrounds were not necessarily regarded as adversely affecting the relationship between adoptive parents and birth parents. Ruth and James, who acknowledged that their son's birth relatives had little in common with them, felt this was an advantage. While still living at home, Peter had needed some time on his own to 'unwind' after visits to his birth relatives, but had seemed to adjust fairly easily to two very different lifestyles. For their part, Ruth and James felt it was better not to interact too much socially with Peter's relatives (although they had attended some family celebrations with their son). By contrast, adoptive parents in two other families felt that they and the birth parents had similar backgrounds and this had made it easier for the two families to relate.

Neither Anil nor his adoptive parents remarked on whether differences in ethnicity and culture had inhibited the development of an ongoing relationship with his birth parents. Their first language was not English and Anil's birth mother had very limited English, although his father was fluent.

Sally, Melanie's adoptive mother, described an improvement in her relationship with Anne since the first interview. Rivalry had been a feature of their relationship during the early years of the placement. Sally explained that she had experienced more rivalry as her relationship with Melanie deepened and this had been exacerbated by Melanie repeating remarks allegedly made by Anne which were critical, for example, that she was too strict. Sally had often felt quite hurt. There was said never to have been rivalry between Anne and Alun. In 1987, Sally and Alun were feeling that the rivalry between Sally and Anne had diminished over time, and adopted a generous attitude towards the birth mother, believing that Anne did not understand Melanie's needs, not that she was malicious.

Sally and Alun acknowledged how hard it had been for Anne when Melanie had begun to call Sally 'mum'. They described her as having 'mellowed' over the years, particularly when she realised how difficult Melanie could be. In 1991, Sally and Alun believed contact had helped Anne realise that she could not have coped with Melanie and she was appreciative of the adoptive parents' efforts, and concerned for Melanie. Sally had by then found sharing easier. At Christmas in 1990, Melanie had said that she could not put 'mum' on the card for Anne. Sally had explained to Melanie: 'Yes, you can. We've sorted that out. She's your natural mum and I'm your mum.' In 1991, Sally described her relationship with Anne as 'good pals at a distance'.

Ongoing contact

Adoptive parents in six families described, both in 1987 and again in 1991, a good relationship with their child's birth parents which was sustained by face-to-face contact in five instances and through letters and telephone calls in the sixth.

Adoptive parents in three of these families described the progress of their relationship with birth parents in quite an uncomplicated way: these placements have been described in Chapter 4 from the birth parents' perspective.

Stephen's adoptive parents, Doreen and William, acknowledged that they had been apprehensive prior to the pre-placement meeting, anticipating that Stephen's birth parents, Eve and Gerald, might be 'posh'. Later, having invited them to visit Stephen some months after the adoption, they worried that their busy household might seem not good enough. However, their anxieties had been unfounded: 'We got on well from the start. They're just like relatives. They mix in. The relationship is very good. They make themselves at home.' Doreen and William had never found sharing hard: 'There's no rivalry. They support us as parents and never interfere.' Doreen particularly appreciated their thoughtfulness in buying presents for all the children, not just for Stephen. She added 'Eve treats me like a sister, except I haven't got a posh home!'

Jamie's adoptive parents, Rob and Carol, said that sharing had never been a problem for them. They had, by 1991, developed a friendship with Jamie's birth father, Ian, which was independent of his contact with Jamie. Their contact with Anna had become less frequent over the years, but they nonetheless regarded her as a friend. Although Anna was from a different ethnic and cultural background, they shared the same religious beliefs and this had been important to both families. They did not think Anna's decreasing contact was to do with their being white, but rather resulted from her pain at recognising Jamie's lack of response to her and his deteriorating health.

Claire's adoptive parents, Helen and Chris, explained that they had developed a good relationship with Beverley before she had requested that they adopt Claire. Helen commented : 'It's a very easy relationship to keep going. There is mutual trust.' 'Beverley had never visited or telephoned other than as agreed nor had there been any disagreements regarding child care or other issues. Helen had always been willing to forward news: 'Beverley has never been a threat. There are no feeling of possessiveness or jealousy.'

Gareth and Jane, Rachel's adoptive parents, acknowledged that there had been some tensions and 'mutual suspicion' at the outset of Rachel's placement. There had been no initial meeting between Gareth and Jane and Cathy until several months after placement. They all later wished this had taken place sooner. Gareth and Jane had subsequently adopted a second child and had met his birth mother before introductions began.

They had found this very helpful in developing a good relationship.

Early on, Gareth and Jane had been (unnecessarily) anxious when Cathy and her husband had moved nearer. Potential difficulties were exacerbated by Rachel occasionally playing off one parent against the other. The 'you're not my real mum' ploy had initially been quite hurtful to Jane, but by 1987 she and Gareth were able to describe a good understanding between themselves and Cathy, whereby they felt she would support them. This had the effect of reducing Rachel's manipulativeness. In 1991, Rachel was living semi-independently and Gareth's and Jane's contact with Cathy was much reduced. On balance, however, they felt their relationship with her was good and that there were no significant differences between them on important issues.

However, as was apparent from the interviews with Rachel, Cathy, Gareth and Jane, all parties acknowledged the significance of the gender issue: Rachel found it easier to say to her adoptive father than to her adoptive mother that she was going to visit her 'mum'; Jane referred to awareness at an early stage of 'another mother shadowing'; and Cathy described a less relaxed relationship with Jane than with Gareth because 'we're both Rachel's mum'.

On the other hand, continuing contact had enabled the participants to have a good understanding of each other's perspectives: Gareth and Jane had a clear picture as to the difficulties which had led to Rachel's placement in care and Cathy's reluctance to agree to adoption; Cathy felt reassured that Rachel did not feel rejected, and commented that Gareth and Jane provided excellent care for Rachel; while Rachel herself had a very clear picture of the family history, did not 'blame' Cathy or herself, and interpreted Cathy's reluctance to agree to adoption as deriving from her concern and care. In the absence of contact there could have been less sympathetic or more distressing interpretations – a "difficult" birth mother holding up the adoption proceedings; a "possessive" adoptive family turning Rachel against her birth mother; and a "rejecting" birth mother. Rachel would not have been able to experience the sense of her parents working together in a co-operative relationship and the fantasies the adults had about each other would not have been dispelled.

The difficult beginning of the relationship of Martin and Joy and their children's birth parents, Shelley and Sam, has already been described. At the time of the 1987 interview, Martin and Joy said they had built up a good relationship with the birth parents over time: 'We are friends. They are very appreciative (they always get a good dinner here!) They love the kids and they love us as well.'

Although Martin had initially felt less welcoming of contact in the adoptive home, he had been won round and commented: 'There's no rivalry. We know Shelley wants the children to be here.' Although Martin and Joy described themselves as being from a working class background, like Shelley and Sam, their experience of family life had been very different. Shelley was said to be happy with the way her children were being cared for: 'Shelley likes our values. She had an unhappy childhood herself and wants things to be different for Michael and Sara. She's pleased they belong to church clubs and activities.'

When Martin and Joy were reinterviewed, contact was less frequent – two or three times a year. However, Joy still felt they were regarded by Shelley and Sam as 'members of their extended family'. She explained that Shelley would ring sometimes for advice and 'share her troubles'. Sara had commented: 'Mummy Shelley says mum's her best friend! But mum's got loads of other friends. Shelley's not her best friend.'

In summary, adoptive parents in 13 families who had described a good relationship in 1987 felt this was still the case four years later, although in some instances contact had decreased. Adoptive parents in three families who had described some tensions in the relationship when first interviewed, spoke of now being on more friendly terms with their children's birth parents. Only Hayley's adoptive parents described no improvement in what had been a poor relationship before contact ended.

IV ADOPTERS FEELING CONFIRMED IN THEIR IDENTITY AS ADOPTIVE PARENTS

This section explores the extent to which adoptive parents felt confirmed in their identity as adoptive parents and how far contact had enhanced or detracted from their "sense of entitlement". Six aspects of their experience as adoptive parents are considered: the attitude of the birth parents to the adoption plan and to them as parents; their perception of the feelings and experience of birth parents; their feeling able to manage contact in the way they wished; their relationship with their child; their handling of the additional tasks which adoption entails; and the attitudes of friends and relatives.

Attitudes of birth parents to the adoption plan and towards the adoptive parents

In Chapter 4, the feelings of those birth parents who had been interviewed have been recorded, together with what were thought by some of the adopted children and the adoptive parents to be the attitude of other birth parents to the adoption plan. However, because of the importance to adoptive parents' experience of adoption of their perception of birth parents' feelings about their child being adopted, this aspect is explored here from the adoptive parents' perspective.

The agreement of birth parents to adoption (emotional as well as legal) had been identified by adopters in 1987 as important in enhancing their confidence to undertake their special role as adoptive parents. The adoptive parents in nine of the 18 families who were reinterviewed had initially been prepared for the possibility of a contested case or for agreement to be withheld. In one such family, Martin and Joy still recalled in 1987 the strain and tension they had experienced when Sara and Michael were being taken by their social worker to visit relatives on neutral territory, and the anxiety they had felt when the timing of the adoption was uncertain. In that context, the birth parents' approval of them as adoptive parents was particularly valued: 'It feels great to know they're not worried about the children being with us.'

While Ruth and James had not anticipated a contested adoption, since Peter's birth mother and grandmother had requested that he be found a permanent home, they commented that the sense of feeling approved as suitable adoptive parents was important not only to them but also to Peter. And a couple who had been selected by their son's birth mother and who had explained in 1987 that 'We felt good to know his birth mother chose us', added four years later: 'We feel privileged that she chose us after meeting two other couples.'

By contrast, there were adoptive parents whose application had been agreed (although sometimes at a very late stage or during the hearing) but who were nonetheless aware in 1987 of birth parents continuing to be negative about the adoption. Hayley's adoptive parents, Ken and Barbara, had been shocked when they first met her birth mother, Mary, to realise the strength of her opposition to the adoption plan. Initially, they had experienced this as very stressful, particularly as they felt that Mary was trying to sabotage the placement. Their sense of Mary's disapproval and the protracted legal proceedings had 'left their mark'. However, in 1987 they said that their contact with Mary demonstrated to them the appropriateness of Hayley being adopted. Four years later, they were satisfied that subsequent events (especially Hayley's rejection of any contact with her birth mother once she reached 16) had confirmed this.

The experience of Melanie's adoptive parents, Sally and Alun, had been similar at the time of the 1987 interview, although her birth mother, Anne, had withheld her agreement to adoption. Like Ken and Barbara, they had endured protracted legal proceedings and were aware of undermining remarks made by Anne, such as 'If you don't like it where you are, I'll ring the social worker and get you moved', although their interpretation was that Anne was concerned about Melanie rather than deliberately trying to sabotage the placement. However, four years later, although they had great anxieties about Melanie's emotional and behavioural problems, they reported that Anne had spoken of her appreciation of their care of Melanie (and their daughter was aware of this). Anne's approval of them as adoptive parents was important in giving them confidence to act as they thought best without fear of her criticising or holding them responsible for Melanie's difficulties.

In 1987, there was still a considerable amount of debate about transracial adoption. White adoptive parents in four families had had face-to-face contact (in two instances on an ongoing basis) with their children's black birth parents. The children placed in three of these families had been adopted at the request of their birth parents because of their disability; their adoptive parents did not describe having sensed any concerns on the part of birth parents that their children had not been placed with adoptive parents of the same ethnic, cultural and religious background (although they alluded to concerns expressed within some agencies). The approval of birth parents (in one instance the birth parents had selected the adoptive parents) was seen as more relevant by the adoptive parents than the criticisms of transracial adoption by some commentators.

Adoptive parents in the fourth family (Malcolm and Jan, who had adopted Paul and Nicola as well as Maxine, all of African-Caribbean descent) were particularly sensitive to adverse comments about transracial adoption since Maxine, as a teenager, had felt unhappy about being black. By 1991, however, then aged 19, she was expressing more confidence about her identity as a black person. Jan and Malcolm were pleased and relieved that they had always been made welcome by the birth parents and extended family of Paul and Nicola, but they had wondered whether Maxine's birth mother had given agreement to the adoption in the expectation that at 18, Maxine would leave her adoptive family to live with her. This had certainly unsettled Jan for a few months during 1988.

Adoptive parents in a further three families were aware that although agreement had been given, birth parents had found relinquishing their child for adoption distressing. Antoinette's adoptive parents' concerns about this seemed balanced by their having enabled their daughter and her birth mother to stay in touch, while Stephen's adoptive parents believed that contact had helped his birth parents become reconciled to the adoption. Their feelings about this had not changed between 1987 and 1991. However, Naomi, the adoptive mother of Janine and Andrew, had expressed criticism in 1987 of their birth mother, Paula, because she showed her distress about the adoption at access meetings. Naomi felt that Paula was unappreciative of what the children were being offered in the adoptive home, as well as concerned that Paula's distress was unsettling Andrew. By 1991, Naomi and Alex appeared to feel that Paula was more accepting of the adoption and this had apparently helped Naomi to be less possessive of the children.

Placements in which adoptive parents had sensed lack of approval by birth parents, even though they had given agreement to adoption, have been described in some detail. However, there were many examples of adoptive parents in other families quoting very supportive comments by birth parents: 'He says she's lucky to be living with us' and 'They've praised us for the care we've given him'. In addition, some adoptive parents had received appreciative comments or letters from other relatives, particularly grandparents (and from one great grandmother!).

Overall, adoptive parents confirmed that they (as well as their children, directly or indirectly) benefited when birth parents conveyed approval, and those who had been aware of birth parents' earlier opposition to adoption particularly valued this. At the time of the 1991 interviews, according to the information provided, only Hayley's adoptive parents, Barbara and Ken, had not been able to establish a relationship with their daughter's birth parents which contained at least a degree of mutual understanding and acceptance.

Perceptions of the feelings and experiences of birth parents

With the greater recognition in the media and within social work of the distress birth parents are likely to experience when their child is adopted, and having had an opportunity at some stage to meet one or both birth parents of the children, it was not surprising that the great majority of adoptive parents interviewed were so sensitive, in varying degrees, to the feelings and experiences of birth parents. An adoptive mother commented: 'It's sad to realise that our having children is another family's tragedy.'

However, in 1987, adoptive parents in two families (whom I had assessed as "less open") had appeared to find justification in a "rescue" attitude – particularly in highlighting the child's material gains through adoption and underplaying the possibility of emotional loss. Furthermore, Naomi appeared to have sought to validate her role as a parent by denying that Janine's and Andrew's birth mother was also a parent and by criticising her. Other adoptive parents had handled their sense of birth parents finding adoption difficult or having been opposed to the plan, by emphasising that the child had wanted to be adopted or by their strong feeling that adoption was right for the child. By 1991, only the adoptive parents of Hayley did not feel that the birth mother had accepted the fact of adoption. In other placements, adoptive parents believed birth parents had become to some degree reconciled to adoption.

In addition to the importance of knowing that birth parents were reconciled to adoption and that they approved of the adoptive family, it emerged that some adoptive parents had been concerned to know what service had been offered to birth parents in the period leading up to the placement for adoption – whether the birth parents had initiated this or whether it had been planned while the child was being looked after by the local authority. It was important that they did not feel birth parents had been wrongfully deprived of their children.

Adoptive parents in two families were sensitive to the poor material circumstances and social functioning of the birth parents of their children and were not sure how much assistance had been received. One adoptive mother said in 1991: 'We don't see ourselves as "rescuing" children. We accept that in a perfect world adoption would be second-best. The birth parents of our children seem to have had the odds stacked against them.'

Jan and Malcolm, as transracial adopters, had been particularly aware of the criticisms of the poor service offered to black families during the early 1980s, when their children had been removed from their parents' care. Adoptive parents in three other families who had adopted transracially were aware that adoption had been requested because of their child's disability and they did not seem to feel that lack of support to the parents as black people had been a factor.

Adoptive parents in three families had been aware of family members who had either expressed an interest in caring for the children at an earlier stage or who perhaps might have been encouraged to do so. In two families, continuing contact had later reassured adoptive parents that the adoption decision had been right. Adoptive parents in the third family, however, still felt in 1991 (by which time their son was living independently) that placement within the birth family might have been possible (although neither their son nor his birth relatives had raised this as an issue as far as they were aware). This had caused them some concern.

Doreen and William expressed the view that in the light of Stephen's severe disabilities, his birth parents had not been offered adequate support services – certainly they had had less help by way of respite care than the adoptive family. In this context, they felt that the adoptive decision had been 'a bit drastic', and that enabling Eve and Gerald to have continuing contact offered some reparation.

This was one of ten instances of adoptive parents feeling more at ease with the adoptive decision (or having had their feelings of concern about birth parents or other relatives lessened) as a result of continuing contact.

For these adoptive parents, contact had confirmed the appropriateness of adoption as events unfolded subsequently; or had shown them that birth parents were coping with the pain of parting with their child; or, they felt, had reassured birth parents that the child was thriving and had benefited from adoption.

An example of how contact proved helpful to adopters was provided by the adoptive mother of a child with learning difficulties, who had found the initial, pre-placement meeting with their son's birth parents a moving experience: 'I was very aware of the mother's distress. I think she would not have wanted to part with him if her husband had been more supportive.' The adoptive mother described having been 'haunted' by the birth mother's sadness and so she had felt reassured when, having initiated a meeting 18 months later, she found that the birth mother had given birth to a second child and seemed much happier and more relaxed. It was only after the second meeting that the adoptive mother had recognised how troubled she had felt about the birth mother's sadness, although she and her husband had offered to arrange a meeting in order to "help" the birth parents.

In a somewhat similar vein, Joy, adoptive mother of Michael and Sara, commented that she 'would have felt really guilty' if contact had not been maintained with the children's birth parents because 'they really love them. There's been no abuse or neglect.'

Thus, overall, contact had proved helpful to the majority of adoptive parents in reassuring them that the child had been appropriately placed with them.

The importance of adoptive parents feeling secure and in control

Although in no case in this study had there been a condition of access attached to the adoption order, not all adoptive parents had felt they were entirely in control regarding contact in 1987. In a few cases there had been an understanding or informal agreement at the time of the adoption order by which adoptive parents subsequently felt morally, if not legally, bound.

The adoptive parents who, in 1987 and again in 1991, had described positively their feelings about adoption with contact all had in common that they had themselves offered to maintain contact after adoption or had initiated contact at some stage after adoption. Furthermore, they or the adopted young people negotiated contact arrangements with birth parents. Adoptive parents in only four families had originally approached the adoption agency with the expectation of maintaining some form of contact.

The comments of Ruth and James, Peter's adoptive parents, illustrate this unusual (in the early 1980s) degree of openness: 'During our assessment we were asked about family contact and we felt from the outset that this was something we would try and maintain . . . we felt strongly that a child should not be cut off from earlier relationships, providing these were reasonably positive . . . we hoped we could adopt a child where good family links could be kept.' Ruth had some professional involvement in the child care field and was aware that at that time, the prevailing wisdom was that earlier relationships should be relinquished: 'Nevertheless, we still had a strong "gut feeling" that good ties should not be entirely severed.'

At an initial meeting during the introductions, Ruth and James came to an agreement with Peter, his mother and grandmother, about the level of contact after adoption. The two families lived in London, the journey between them taking about 45 minutes by bus. In 1987, Ruth and James felt satisfied with the way contact was occurring, with visits being planned in advance, although occasionally a relative would arrive unexpectedly to collect Peter. When reinterviewed in 1991, control in relation to contact did not arise, as Peter had moved away to live independently.

By contrast, Martin and Joy had not anticipated when Sara and Michael were placed with them that there would be any ongoing contact after adoption: 'Initially we wanted no contact. We didn't want to know the "other" parents.' They had known when Michael and Sara were placed that legal difficulties were likely. However, they had been led to expect that contact was about to be terminated. In 1987, Martin had been full of praise for Joy's initiative in having invited Sam and Shelley to visit the children in the adoptive home. He commented: 'I've learned a hell of a lot from Joy.' However, Martin acknowledged that at first he had found Joy's wish to invite Sam and Shelley to the adoptive home very hard to accept, fearing loss of control. On the first few occasions when Shelley and Sam were due to visit, he had deliberately planned not to be there.

The children had eventually been adopted, with the agreement of Shelley and Sam, just a few weeks before the first interview. By then both Joy and Martin were happy that Shelley and Sam would be continuing to visit every six weeks or so. Four years later, Martin and Joy had no regrets about their involvement in adoption with contact, which had gradually reduced to about three times a year – Shelley's mental health had apparently deteriorated and she and Sam were only able to visit if accompanied by their landlord, who had a protective attitude towards them and whom Joy and Martin trusted. Shelley and Sam had never visited without an invitation and arrangements were always amicably negotiated; for example, during 1991 the children had gone with Shelley and Sam and their landlord on outings to the coast. When I met Sara, then nine years old, she had a good understanding of her birth parents' difficulties and had commented: 'Mum and dad will only let us go out with mummy Shelley and daddy Sam if Desmond (their landlord) takes us.'

Clearly Martin and Joy had moved a long way over time in their ideas about contact, largely guided by what they thought would be helpful to Michael and Sara and by their learning from experience that contact had not undermined them in their role as parents by reducing their control.

How to manage contact in a way which did not diminish their identity as parents was discussed by a family with five adopted children. They had, since 1987, re-established contact with the birth parents of two of their other children, in addition to the boy who had been included in the 1987 sample. They had taken this initiative because they 'would like the children to grow up feeling adoption is not something to be ashamed of' and they did not want them 'to feel bitter about the past'. However, with a total of five adopted children, all with some form of family contact, they had felt the need of "ground rules" and had established with birth relatives that telephone calls were not to be made "out of the blue", although letters were welcome at any time and telephone contact did occur in relation to arranging face-to-face contact. The birth relatives had complied with this, so the adoptive parents felt contact was not outside their control.

Feeling in control of contact was important for Anil and his adoptive parents. Sue and Dave had had no expectation of contact following Anil's adoption. When they learned that his birth parents were making enquiries about him, they had gained Anil's agreement before inviting them to visit. Subsequently, it seemed to be Anil, rather than Sue and Dave, who felt some anxiety about the way in which contact was to be maintained.

Following the birth parents' visit, when Anil was twelve, there had been letter contact between the two families. The birth parents had written early in 1991 to ask about a further visit. Sue and Dave had asked them to telephone to make arrangements during school holidays. However, six months later, the adoptive family moved to another town because Dave had changed his job. They did not have an address for the birth parents who frequently travelled between the UK and their country of origin. Subsequently, when the birth parents, unable to get through by telephone, visited and found the house up for sale, they asked the estate agents to forward a letter.

Anil was wanting to stay in contact with his birth parents but not wishing to meet them again when interviewed in 1991. He asked his adoptive parents not to forward the new address 'in case they just turn up'. Anil's way of remaining in control of contact was to plan to correspond via the voluntary adoption agency through which one of his adopted sisters had been placed. His adoptive mother speculated that perhaps there was a more informal attitude to adoption within the birth parents' culture and therefore 'the boundaries might be different'.

Overall, adoptive parents in the 13 families who had felt positive about adoption with contact both in 1987 and again in 1991, had continued to feel that contact had not diminished their sense of control as adoptive parents. There had been some significant changes in the pattern of contact, with negotiation about arrangements in several families being undertaken by the young people themselves. Adoptive parents were supportive of this.

Adoptive parents in four families, who were reinterviewed in 1991, had conveyed in 1987 that adoption with contact had to an extent been imposed on them. They had gone along with this with varying degrees of acceptance, and some diminishing of their sense of control.

Among these were Alex and Naomi, adoptive parents of Janine and Andrew. As described in Chapter 3, adoptive parents had been sought for Janine and Andrew who would maintain contact after adoption – and indeed Alex and Naomi had written to the children's birth parents prior to the adoption to confirm their willingness to do so. Later, Naomi particularly had felt resentful of this undertaking and had queried the need to comply with it. In 1987, she had stated that her reason for agreeing to be interviewed was because she felt angry that she and Alex were being used as "guinea pigs" by the agency, which had not adequately prepared them for the complexities of adoption with contact. However, by 1991, Alex and Naomi seemed happy to leave Janine and Andrew to negotiate contact direct: 'The ball is now in the children's court.' This appeared to be much less threatening to their sense of control and they no longer experienced contact as being imposed by others outside the adoptive family.

The adoptive parents in the two families who had adopted Hayley and her brother Craig had also felt under an obligation to maintain contact until the children were 16, having offered to do so in the High Court. Hayley's adoptive parents had agreed to a placement with continuing contact at the outset because it had been part of the "package". Craig's adoptive parents had described some difficulties associated with contact but believed it was important for him to maintain it. Looking back, Hayley's adoptive father felt that having to maintain contact had made their task as adoptive parents more difficult. They were more ready to acknowledge in 1991 than in 1987 that they had always been reluctant to maintain contact: 'We never thought it was right. We were pushed into it.'

Although they had been among the group of adoptive parents in six families who had described some reservations about contact, Melanie's adoptive parents, Sally and Alun, had become involved in adoption with contact through their own choice, unlike the adoptive parents of Janine and Andrew and of Hayley. Melanie had been adopted only a few months before the 1987 interview, when aged 13, and Sally and Alun had offered to take her to visit her birth mother and brother twice a year. Although this commitment to contact added complications to a placement which was far from straightforward, they had commented in 1987: 'We'd be reluctant to stop access. It seems like one more stressful thing to cope with at the time, but it may pay dividends later.'

Because in the early years of the placement there had been a tense relationship between Sally and Anne, Melanie's birth mother, Alun had usually negotiated contact (in consultation with Sally). They had not felt under pressure to continue contact, as Melanie had appeared at times to be indifferent to contact and Anne did not make unreasonable demands to see Melanie. Following a very difficult visit by Melanie to Anne in 1989, when Melanie was described as having 'gone berserk', Anne had felt she could not control Melanie and had asked Sally and Alun not to leave Melanie with her for the whole day, as had been the pattern in the past. Melanie, for her part, had declined to visit Anne subsequently, although there was letter and telephone contact. In 1991, Sally and Alun were maintaining contact with Anne independently of Melanie. Overall, they had felt in control of contact since Melanie had been placed eight years earlier, although in the past, Melanie had used contact to be manipulative.

Thus one of the themes which had emerged from the 1987 interviews – the importance to adoptive parents' satisfaction with contact after adoption of their having some sense of control of contact – was confirmed by the second interviews. Adoptive parents felt in control when they had initiated or offered to maintain contact and when they and/or the adopted young person negotiated contact direct with birth relatives (as had happened increasingly over the years). They wished to have the freedom and flexibility to determine contact in accordance with the child's wishes and their perception of her or his needs. Adoptive parents experienced a diminished sense of control and were more likely to feel resentful of contact if they did not share the agency view about the benefits of contact or felt unhappy or threatened by a child's wish to maintain contact.

Adoptive parents' relationship with their child

As described in Chapter 3, although for many of the 26 children there were significant pre-placement barriers to their becoming attached to adoptive family members, the adoptive parents on the whole expressed satisfaction with the degree of their child's attachment to them.

In those instances reported in 1987 in which children had not seemed to be well attached nor to relate like a full family member, they had all joined their families at seven years or more after a difficult pre-placement history. The adoptive parents in two families reinterviewed in 1991 who had thought in 1987 that contact might have affected their children developing an attachment, felt more confident of their children's affection four years later.

Melanie's adoptive parents had not believed in 1987 that her twice-yearly contact with her birth mother had affected her attachment (which at that time seemed to have more than a degree of ambivalence): 'Contact is a side issue.' Four years later, this was still their view. From their account of Melanie, then accommodated by the local authority at their request, she still had mixed feelings towards her adoptive parents, although they commented: 'She does show some sensitivity to our feelings and is a pleasant family member when not under pressure.'

Doreen and William were typical of adoptive parents of older placed children who had realistic expectations emotionally. They described Stephen as 'not demonstrative' in the way that an adopted younger-placed sibling was – he did not show the same 'depth of attachment'. However, they thought this was due to the number of pre-placement moves and separations he had experienced – 'he had loved and lost so many times' – and not to contact. They did not feel frustrated or dissatisfied with his lack of demonstrativeness, which they did not believe was affected by his learning difficulties.

Malcolm and Jan felt happy with the extent of their children's attachment: Paul and Nicola had become attached relatively quickly and contact did not appear to have interfered with this. Nicola was described as sensitive to her adoptive parents' feelings about their having contact with Corine as she had asked: 'Do you mind my having another mum as well?' Maxine, on the other hand, had 'needed a long time before seeing us as mum and dad'. Placed at the age of eight, she was still calling Jan and Malcolm by their first names in 1991, having explained to them: 'I've had too many mums.' They felt that earlier rejections and placement breakdowns, not contact, had led to Maxine's wariness about becoming attached.

Ruth and James commented of Peter: 'There would have been limitations anyway with an older child's attachment – grafting him on to a new family at the age of 13.' They added that Peter would 'never have settled without contact'.

None of the adoptive parents of children placed while under the age of seven felt that contact had affected the children's attachment and all felt satisfied that their child was, as one adoptive family expressed it, 'emotionally a full member of the family'. Joy, adoptive mother of Michael and Sara, commented: 'If the children are little when placed, why should contact make a difference?' And Claire's adoptive mother recalled her sometimes having said that 'she wishes she'd come from my tummy'.

In 1987, none of the adoptive parents believed that the development of their attachment to their child had been delayed or impaired by contact.

Adoptive parents more often said that contact had helped them to develop a close attachment to their child in the early stages.

Four years later, and with the advantage of looking back over a longer period, adoptive parents still felt that contact had not inhibited their becoming attached. Joy, who had had no children born to her, said of her feelings for Sara and Michael: 'I don't think I could love them any more if I had given birth to them.' Some adoptive parents acknowledged that it took time to develop an attachment to an older-placed child but did not link this with contact. Doreen made a comparison with the type of attachment she felt for her daughter placed as a baby, but related this to age at placement, not to continued contact: 'I don't see myself as the "exclusive" parent of Stephen that I feel I am with (my daughter) – but then she was placed as a baby. I've always felt that because Stephen had spent so many years with his birth family that he still belongs in part to that family. But this has not stopped me loving him.'

In 1987, none of the adoptive parents (including, ironically, the adoptive parents of Craig, who was to leave the adoptive home weeks later) anticipated that their son or daughter would be more likely to return to the birth family because of contact. On the contrary, a number felt that this was a less likely outcome because the child would have a more realistic picture of the birth relatives and would not be impelled to leave because of unsatisfied curiosity and/or a feeling that barriers were being put up by adoptive parents. Moreover, several adoptive parents had acknowledged that in all kinds of families young people might leave precipitously or with their parents' reluctant approval, although separation is often regarded as more difficult for adopted children who have had hurtful experiences of separation earlier in their lives.

Melanie was being accommodated by the local authority and her adoptive parents pointed out that during all the stress and turmoil of the previous two years, Melanie had never run away to, or asked to live with, her birth mother – although they thought she might have done if contact had not helped both Melanie and Anne understand the difficulties they had when spending time together.

Peter had in fact spent time living with his uncle. Ruth and James, when asked in 1987 whether they had any concerns that contact might increase the likelihood of Peter returning to live with his family of origin, had commented: 'Any child might want to leave home at 16 plus. We would still have enjoyed having Peter as a member of our family for several years.' However, they had been taken aback when Peter, at the age of 17, 'had announced he wasn't very happy with us, and wanted to go and live with his uncle'. Having moved out, Peter didn't make any contact with them at Christmas, a few months later, which caused them much hurt and sadness. However, in the New Year, Peter had requested that he come back and after some negotiation, 'he settled into his room as if he had never been away'.

Looking back at this two years later (by which time Peter, aged 20, was living independently with his girlfriend), Ruth and James felt that Peter's being in touch with birth relatives provided a "safety net" – somewhere safe where he could go when he needed to test out and experience some independence. At the time of the interview there had been enormous publicity about a teenage girl who had left home and had been murdered while homeless. They were aware (through their adoptive network and Ruth's professional experience) of the difficulties some adoptive children have in achieving separation: they did not believe that Peter's continued contact with birth relatives had led to his departure; indeed, they felt he would never have settled with them initially without contact. Ruth and James were reassured that Peter had felt able to ask to return when he needed to, saying himself that they were 'his parents' (Ruth quoted a 'classic note' left by Peter on one occasion when he went to visit his birth mother: 'Mum – I've gone to see mum').

The adoptive parents of the seven young people aged 16 or more who were still living at home did not feel in 1991 that contact was undermining their sense of security. This had never been an issue for the adoptive parents of younger-placed children, but adoptive parents of children placed at seven years or older were likely to feel that they had become more confident as time had gone on and their child had developed greater attachment.

The comments of adoptive parents whose adopted children were under 16 were similar. Joy and Martin thought Michael and Sara would not be more likely to leave their adoptive family because of contact: on the contrary they would have no need to check out the reality for themselves (as had a foster child placed previously with Joy and Martin who had lost contact with her birth parents).

Malcolm and Jan wondered whether either Paul or Nicola might go to live with or near their birth relatives when they reached their late teens in order to live in an area where there were more black people. Jan added: 'If so, I hope I'll be able to let them go. Then they're more likely to come back.' This possibility was considered not because of continuing contact as such, but because Jan and Malcolm were aware of being transracial adopters in an area with few black people.

The additional tasks of adoptive parents

There was some discussion with adoptive parents about the effect of contact on the acknowledgment of the differences between parenting by birth and parenting by adoption, and on explaining to the child the circumstances of adoption.

Adoptive parents in four of the families who had adopted transracially commented in 1987 that their recognition of the child's different racial background was a tangible reminder that he or she had not been born to them, and contact therefore had little impact in this respect. They and other adoptive parents expressed a positive view about building a family through adoption. A typical comment was: 'We have never pretended that he was born to us or that adopting a child is the same as giving birth to one.'

However, two adoptive fathers had acknowledged in 1987 that continuing contact had highlighted the painful fact of infertility: one admitted that when the child's birth parents first had contact in the adoptive home, he had avoided being there when they visited because he did not want to acknowledge that the children had parents who had given them birth. He had gradually become reconciled to this, however, as he did not experience the birth parents' visits as any threat in reality. Referring briefly to this emotion again in 1991, he added: 'You get used to it.'

The second adoptive father acknowledged having found his infertility in the early stages of the placement more difficult than his wife: it had emphasised his sense of "guilt" at not being able to give his wife a child. However, he had overcome this with the help and understanding of his wife and because of his confidence in the security of the relationship they had with their adopted child. He did not refer to this again when reinterviewed.

An adoptive mother had indirectly acknowledged in 1987 that contact with her children's birth mother raised the issue of her infertility for her when she explained that her husband did not feel jealous or resentful of the birth parents because he had had children born to him in a previous marriage. By 1991, with increased confidence in her relationship with her children and their perception of her as their mother, this sense of jealousy appeared to have diminished.

Adoptive parents in twelve of the families had not had children born to them and all had therefore chosen to adopt as an alternative means to achieving parenthood (although a few said that they had considered adoption before they realised that conception was not a possibility). The fact that so few adoptive parents, whether they had children born to them or not, acknowledged that contact had highlighted in a negative way the fact that their children had other birth parents, could have been because of their exceptional degree of openness of attitude, the preparation by the agency, their positive experience of adoptive parenthood, the reassurance that contact provided, or a combination of some or all of these.

Acknowledgment of difference also entails recognising the significance of heredity in a child's development. Two adoptive mothers said in 1987 that they had thought more about this as a result of contact. One acknowledged that she had found it quite hard to move from her belief in the supremacy of environmental factors. In 1991, she was even more aware of similarities between her adoptive daughter and her birth mother and viewed this largely in a positive sense. Knowing some of the more difficult aspects of the birth mother's personality, she had sometimes been tempted to think 'just like your mother!' However, she was also aware of the birth mother's warm and likeable qualities, which her daughter had also possessed.

On the other hand, comments made by other adoptive parents in 1991 indicated the opposite view, that it was easier to ascribe negative qualities to heredity if one did not know a birth parent at first hand and perhaps had a stereotyped or prejudiced view. In addition, a few adoptive parents drew attention to positive traits which they believed were derived from birth parents. Claire's adoptive mother felt pleased to see that she had inherited her birth mother's musical ability and made a point of drawing this to Beverley's attention.

With regard to helping the child understand the circumstances of adoption, all the adoptive parents felt that having first-hand knowledge and background information (and, also, in some instances, a liking and regard for the birth parents) was helpful to them. Hayley's adoptive parents, who had largely negative views about continuing contact in her case, explained in 1991 that this had enabled Hayley and themselves to make their own assessment of the overall situation. And Alex and Naomi, who had felt in 1987 that Andrew had a fantasy picture of a "fairy tale" birth mother, stated in 1991 that contact had enabled them to help him have a more realistic understanding.

Because of their openness in attitude, it seemed likely that most of the adoptive parents in the sample would have brought a great deal of understanding, honesty, and empathy to the task of explaining the adoptive circumstances. However, their view was that contact had assisted them in this task, and this was felt particularly strongly by most of the adoptive parents who had experience of both open and closed adoption.

The attitude of relatives and friends and the impact of this

In the main, adoptive parents said friends and relatives had been supportive of adoption with contact although adoptive parents in five families referred to some initial anxieties on the part of adoptive grandparents. Martin described how his parents 'held back' early on because they were worried that he and Joy would 'lose' Michael and Sara: 'They cried when the adoption went through.' The grandparents had eventually met Shelley and Sam and would say on occasion to the children: 'Mummy Shelley loves you.' Martin felt this indicated that his parents were now fully supportive.

Only Stephen's adoptive parents, Doreen and William, described some negative comments by friends (who were also adoptive parents, but without contact): they had suggested that Stephen's birth parents might wish to reclaim him once he reached 18. Although the adoptive parents thought this unlikely, the adoptive mother said that it did cause her to worry fleetingly from time to time.

The approval of their relatives and friends was important to adoptive parents in different degrees, depending on the closeness of the relationship and their confidence as adoptive parents. In general, adoptive parents felt they had the support of people important to them, and that any reservations about the contact had derived from concern for them.

Overall, adoptive parents indicated that contact had enhanced, rather than detracted from, their confidence and sense of identity as adoptive parents.

Perceptions of the effects of contact on the child

While most adoptive parents assessed the effects of contact on the child primarily in terms of the child's "best interests", its impact on their relationship with their son or daughter was also important to them. Adoptive parents' feelings about their child's attachment to them have been described above. In most instances, contact was regarded by adoptive parents as having had a mainly beneficial effect, whether direct or indirect, on their child's well-being.

Adoptive parents in three families, including the "mixed race" couple, whose children had been placed while under the age of two, felt particularly strongly that as well as having greater understanding of the circumstances of adoption, their child was reassured that contact at any stage in the future would be welcomed. Claire's adoptive parents compared her situation with that of her older adoptive brother: 'We'll always have up-to-date information, and know that Beverley would be welcoming of face-to-face contact at any time.' Furthermore, 'Any meeting will be based on reality – Beverley is not an anonymous figure.' By contrast, they had no direct information about their son's birth father and very little about his birth mother. He was longing to make contact with her but they had no clues as to her whereabouts, nor did they know whether she would welcome contact. They feared his experiencing disappointment or rejection.

Likewise, Joy and Martin felt that contact had been helpful to Michael and Sara. Martin referred to 'genetic continuity': 'It would be a nag in your mind, not knowing. Even at my age I'd need to know if I found out I was adopted. Michael and Sara can see for themselves. They know it's not their (Sam's and Shelley's) fault.' Joy and Martin had previously fostered two boys who had harboured unrealistic fantasies about their birth parents, and they felt it was important that Michael and Sara were growing up with some idea of their parents' psychiatric problems: 'Michael and Sara do have an understanding of their parents' difficulties. Michael especially is a very caring and sensitive child. I think possibly in this way their lives are richer for it (contact with Sam and Shelley).'

Anil's adoptive parents, Sue and Dave, described in 1987 how contact had not only given their son first-hand knowledge of his birth parents, but had also provided an opportunity for expressing some long-held emotions: they had thought that Anil had accepted their view of his birth parents as not uncaring or rejecting. However, when the opportunity for a meeting occurred, Anil was said to have been initially pleased but then 'exploded with a torrent of angry feelings'. He recalled the occasion when he was about two and his birth mother had visited him in hospital and had not returned, despite having promised to do so. Sue and Dave were shocked by Anil's reaction as they had not realised he had these angry feelings. They felt the meeting had helped Anil to have a 'healthy and balanced outlook', as he had had an opportunity to understand at first hand why his birth parents had been unable to care for him. They did not think this would have been achieved without a meeting.

Anil himself confirmed this. On hearing of his birth parents' enquiry, he recalled: 'I felt angry. Maybe it was a shock. I wondered why now, after all this time? What did they want?' Anil described the outcome of the meeting as enabling him to have 'a clearer picture, even though I'd already seen photos'. He had been surprised at how young his mother had looked and had been pleased by the appropriateness of the present they had brought. Anil realised his birth parents 'still cared'.

While adoptive parents in several families believed contact had helped their son or daughter achieve a greater understanding and a more realistic picture of their birth parents, Ken and Barbara, Hayley's adoptive parents, believed that for her, the process had involved 'further hurtfulness' – Mary had 'shown she didn't care about Hayley's feelings or wishes'.

In considering how contact had helped their children develop a sense of identity, adoptive parents in eight families made special reference to the positive impact of contact on their son's or daughter's self-esteem. Helen commented: 'Claire will know how much Beverley always cared about her.' And the adoptive father of a boy placed as a baby expressed the view that 'contact in the formative years prevents a psychological scar developing'. He felt his son had a 'solid foundation for the future' and would never have the need to 'reproach birth parents'. An adoptive mother of several children, each of whom had had limited contact with their birth parents, commented that the aim of maintaining links was 'to help our children feel better about themselves'.

Antoinette's adoptive parents believed that contact had given their daughter 'continuity and stability', and that Antoinette's self-confidence had been increased because 'Eleanor has told Antoinette she loves her'. Frank and Lorna explained in 1987: 'When Antoinette came to us after several years of being in and out of care her self-esteem was very low. Eleanor's reassurance, initially when she visited and now when she writes, about how precious and much-loved Antoinette is, has really helped her.'

Jan and Malcolm felt that contact provided 'a bridge to the black community' for their children and would enable them to 'take their place' amongst black people later. Living in a predominantly white area, Jan and Malcolm felt it would have been more difficult for them as transracial adopters to help their children develop a pride in their black heritage without contact. They said in 1991 of Paul and Nicola: 'The children belong to both families.' Jan commented that a few years previously she had felt 'guilty' about having adopted transracially. However, given the positive outcome in terms of the children's racial identity, and having explained to the children why they had been placed transracially, she felt more comfortable about having adopted black children.

Sue and Dave appeared to attach much less significance to issues of race and culture in relation to contact. Anil and his adoptive family had been living in an area with a large community from the same minority ethnic group as his birth parents. However, Anil's contact with the wider community had been limited because of his disability. He and his adoptive parents had not been aware of any racism directed towards him. When interviewed, Anil showed little interest in his birth family's racial and cultural background, although the "differences" had contributed to his description of the first meeting as 'like making friends with strangers'.

The opportunity for access to family medical history, often cited as a reason for the opening of files where this is not permitted, was referred to by adoptive parents in only three families as an advantage of contact, presumably because of the adequacy of the information provided by the agency.

On the whole, adoptive parents believed that their child had felt a sense of permanence in the placement. Furthermore, there was a limited number of placements in which children were described as having divided loyalties, most adoptive parents describing mutual acceptance by the adults and a supportive attitude by birth parents. In some cases, this had been achieved after early difficulties: Martin and Joy referred to social workers having 'set up a tug of love situation' at the outset of the placement by arranging meetings on neutral territory without the two sets of parents having had an opportunity to meet and develop a relationship.

However, as described above, there had been a few instances in which birth parents had used contact, whether deliberately or not, in a way which adoptive parents believed was undermining their attempts to help the child feel secure in the placement.

Adoptive parents in several families echoed the comments made by some of the adopted children themselves in highlighting the importance of contact with birth parents as a means of facilitating ongoing contact with other relatives, especially brothers and sisters. However, adoptive parents in one family had under-estimated the importance of sibling contact. The adoptive parents of Jamie and of Stephen, both children with learning difficulties, emphasised the importance of contact with brothers and sisters for their children's future. Rob said: 'Children with disabilities need as many concerned people in their lives as possible.' And Doreen anticipated that Stephen's brother and sister would go on caring about him for the rest of his life: 'Joshua and Louise will always be there for him. They'll be able to see he's OK long after we and his parents are dead.'

Thus in all but one family, adoptive parents were able to identify beneficial effects of contact for their son or daughter, and this contributed to their having a positive view of adoption with contact.

V ADOPTIVE PARENTS' OVERALL FEELINGS ABOUT CONTACT

The feelings of adoptive parents in these 17 families were clearly affected by the extent to which their expectations of adoption had been fulfilled and how far contact had contributed to this, negatively or positively. For adoptive parents in 16 of the families, adoption had been a rewarding experience.

However, Melanie's adoptive parents, Sally and Alun, were feeling hurt and distressed in 1991 by the difficulties which had led to their requesting that their daughter be accommodated by the local authority. Their perception was that the recent problems were not linked to contact. Nonetheless, although they had chosen to maintain contact after adoption, and had felt it was important for Melanie, Sally and Alun described how contact had been associated with some tension and stress in the early years. Sally and Alun had stayed in touch with Anne and planned to continue to do so, while respecting Melanie's wish to limit her contact with her birth mother for the time being.

Of those adoptive parents who described their experience of adoption in positive terms, Hayley's adoptive parents felt this had been despite contact; adoptive parents in ten families regarded contact as having contributed to their positive experience; adoptive parents in two families (earlier described as "less open") had had reservations in 1987 but in 1991 expressed satisfaction with their experience of adoption and felt that contact had benefited their children; and in three families, contact had been limited and had not been a significant part of the life of the adoptive family, although there had nonetheless been benefits.

Among the adoptive parents in ten families who felt contact with birth parents had contributed to making their experience of adoption more positive, were the adopters in five families whose circumstances have been described earlier.

Rob and Carol, Jamie's adoptive parents, commented: 'For us, contact with Ian and Anna, and with Jamie's sisters, Charlotte and Sophie, has been positive.' They explained that it had been helpful to know the family background, to have the reassurance that Ian particularly was readily available to talk about Jamie's needs, and to have the emotional (and in the early days, the practical) support of the birth parents. Because of Jamie's very limited understanding, they found it difficult to assess whether, as a child with one black and one white parent, he had gained from contact with his black parent. In their view, the relationship between the adults was the most important factor in determining whether contact was helpful.

Claire's adoptive parents, Helen and Chris, were not aware of any disadvantages of adoption with contact, and did not foresee any in the future. With their older adopted child increasingly desperate to meet his birth mother, Helen commented that in 1991 she was feeling more strongly about the importance of maintaining contact, or at least knowing how to access up-to-date information, than she had done four years previously.

Joy and Martin summed up their feelings about adoption with contact: 'We're relieved we did it this way . . . we have no worries . . . nothing could be better for Michael and Sara.' They highlighted that what gave them confidence was their perception that Shelley and Sam loved the children and mutual trust had developed. Joy and Martin were aware that as they grew older, the children, especially Michael, were becoming less interested in visits by Sam and Shelley: 'Mentally, they've outstripped their parents in intelligence.' However, Joy felt she would be able to help Shelley understand this.

As described above, Jan and Malcolm had found it easier to establish and maintain a relationship with Paul's and Nicola's birth relatives than with Maxine's, and felt that adoption with contact had been 'especially successful' for the younger two children. In 1987, they had described contact as an 'enriching' experience. In 1991, 'despite some occasional emotional and practical difficulties', Jan and Malcolm said they had 'no regrets' and that for them adoption with contact had been 'largely a success – contact has been worthwhile'. They made comparisons with children in reconstituted families having 'to take on board' new relationships and felt that in adoption with contact, as in divorce, it was the attitude of the adults which was crucial. Jan and Malcolm anticipated continuing to support their children's wishes regarding contact in the future.

Ruth and James, Peter's adoptive parents, while commenting that they 'would not have done things differently in regard to contact', did query the practice of placing children 'as old as 13' for adoption. They recalled that 'adoption had been sold to Peter as the best option' and he had been keen to be adopted. However, looking back, Ruth and James wondered whether this had been right. They pointed out that Peter, now living independently at the age of 20, was in some respects back within the network of his extended family – his girlfriend was related to his cousin's wife!

Alex and Naomi were adoptive parents in one of the two families who had reservations about contact in 1987 but who felt more positively in 1991. Naomi had acknowledged when first interviewed her reluctant (although agreed) participation in adoption with contact and her greater difficulty in establishing an amicable relationship with Janine's and Andrew's birth mother than her husband. Four years later, Naomi recalled that contact had 'caused stress in the early years'. However, both she and Alex felt satisfied that over time, and particularly as the relationship between Paula and Naomi had improved, contact had ceased to be problematic. They believed that overall it had been right to have maintained contact and were content for Janine and Andrew to continue to negotiate their own arrangements.

In one of the three families in which contact had been limited, the adoptive parents who had adopted several children felt able to recommend that other adopters approached their task with 'an open attitude'. In this family, although contact was mainly by letter, the adoptive mother wrote that 'it is more complicated than one would imagine because of the number of children we have and being sure we give each child enough time for this important issue'. However, their comment to prospective adopters was that 'as adopters, you may gain and you definitely won't lose'.

Anil's adoptive parents, Sue and Dave, also felt the limited contact had been beneficial. However, from their own perspective, they were pleased that contact had been within their control and had occurred a long time after placement, when they felt secure in their relationship with Anil. They respected Anil's wish that there should be no face-to-face contact in the immediate future. Anil explained that he would like to have news of his birth family, particularly of his brothers and sisters, but 'that visit's been enough for now'. He described 'not wanting to be over-friendly'.

Finally, what of the impact on other children in those families where some children had contact and others did not (including children born to the adoptive parents and children fostered or adopted without contact)?

Although adoptive parents in five families had had children born to them, their adopted children's contact with their family of origin was regarded as a sensitive area in only one. In this family, there was one child born to the adoptive parents and four adopted children, all of whom were having contact either with their birth parents or with a previous carer. Each child's "Adoption Day" was celebrated with a special meal. The adoptive parents celebrated their non-adopted child's "special day" on the appropriate Saint's Day and ensured that one of his godparents paid extra attention to him. This was clearly understood by all the children in the family. When I spoke to the boy, who was then eight, he was pleased that his brothers and sisters had contact but added: 'Sometimes I feel the odd one out because I've only got one mum and one dad.' However, the adoptive parents did not believe that at this stage the situation was causing their son distress.

Adoptive parents in seven families with experience of "open" and "closed" adoption continued to feel that openness was preferable, although this was qualified by recognition that contact was not appropriate in all circumstances. In one family, two adopted children had sibling contact and had not shown any resentment of the other child's contact with his birth mother. Adoptive parents in the eighth family who had previously adopted on the closed model and had expressed a preference for this in 1987, were able to see some benefits from contact for their older-placed son in 1991.

Adoptive parents in only one of the families with experience of contact with birth parents for one or two children but not for others, felt this had been potentially problematic. In that instance, the adoptive mother said in 1991 that she had 'become an advocate (of adoption with contact), where appropriate, since we last spoke'. She and her husband had adopted two children in addition to the child with learning difficulties whose birth parents had maintained some occasional contact by letters, presents and telephone calls, until they separated when he was four. The adoptive parents said that because of their son's learning difficulties and age, he had not been able to appreciate the significance of the presents and telephone calls.

However, their older adopted son, aged eight by the time the younger boy's contact had ceased, had begun to be 'rather jealous', asking why his birth parents did not send him presents. The adoptive parents forwarded a photograph and news of him to the agency each year, but doubted that there would be any response or that it would be possible to trace the birth mother (the birth father had not known of the pregnancy). The birth mother had been unwilling to meet the adoptive parents or agree to keep in touch with the agency because she had felt the need to keep her pregnancy a secret from her family and community. As transracial adopters, the adoptive parents commented that 'ideally, we would have preferred openness for all three children'. In the event, they felt their middle child had not been affected by the ending of contact, while their oldest son might have found it more upsetting over the years if his brother's contact had continued. They therefore felt 'some relief' that contact had ended, although they would not refuse contact if either of the birth parents were to get in touch in the future.

Adoptive parents who had older children adopted as babies and now in their twenties, wished, looking back, that they had met their birth parents: in one case, the birth mother had in fact requested this, but the adoptive parents had felt 'threatened' by the suggestion and had refused. Twenty six years later, they had spoken to her on the telephone, their daughter having traced her.

Thus on the whole, for this group of adoptive parents, birth parent contact was not creating difficulties for other children in the family, whatever their legal status, at the time of the second interview.

VI CONCLUSION

The interviews with adoptive parents in 18 families provided an opportunity to explore whether and how their feelings about adoption with contact had changed in the four years since the first meeting with them. They now had longer experience as adoptive parents and some of the children were reaching an age at which issues of identity and independence were increasingly important (18 were aged 16 years or more). More young people were negotiating contact arrangements themselves and this included in three instances a decision to end face-to-face contact and in five cases to stay for a weekend with birth parents.

The adoptive parents in 13 families who had felt positively about contact in 1987 continued to do so. In addition, adoptive parents in two families who had previously expressed concerns or unease about contact, were able to acknowledge when reinterviewed that they had ascribed to the effects of contact their earlier dissatisfaction with their child's behaviour and degree of attachment. They now described ways in which contact had been helpful to their child, despite tensions in the relationship between the adults in one instance. The extent and significance of contact for these 15 families varied, but some adoptive parents stated that contact had contributed to their satisfaction with their experience of adoption. All believed that their child had benefited, in some cases indirectly. Contact had not detracted from, and had sometimes enhanced, their identity as adoptive parents, particularly through dispelling myths.

Adoptive parents in the remaining three families had adopted Hayley, Craig and Melanie respectively. Hayley's adoptive parents were alone in stating that contact had been an almost entirely negative experience. Craig's adoptive parents had experienced the pain of his running away at the age of 14, not to return, while Melanie's adoptive parents had struggled for several years to manage her increasingly disruptive behaviour. However, the adoptive parents in neither family considered that these difficulties had resulted from contact, although meetings had in different ways been stressful at times.

The changes which had occurred in the pattern of contact reinforced the need for an open attitude on the part of adoptive parents, within which young people could take responsibility for negotiating contact and/or the adults could make adjustments to take account of changing needs. Contact had worked well when adoptive parents appreciated the value of contact or took the initiative themselves, rather than going along with arrangements less than wholeheartedly. The agency representative through which the two "less open" adoptive families had been recruited commented that with hindsight the importance of contact had not been taken into account sufficiently when children were identified for placement with them. This has implications for agency selection of adoptive parents.

A co-operative relationship with birth parents was also helpful. It did not seem necessary that adoptive parents and birth parents were alike in ethnic and cultural background, nor that they were of similar socio-economic status. However, it could be speculated, particularly in the light of the ease with which the one black family in the sample negotiated contact, that more similarity between the birth and adoptive families may have been helpful in some instances, at least in the early stages.

Social work input prior to placement and adoption had made a significant impact in some cases, suggesting that the benefits of a more open approach can be maximised with appropriate recruitment of adoptive parents, preparation of all parties, and mediation where necessary. The observations and suggestions made by adoptive parents about social work input are reported in Appendix III.

It seemed that, to a large degree assisted by contact, at least half the adoptive parents in the study had achieved 'some sense of kinship with the people who gave their child birth.'[1]

Reference

1. Rowe J, 'The reality of the adoptive family', in Tod R J (ed), *Social Work in Adoption*, Longman, 1971.

6 Discussion and policy implications

The present study, begun in 1985, has been concerned with issues of contact and permanence. It was undertaken in a context in which children for whom permanence was sought were almost invariably placed outside the family of origin on a "closed" adoption model. The purpose of the study at the outset was to explore whether termination of contact was necessary in order to achieve a secure placement and to gain insights about placement options which could accommodate contact. Stage 1 included interviews with adoptive parents in 22 families who described their perspectives of adoption with contact and their perception about its impact on their adopted children and, in some instances, on their children's birth parents. It clearly emerged that contact in some form after adoption did not have the adverse impact on the adoption placement which had been anticipated by most advocates of permanency planning in the late 1970s and early 1980s.

When the second stage of the study was begun in 1990, attitudes regarding contact among agency policy makers and practitioners had been influenced by research findings about the value of contact for children separated from their family of origin and the legislative recognition, especially through the Children Act 1989, of the importance of contact. Stage 2 provided an opportunity to review and add to the conclusions and suggestions for practice which had been derived from Stage 1 and the research then available.

Adoptive parents were able to comment on the effects of contact when their children had reached a later stage of development. Eighteen of the 27 adopted children were aged 16 years or more in 1991. More young people were able to take responsibility for negotiating arrangements. As contact is likely to have different meanings at different developmental stages, the second interviews were particularly illuminating. It was also possible to hear directly from some young people and a few birth parents.

There follows a discussion of the context and meaning of contact in relation to permanent placement, particularly adoption, and the implications for legislation, policy and practice.

I CONTACT: ITS CONTEXT AND MEANING

Contact with birth parents had been made available at some stage after adoption to the children in this study at a time when such arrangements were exceptional. It seems appropriate to consider the meaning of contact in the context of greater openness in society in the UK and at a time when a substantial minority of non-adopted children do not live with both their birth parents throughout their childhood.[1] Children living in adoptive families and having contact have much in common with other children who have complicated family networks. Moreover, there is also now greater awareness and recognition in the UK of the diversity of permanent arrangements ("social" rather than legal adoption) within the extended family and community in some Asian, African and Caribbean communities, in which a child may grow up having continuing involvement with birth parents.[2]

Implications of contact for the nature of adoption

Perceptions of the institution of modern adoption in Western societies began to change with the acceptance of Kirk's analysis of the hazards of the approach which valued "rejection of difference" between parenthood by adoption and by birth.[3] Rejection of difference was often the intended or unintended result of the closed model of adoption. Continuing or potential contact with birth relatives has been made possible by greater acceptance of the need to acknowledge difference but, as the present study demonstrates, has itself had an impact on the already changing nature of adoption. Even quite limited contact was shown to assist the acknowledgment of difference by making unavoidable the reality of the birth family, and, in some instances, highlighting the contribution of heredity to a child's development and personality.

It was noted in Chapter 1 that there is now greater recognition of adoption as a lifelong process. The closed model was developed during the period when adoption was seen 'as a brief process to meet an immediate need'.[4] This study has shown that the opportunity for contact enabled the adopted young people to develop or maintain relationships with birth relatives into adult life without the stress of the "search" and "reunion" which can create so much (usually needless) anxiety in a closed adoption. Contact also enhanced a young person's connection with a wide range of birth relatives, including brothers and sisters whose existence may not have been known without communication between the birth family and the adoptive family after adoption. The availability of contact means that these adopted young people will have some control in the future about maintaining contact or not with brothers and sisters. For many people, sibling relationships may be the most enduring, but a closed adoption has usually denied this possibility to children who have been adopted and to their non-adopted siblings.

Until the late 1960s, when the research findings of McWhinnie,[5] Kornitzer[6] and Triseliotis[7] were published, an adoption in the UK appears to have been regarded as successful, at least in the eyes of the adoptive parents, when a child fulfilled the "as if" role and showed no curiosity about her or his family of origin. The present study confirmed research and practitioner emphasis on the importance of greater openness within adoptive families about the family of origin.[8,9,10] A number of adoptive parents in this study indicated that contact had helped them to create an emotional climate in which family members felt comfortable to talk about the family of origin. There was an exceptionally "open" atmosphere in many of the households – the sense of openness was related more to the attitude of the adoptive parents than to the amount of contact.

Adoption in which children continue to maintain contact with birth parents represents a major departure from the concept of adoption which has prevailed in the UK since the late 1940s. Although it is often suggested that contact or the possibility of contact increases anxiety and insecurity, particularly on the part of adoptive parents, the evidence from this study is that by undermining secrecy and fantasy, well-managed contact can reduce such feelings.

The meaning of contact

As this study has demonstrated, contact can have a different meaning and fulfil a different purpose for each of the family members involved. Furthermore, it is important to recognise that contact encompasses a broad range of means of communication. The meaning of contact is considered here in relation to what are described by Howe and Hinings as 'two important and demanding matters' – 'the additional developmental tasks posed by adoption and the personal relationships within the family that have arisen out of the experience of loss'.[11] The themes of identity and loss are common to all parties in adoption and are being increasingly acknowledged.[12, 13]

The adopted person

The significance of contact for an adopted child will vary depending on the child's age and stage of development; the relationship with the birth relative with whom she or he is in touch; the role that contact is fulfilling at that time; and the extent of contact. Burnell has drawn attention to the likely changing meaning and value of contact over time.[14]

The variety of meanings can be illustrated from the present study. Thoburn has argued that children's well-being depends not only on the meeting of basic physical and psychological needs (which adopted children share with all children), but on the provision of 'a sense of "permanence" and also a sense of their own "identity".'[15] As described above, contact appeared or was stated to have been significant in relation to the development of a sense of identity for all the 15 children and young people interviewed, particularly for two of the African-Caribbean children placed transracially, although the extent of, and expressed wish for, contact varied greatly.

While for four young people, contact had fulfilled the need for information, contact had in addition provided continuity and had maintained an ongoing relationship for the other eleven young people, although their feelings about the relationship and the strength of the attachment varied. Furthermore, for one adopted young person, her contact with her grandparents seemed more significant than that with her mother, while for another, contact with siblings was more important. A young woman who had ended contact stated that it had been useful in helping her clarify that she wished to put down roots in her adoptive family, whereas contact had become more important for another young woman as she reached adulthood – her source of security and self-esteem.

Brothers and sisters placed together sometimes negotiated different levels of contact. Some of the older-placed children had been able to maintain what seemed a significant relationship with their birth parent while nonetheless wanting to be part of the adoptive family legally and emotionally. Contact, or the opportunity of contact, provided a range of choices for the adopted people in this study, which would have been denied them in a closed adoption. The extent to which young people were negotiating contact, including to end contact, demonstrated that an atmosphere of openness can lessen the powerlessness which adopted people, adults as well as children, have sometimes described.

Contact was not thought to have adversely affected the attachment of any of the children placed while under seven years of age, nor to have given rise to divided loyalties, even when there had been fortnightly face-to-face contact. Some of the older children were described as being more wary or taking several years to show a strong attachment. However, none had chosen to move to live with birth families on a permanent basis once reaching 16 or on leaving home. Adoptive parents were satisfied with the degree of attachment, being realistic about what were reasonable expectations, given the age of the children at placement and the impact of their earlier experiences.

The adoptive parents whose son had left their family believed that he *had* become attached to them, but that in adolescence, the pull of the "genetic bond" had been too strong, and he had felt that 'his loyalties lay with his birth family'. They thought with hindsight that fostering would have been a less difficult option for him than adoption, and that the disruption was caused not by contact but by a 'crisis of identity'. It should be noted that lack of or limited attachment is not unusual when children are placed later. Studies of *closed* adoption placements in the 1980s have shown that attachment difficulties are the major source of dissatisfaction and disruption for adoptive parents.[16,17,18]

Among the children not interviewed, contact seemed to have had different meanings for the children with learning difficulties. For example, face-to-face meetings provided continuity for one child, and would enable support to be provided in the future from his brother and sister.

There is no way of measuring how far contact may have helped the adopted children in this study come to terms with the loss inherent in adoption – the implicit (and sometimes explicit) rejection and becoming 'disconnected from one's ancestry'.[19] However, some of the older young people who were interviewed were clear that this had been one of the beneficial effects of contact for them, and this view was shared by many of the adoptive parents also.

A few young people appeared to draw some comfort from their perception that contact was helpful to their birth parents who had found adoption upsetting – a reassurance which is not available for children in a closed adoption who are aware at the time of placement or adoption of their birth parent's opposition or distress.

The birth parents

As outlined by Howe *et al*, the additional tasks required of a birth mother who has lost a child through closed adoption are concerned with 'living with loss'.[20] In picking up the threads of her life, she has to consider whom to tell – how to manage her 'spoiled identity'. It emerged from the interviews with birth parents in this study that despite greater social acceptance of adoption and more openness, discussing the loss of a child through adoption, within as well as outside the immediate family, was difficult, in varying degrees. However, the sense of loss was mitigated for all the birth parents by the reassurance contact provided, particularly the knowledge that the child was benefiting from adoption and the hope that the child would not feel rejected. This was particularly strongly felt by the birth mother with experience of both open and closed adoption.

There are additional adjustments implicitly or explicitly required of a birth parent in an adoption arrangement in which there is some continued contact, including adapting to a non-parental role in relation to the child and endeavouring to ensure that her or his contribution is beneficial to the child and acceptable to the adoptive parents. The birth parents interviewed were sensitive to this and clearly the costs involved in making this adjustment were outweighed for them by the positive aspects of contact, including enhanced self-esteem which derived from not feeling excluded. However, it seemed clear from the observations of one young woman and her adoptive parents that her birth mother had regarded contact as a possible means of retaining her parental role. This highlights the importance of seeking to understand what the opportunity of contact means to the different parties when an agreement for contact is negotiated and undertaking the necessary preparation and support.

The adoptive parents

The additional tasks of adoptive parents include achieving confidence in their identity as parents in relation to a child with whom they have no biological connection (and who may have been cared for in the early years by their birth parents or other significant carers); helping the child develop a sense of identity which incorporates valuing her or his heritage; and acknowledging the significance of the child's origins. Where there is contact, the reality of the birth family is more tangible. Overall, the majority of adoptive parents interviewed felt that their identity as parents (their sense of "entitlement") had been enhanced through greater openness and through contact. However, contact, whether through indirect or face-to-face contact, entails some degree of "sharing", which had been difficult for a few adoptive parents during the early stages, because of their need to feel that they were the child's only parents.

An experience of loss which characterises many (although by no means all) adoptive families derives from involuntary childlessness, and it was noticeable that adoptive parents in five of the six families who had described reservations or difficulties in relation to contact in 1987 had had to deal with issues arising from infertility. Where rivalry at some stage between adoptive and birth parents had been described by adoptive parents, this always concerned the feelings of an involuntarily childless adoptive parent in relation to the birth parent of the same gender. Even for adoptive parents who have experienced no difficulties around infertility, it is commonly suggested that adoption nonetheless entails loss – the lack of a shared heritage with the child and, possibly, no participation in her or his early life. Depending on the way adoptive parents are dealing with this loss, and particularly if their expectations of adoption are as a resolution of loss, contact may mean a heightened awareness of unresolved issues. However, according to the accounts of adoptive parents in this study, time and their increased confidence as parents lessened the impact of contact on their sense of loss through infertility, and their feelings of rivalry subsequently diminished.

For adoptive and birth parents, as well as the child, continuing contact involves an extension of family networks. Some adoptive parents very much welcomed this and were involved in visits or meetings with their children's birth parents and other relatives. This became quite complex in four families in which there were unrelated adopted children each having contact. In other arrangements, contact was more limited, or the adoptive parents did not become involved directly in their child's contact.

Factors affecting the experience of adoption with contact

The interviews in 1991 provided an opportunity to review the factors identified through the earlier interviews as being likely to result in a more positive or more negative experience of adoption with contact for the adoptive parents, and to obtain the perspective of the other participants. Factors associated with adoptive parents are considered first, since, as in the closed model of adoption, their attitudes and wishes were generally the most powerful determinant of the possibility and the extent of contact. It is important that the factors described below are not regarded as a list of indicators as to whether contact is desirable or feasible, since each case will need to be considered individually and social work practice can make a difference, as discussed below.

Factors associated with adoptive parents

Openness of attitude on the part of adoptive parents was confirmed as a prerequisite of their experiencing contact positively, and this quality also emerged as important to the adopted children and birth parents. Adoptive parents in two families, earlier assessed as less open in attitude, viewed contact more favourably when reinterviewed. They acknowledged that their previously negative perception of contact had been the result of their having been less than wholehearted about adoption with contact and their having ascribed to contact the dissatisfaction they were then experiencing in relation to their child's attachment. In families where contact had been very limited, but where the young people were encouraged to consider contact and/or talk openly about their adoption, they valued this. The birth parents who were interviewed were appreciative of adopters' openness of attitude – particularly their valuing of contact. Being able to maintain contact had made a great difference to their lives.

Being in control of contact was emphasised as important by adoptive parents in 1987, but less so in 1991, by which time young people themselves, particularly in the families in which there had previously been tensions, had taken responsibility for negotiating contact. Feeling in control was associated with having the legal security of adoption and with having offered to maintain contact rather than having had contact imposed through a court order. By far the largest group of adopters, in asserting their wish to be free to manage contact, had a child-focused approach – they wanted their child to feel free to participate in contact or not depending on her or his needs or wishes, which they knew would change or had changed with time. Within this framework, the nature and extent of contact was sometimes clearly within the control of the adopted person and, in other cases, birth parents were able to initiate contact.

Adoptive parents in five of the families interviewed in 1987 did not feel they had control of decisions about contact. Adoptive parents in three families had entered into an informal arrangement to continue contact and, when first interviewed, were not wholly convinced that this was right for them or their child and expressed varying degrees of resentment. Agencies selecting new families for the four children placed with adoptive parents in these three families appeared not to have given sufficient weight to the child's need or wish to maintain contact. None of the adoptive parents in these five families had initially wanted adoption with contact, but adoptive parents in two families had been able to adjust to the expectation of contact in a child-focused way. As contact arrangements in 1987 for the children placed in these five families were all negotiated and supervised by a social worker, the adoptive parents' sense of control was further diminished. It is possible that if adoptive parents who were willing to maintain contact had been specifically recruited for this group of children, direct negotiation between the parents would have occurred and discomfort with contact lessened.

Factors associated with birth parents

The agreement of birth parents was very important to adoptive parents, particularly those who had earlier anticipated a contested case. It was also clear that at least three of the young people would not have wanted to be adopted had their birth parents not agreed, and others were relieved that agreement had been forthcoming eventually. It emerged from the interviews with birth parents that those who were initially reluctant to agree to adoption did so because they felt they were being listened to, had some involvement or promise of involvement, and knew that they could maintain contact or at least receive news of their child's progress. Some of the adoptive parents who were interviewed acknowledged how hard it must be for birth parents to give agreement without having met their child's adopters and without any expectation of receiving news in the future. This study thus provides some indicators as to how social work practice can reduce the need for contested cases.

Birth parents' approval of the adoptive parents was a related but separate factor. Having been chosen by birth parents or believing that birth parents are confident in them as suitable parents for their child enhances adoptive parents' sense of identity as adopters and confirms them in their role. Birth parents who are upset or unhappy about the plan for adoption, may feel able to give their agreement because through contact they recognise that their child's welfare will be safeguarded by the adopters who have been selected. Knowing their birth parents approve of their adoptive family may help children adjust to being in an adoptive family and/or be a source of satisfaction to them. Adoptive parents in a few families who had been aware of birth parent disapproval at some stage had felt undermined by this initially.

In two placements, adoptive parents reported that by 1991, their children's birth parents had expressed appreciative comments about their care of the children – contact can enable birth parents to distinguish between the adoptive parents and the agency. It is noteworthy that in the two instances in which approval was perceived not to be forthcoming (even though agreement to adoption was given), one young woman chose to end contact, and her brother, adopted separately, left his adoptive family to return to the care of his birth mother. This highlights the importance of working to avoid a child potentially feeling disloyal to one set of parents or the other.

The role adopted by birth parents is seen as supportive by adoptive parents when they do not feel their function as parents is undermined. This is likely to follow from a good relationship in which there is scope for negotiation and mutual respect. The birth parents who were interviewed were particularly sensitive on this point. One birth parent had been helped by social work input to clarify her role after adoption, while the others had negotiated this with the adoptive parents without social work involvement. Participants' views about social work input are given in Appendix III.

Factors associated with the child

The age of the child at placement is particularly important. Contact is more likely to be experienced positively by adoptive parents when children are seven years or younger at placement, although the study indicated that older children can be successfully placed with continuing contact. Contact may be perceived as problematic in the case of older children who have had adverse pre-placement experiences such as long periods in residential care; many changes of carer, including previous disrupted "permanent" placements; emotional and behavioural problems at placement; placement separate from brothers and sisters; and erratic, rather than consistent, contact with their birth parents. These features are known to be likely to affect adversely a child's ability to attach in closed adoptions, which itself is linked to adoptive parents' satisfaction with their experience of adoption.[21,22]

When adoptive parents felt their child's attachment to them was limited, they were more likely to describe tensions around contact. However, adoptive parents in only one family believed that, with hindsight, their daughter's contact with her birth mother should not have continued. There was no evidence in this study that contact in itself led to difficulties for the child in becoming attached to the adoptive family. Adoptive parents in six families who had expressed reservations regarding contact in 1987 were struggling with their child's behaviour or were experiencing dissatisfaction with their child's level of attachment. Adoptive parents in three families believed their child's difficult behaviour was more marked before or after face-to-face contact once or twice a year, but adoptive parents in the other three families did not attribute difficulties to contact. It could be that at least some adoptive parents ascribed to contact their disappointment with some aspects of their experience of adoption. Contact was seen as unproblematic in the case of younger-placed children and this may be related to the fact that adoption, whether closed or with contact, is on the whole more "successful" for the younger group; in particular, younger children are likely to have fewer obstacles to becoming attached.

Limited understanding/acceptance of the reason for adoption may inhibit a child's adjustment to the adoptive family. It is striking that all eight children in the six families whose adoptive parents expressed reservations in 1987 had a brother or sister who remained at home with a birth parent, and a few adoptive parents commented that this had been a source of confusion for their child. Other young people only developed a fuller understanding, with the help of contact, as they reached adolescence. In this context, contact may highlight unresolved issues, although it is relevant to point out that difficulties and disruption due to identity issues and limited understanding of the circumstances of adoption commonly occur in closed adoption, particularly in adolescence.[23,24]

Relationships between birth and adoptive parents

The establishment of a good relationship between the adults, which was so important to all the participants who were interviewed, may develop over time. Some adoptive parents felt that social workers had not done enough early on to make it possible for them and their children's birth parents to develop some mutual understanding, for example, by providing opportunities for them to meet together. Clearly the establishment of a good relationship was likely to be easier when birth parents had requested adoption and been involved in the choice of adopters. However, this study demonstrates that a child-focused approach by both sets of parents, together with an openness of attitude on the part of adopters which acknowledges birth parents' concerns, can result in a good relationship, despite the adversarial nature of proceedings between the birth parents and the local authority prior to placement. Social workers had sometimes, but by no means invariably, assisted in this process.

A good relationship between their two sets of parents is valued by children and young people and is helpful to their self-esteem. Three young people described vividly the tensions at meetings when their parents had not achieved mutual acceptance. Although social workers "supervised" these meetings, it did not appear that there had been any attempt at mediation between meetings, nor any consideration of alternative ways of managing meetings.

The birth parents who were interviewed had responded positively to the openness of attitude of their children's adoptive parents, so that a relationship was established which was valued by all the adults. This quality of openness in adoptive parents is essential, and likely to evoke a co-operative response from birth parents who usually feel powerless in comparison with prospective adopters, especially when they are losing their children through adoption against their will.

Differences in ethnicity, culture and class were generally not in themselves significant in the relationships established and the satisfaction experienced, according to the accounts of the respondents. However, the one black family in the study attributed their good relationship with their son's birth relatives to a shared cultural understanding about the possibility of adoption with contact, and some adoptive parents may have underestimated the effect of differences from the perspective of birth parents. More significant was openness of attitude and a shared understanding about the needs of the child. Where these were absent, differences in background became more apparent. However, as in all relationships, the "chemistry" between people was important, as evidenced by the fact that adoptive parents in four families who had contact with more than one set of birth parents, found some relationships developed more easily than others. The adopted people were less likely to mention differences in background than their parents.

The perception of the impact of contact on the adopted child

It is important to birth and adoptive parents alike that contact is perceived to be of benefit to their child. Benefits may be direct or indirect, for example, in the case of some children with learning disabilities or younger-placed children where contact after adoption has not been ongoing. Children may gain in different ways at different stages. The adoptive parents who described benefits for their child's emotional well-being most commonly referred to their sense of identity and self-esteem; their greater understanding of the circumstances leading to adoption and of their heritage; their feeling a connection with birth relatives; and, in the case of some older children, their having had permission to develop attachments in their new family. None of the adoptive parents believed that contact had interfered with their developing an attachment to their child. The birth parents who were interviewed felt strongly that their involvement, and that of brothers and sisters, in the lives of their children, was beneficial to them currently and would be so in the future.

The process

The satisfaction of adoptive parents with the experience of adoption with contact is associated with the stage at which the need for contact has been identified and by whom. Adoptive parents who take the initiative to instigate or maintain contact, and those who believe it is important to maintain contact in accordance with the wishes of the child and/or the birth parents, are likely to regard their experience of contact positively. Where children needing placement are having ongoing contact which is planned to continue after adoption in some form, prospective adopters should be appropriately selected. Adoptive parents reported feeling particularly strengthened in that role when they had been chosen by birth parents.

The birth parents who were interviewed had been able to remain in touch with their children only because of the willingness of the adoptive parents. Adopters had *not* been selected by the agency on the basis that they would maintain contact. Two birth parents felt strongly that the initial decision as to whether contact should continue should not depend solely on the wishes of the adoptive parents, irrespective of the wishes of the birth family and the needs of the child. It is important to note that some birth parents needed time to come to accept the plan for adoption and that the attitudes of adoptive parents and of social workers were an important part of this process.

The most satisfactory way of arranging contact from the perspective of all participants in the study was by direct negotiation, whether between the adults (as tended to happen with younger children or those with learning difficulties); or involving the child and the adults; or between the adopted young person and her or his birth family, with the approval of the adoptive parents.

Social worker input

In some cases, contact arrangements had developed in a positive way despite, rather than because of, social worker input (see Appendix III). In others, an agency's or a social worker's belief in the value of openness and contact had influenced the recruitment and preparation of prospective adopters and (less often) the work with the birth parents and the child. In a few cases, it seemed that mediation might have reduced the stress reported by adoptive parents. Clearly social work input can make a difference. The implications of the study findings for social work practice are discussed below.

It can be seen that a number of overlapping variables obtained in those placements in which a less positive experience of adoption with contact was described. An older child at placement may have problems in attaching, perhaps combined with behaviour difficulties, which make the experience of adoption, whether "open" or "closed", less rewarding to adoptive parents. Contact in itself does not impede attachment. However, contact may be perceived, particularly by "less open" adopters, to be the reason for a less satisfactory adoption, when there might have been the same outcome without contact. All studies show older child adoptions to be more problematic, and most concern "closed" adoption.

A factor which did not affect the experience of adoption with contact was the nature and extent of contact. In some of the placements described most positively by adoptive parents (and in one case by the adopted person and her mother also), face-to-face contact had been frequent, at least once a month. In most, contact had been more limited or had ended by 1991 but might nonetheless be described in positive terms by participants. In those placements in which contact had been described as problematic, contact had been relatively infrequent, ranging from one to three meetings a year.

The child's participation in decision-making

Fox Harding has described the 'manifestations of a children's rights perspective' in English child care policy in the 1980s.[25] Southwell, in her study of applications made to juvenile courts in the North of England during 1987–88, asserted that access (the term in use prior to the Children Act 1989) 'is the right of the child'.[26] Section 10(8) of the Act gives children of 'sufficient understanding' the right to seek leave to apply for a section 8 order (which could include a contact order). *The Guardian*, in May 1993, described a case in which a brother and sister aged eleven and ten years respectively had been granted legal aid for their application for an order that their father have more contact with them. However, Weyland 1992 has pointed out that it 'has never been stated judicially that access is a right of a child in care'.[27]

A number of the young people interviewed in the present study expressed the view that contact, or the availability of contact, was the right of an adopted child, while the brother and sister of an adopted child believed that they should have had the right to maintain contact with him. One of the possible conclusions of pursuing this view is that the closed model of adoption infringes the child's right by removing or by making very difficult the potential for contact. However, even if the possibility of contact is regarded as the right of adopted children, they, like other young people, will continue to rely on adults to a greater or lesser extent to exercise their rights.[28]

The importance of ascertaining and taking account of children's wishes and feelings is emphasised in the Children Act 1989. Hinchliffe argues that under earlier legislation, children's wishes and feelings received more attention 'if they happened to conform with the professional view', with a child who wanted no contact with birth relatives being more likely to be listened to than a child who wanted to keep in touch with them.[29] There were examples in the studies conducted by Thoburn, Murdoch and O'Brien, and Southwell of children's wishes regarding contact being disregarded.[30,31]

In the present study, only one young person stated that her wishes regarding contact (in her case to end contact with her birth mother at the time of the adoption hearing) had not been sought. Another young person estimated that 99 per cent of children would wish to remain in contact with their birth relatives. Ascertaining the wishes and feelings of children is a skilled task, particularly when they may not accord with the wishes or views of their carers and/or the worker involved. In most cases in this study contact had occurred or was agreed when the children were not of sufficient age or understanding for their wishes to be sought. In those instances, decisions had been made in relation to the perception by adults of the child's welfare.

The Children Act 1989 requires that the child's welfare is the paramount consideration in all decisions affecting her or him. However, as the Stage 1 interviews with agency representatives demonstrated, the views of social work professionals as to what will best promote a child's welfare are influenced by agency policies and individual attitudes, rather than by the circumstances of a particular case. And Weyland, reviewing case-law in different legal contexts, has pointed out that the concept of the welfare of the child is 'capable of being filled with different meanings on account of its indeterminacy and vagueness, and these change with the passage of time under the influence of an expertise which is constantly open to revision.[32] While most of the birth and adoptive parents interviewed in the study had both a child-focused perspective and an openness of attitude regarding contact, there were a few instances of adoptive parents finding it difficult to set on one side their own wishes and feelings when considering whether contact was helpful to their children.

Positive feelings about contact in some form were expressed by all but one of the adopted people interviewed. Furthermore, the adopted people and/or their parents believed they had benefited from contact and would continue to do so in adulthood. This suggests that the Children Act presumption that contact will usually be beneficial should guide policy makers and practitioners when contact is being considered in relation to a child whose wishes cannot be ascertained because of their age or level of understanding.

Traditionally, as Hartman and Laird have pointed out, adopted children are 'the most disempowered' of all those involved in adoption, 'having generally had no opportunity to participate in the decisions that have so powerfully shaped their lives and their identities'.[33] Although Hartman and Laird were writing of the experience of adoption in North America, it is applicable in the UK.

The Children Act 1989 has emphasised the importance of children's participation in decision-making. Some well-publicised cases have given an indication as to how far children can be regarded as able to participate. An eleven-year-old girl was assessed by her solicitor as being of sufficient age and understanding to seek leave to apply for a residence order to enable her to leave the home of her birth mother and live with her former foster carers; an interim residence order was granted.[34] And a girl of 13 was allowed by the Court of Appeal in May 1993 to proceed with an application for a residence order authorising her to leave her adoptive parents and live with her birth mother's sister.[35]

In practice, as studies of permanent placements show, most children who are adopted are under ten years when placed. How far can children in that age group be fully informed about adoption and contact and any alternatives available so as to enable them to participate in decisions? And are they likely to be assessed as having sufficient understanding to be consulted? The competence of children aged eight and over to agree to or decline orthopaedic surgery is discussed by Alderson.[36] The nature of decision-making in relation to the kind of surgery which Alderson has studied (painful and disabling in the short term, but with the possibility of improved mobility in adulthood) has some parallels with the decision-making undertaken by professionals as part of permanency planning, when children's contact with birth relatives was routinely severed, irrespective of their wishes – 'the price that has to be paid to achieve permanence'.[37] In both situations, adults' 'belief in their superior wisdom' is used to justify over-riding or not listening to children's wishes for the sake of their putative future interests. Alderson asserts that adults have to 'give away power before children can assert more control over their own lives'.[38]

The draft Adoption Bill proposes that children of twelve years and older should be asked to give their agreement to adoption. This proposal has met with mixed responses, with some concern expressed about the possible effects on the child, in the short and/or longer term, of having to consent to an arrangement which severs the legal connection with her or his birth family. There were three instances in this study of adopted people regarding (or being said to regard) adoption differently at a later point in their lives: one adopted child left his adoptive home at 14 although at the age of 11 he had written to the court asserting that he wished to be adopted; a young woman who had requested that she be adopted at 13 had said when she was 17 that she wished she had never been adopted; and a young woman described how adoption after many years as a foster child may have been a mistake because this changed her adoptive parents' emotional expectations of her.

Many different interpretations could be offered for these apparently changed feelings about adoption. It may be pertinent that in all three instances, birth parents were reported to have been opposed to adoption or to have had reservations or to have felt distressed. These reported comments indicate both how subsequent events may alter perspectives and how difficult it must be, even for children over twelve, to consider fully the long-term implications of adoption decisions. This would not justify disregarding children's wishes and feelings in decision-making. However, it is important that children are not left feeling totally responsible for decisions with lifelong implications, particularly if those decisions may currently or at a later date be construed as implying disloyalty or ingratitude to one or other set of parents.

Particularly in relation to very young children, who are clearly unable to participate in decision-making, but also in the case of older children, given that feelings about contact change over time, it would seem that their welfare can best be promoted by placement with adoptive parents who are open in attitude and open to the possibility of some form of contact in the future. This has implications for policy and practice.

II IMPLICATIONS FOR LEGISLATION, POLICY AND PRACTICE

Before discussing the findings of this exploratory study in relation to legislation, policy and practice, it is important to consider how far generalisation would be justified.

The finding from the 1987 agency interviews which is of particular relevance in terms of current policy and practice, was the marked impact of agency policy and workers' attitudes towards adoption and openness on the sort of placements effected. Although only about one third of voluntary adoption agencies, and no local authority agencies, were included in the sample, this finding is likely to be applicable more generally. Other UK studies have highlighted differences in the way legislation is implemented,[39] while studies in the US and in New Zealand have demonstrated how agency attitudes influence the degree of openness sought or offered by birth and adoptive parents.

Generalisation from the interviews in 1987 with adoptive parents in 22 families about adoption with contact was acknowledged to be limited because the sample was too small to allow for statistical analysis. Furthermore, the sample was likely to have been biased; adoptive parents may have tended to diminish any sense of dissatisfaction with the effects of contact; the picture conveyed by adoptive parents was essentially a "snapshot"; and the evaluation of openness was based on the perspectives only of the adoptive parents.

Despite these limitations, it could nonetheless be asserted on the basis of these interviews, conducted at a time when severing contact prior to adoption was still the usual practice in the UK, that continuing contact did not appear to jeopardise the achievement of permanency through adoption. On the contrary, when considered in the context of the quantitative study from which the samples were derived, contact emerged as a protective factor. This finding is consistent with those of the Lothian study[40] and the sibling placement study by Wedge and Mantle.[41] It is relevant to point out that there have been no studies focusing on the effects on children of the severance of contact which the closed model of adoption requires. The interviews with adoptive parents enabled some tentative suggestions to be made as to the factors which were likely to result in contact being experienced positively by the adoptive parents.

The further interviews in 1991 with adoptive parents in 18 of the 22 families reduced the "snapshot" effect, in that adoptive parents were able to draw on longer experience of contact and the majority of their adopted children were by this time teenagers or young adults. All but two of the 27 children in those adoptive families who had had some form of contact with birth parents could be judged as having been successfully placed, using Thoburn's criteria.[42] However, the limitations outlined above in relation to the 1987 interviews with adoptive parents were applicable to the interviews with adopted young people and birth parents: even smaller numbers; biased samples (all had agreed to be interviewed, and the adoptive parents had been able to determine which children were invited to participate); and the adopted young people particularly would have been susceptible to responding to the interest of the interviewer.

However, some useful insights emerged from these additional interviews which, taken together with the initial interviews with adoptive parents and the increased literature now available about openness and contact, could be useful to policy makers and practitioners. This study explored aspects of contact not available from studies in New Zealand and the US, which have been mainly concerned with adoption of infants voluntarily relinquished. And while the interviews focused on contact with birth parents, the insights for practice could be applied in relation to contact with non-parental relatives, since similar, but potentially less complex, issues arise.

Legislation

The present study has demonstrated that more open practice, including adoption with contact, is achievable within the framework of the Adoption Act 1976. All the contact arrangements were the result of voluntary agreement, rather than a condition of access, and were put in place largely as a result of the openness of attitude of the adoptive parents and, to a lesser extent, the identifying by some agency workers of a child's need for contact. The philosophy and attitudes of professionals would seem to be more significant than the legislative framework, as highlighted by Jackson in her review of the implementation of the Children Act 1989 from the perspective of families.[43]

However, primary legislation, and particularly accompanying Guidance, have the potential to alter the balance of power – the Guidance accompanying the Children Act 1989 acknowledged the need to redress the previous imbalance between birth families and local authorities in respect of contact.[44] Furthermore, the decrease since implementation of the Act in 1991 in the number of children looked after by local authorities following compulsory proceedings[45] should reduce the number of contested cases, since such proceedings have been shown to lessen co-operation between the local authority and the birth parents.[46]

The proposals regarding legislative changes contained in the draft Adoption Bill appear not to take account of studies which indicate that contact tends to be a protective rather than a destabilising factor. There is no reference to the potentially positive aspects of contact, described by the majority of respondents in this study, nor to the fact that birth parents on the whole wish through contact to contribute to their child's well-being, rather than to jeopardise it. Underlying the attitudes to contact in the Adoption Bill, in contrast to those informing provisions in the Children Act 1989 and the interdepartmental Review published in 1992, there appears to be a revival of the Victorian notion of the "deserving" and the "undeserving": the wishes of the "new parents", it is implied, are more worthy of respect in regard to contact than those of the birth parents or even the child.[47]

Agency policy and attitudes

In seeking to develop more open practice, it is important that agency workers acknowledge the power they hold in relation to all parties in adoption and in determining the sort of placement achieved for a child. The powerlessness of birth parents in the UK system has recently been better understood (although in jurisdictions in which independent and private placements are permitted, such as certain states in the US, a birth parent will have greater power to choose adoptive parents and request contact). Once a child has been placed, adoptive parents are usually regarded as the most powerful of the parties personally involved in adoption. It was suggested following the 1987 interviews, and now seems to be confirmed, that in order to achieve greater openness in their practice, professionals need to relinquish to the parties personally involved, particularly the child and the birth parents, some of the power which they have increasingly assumed since the first UK legislation in 1926.

Given the concern of some of the adoptive parents and young people interviewed regarding the availability of services to birth relatives, and their sensitivity to birth parents' feelings about the adoption, it is important that agency policies create a context in which the need for adoption can be negotiated, understood and accepted by birth parents and the wider family, and in which contested cases occur only in exceptional circumstances. Policies should be sensitive to cultural differences and to race, religion and language and should:

- *ensure that the resources of the wider family are fully explored*, as required by the Children Act 1989, and that services are provided to birth parents and other relatives so as to avoid the need for a placement outside the family of origin. The Family Rights Group is currently pioneering a system of "family conferences", based on the New Zealand model, in order to achieve this.[48]

- *incorporate a less eurocentric view of permanence*, valuing the experience of other cultures, so that adoption, and particularly closed adoption, is no longer regarded as a superior form of permanence.[49]
- *recognise the range of forms of communication*, with birth parents and/or other relatives, that can be beneficial to adopted children and both their families, particularly acknowledging the strong feelings of children in this study, both those living in adoptive families and those remaining with their birth parents, about the importance of contact with brothers and sisters. However, it is important that the rigidity of permanency planning in its extreme form is not replaced by assumptions that contact will always be appropriate, irrespective of individual circumstances and cultural backgrounds, or that any one form of contact is likely to be more beneficial than another. Baran and Pannor, advocates of more open adoption in the US for two decades, highlighted the importance of a framework which permits 'whatever is necessary and meaningful for the individuals involved'.[50]
- *not assume that there are inevitably conflicting needs and wishes* regarding contact as between adopted children and their two sets of parents and between adoptive and birth parents. This study and that of Ryburn[51] demonstrate that with good will, a child-centred approach and skilled mediation, positive contact arrangements are possible even after the prospect or experience of a contested case.

These policies and attitudes would seem to be essential if agencies are to work towards practice which enhances the likelihood of contact being experienced positively.

Agency practice

This study indicates what factors are likely to contribute to positive experiences of openness and contact for participants, and how agency practice can enhance the benefits of contact.

Exploring the possibility of contact

The possibility of some form of contact or potential contact with a birth relative (not necessarily a parent) should be considered in relation to all adoption placements, taking into account children's wishes and feelings and recognising that these may change over time. A presumption that contact is likely to be beneficial may make it more acceptable for children to express a wish to have contact with a birth relative without feeling that they will jeopardise their opportunity to be adopted, as used to be the case, or that they are being disloyal to their adoptive parents. In this study, contact for children under seven at placement proved to be relatively uncomplicated. However, such children, and others who have learning difficulties, may be unable to express their wishes and feelings, and it would be the responsibility of agencies to consider and discuss with prospective adoptive parents and birth relatives the potential benefits of contact arrangements which this study has highlighted.

Although adoptive parents were more likely to express reservations about contact in relation to older-placed children, there was no indication that problems in attaching, or behaviour or emotional difficulties, would have been fewer in a closed adoption, nor that they were significantly exacerbated by contact. Moreover, there were some examples of particularly successful placements with contact of older children: the key factors seemed to be the the child's pre-placement experiences; openness of attitude of adoptive parents; the ability of birth parents to indicate, over time, their acceptance of the adoption plan; and whether work around separation and loss had been undertaken with the child and the birth parents. Social work input in some of these areas could effect some change in outcome.

Involving birth relatives in the process

Birth parents and other relatives have tended historically to receive least attention and respect, and the experience of the birth parents interviewed reflected this. Assuming that alternatives to adoption have been thoroughly explored and that placement of a child for adoption is significantly better than any other option, the evidence from this study is that it is helpful to involve birth parents (and/or possibly other relatives) in the choice of adoptive parents, with particular emphasis on the degree of contact requested by the birth relatives. Clearly agreement to such a request should be consistent with the welfare of the child, but it should not be determined by the availability or otherwise of prospective adopters willing to consider contact: this and other studies have shown that "open" adopters can be recruited by agencies which value a child's connection with her or his family of origin.

However, contact should not be offered only as an inducement to persuade a birth parent to give agreement to adoption. Although it was true for some birth parents interviewed that the reassurance provided by contact enabled them to give agreement, or give agreement more willingly, contact was offered because it was thought to accord with the child's wishes or be likely to promote her or his welfare. Birth parents may oppose or withhold agreement to adoption (there was one example of the latter in this study) and nonetheless maintain contact co-operatively.[52]

It is to be hoped that agencies will regard birth parents as being entitled to be treated with courtesy and sensitivity – as the White Paper proposed in the case of prospective adopters. In the great majority of cases skilled counselling and the participation of birth parents in the process are likely to reduce the possibility of a contested case, which, as this study indicates, would be beneficial for all parties. However, a birth parent may, understandably, only be ready to give agreement once he or she is satisfied through contact that the child is making good progress in the care of the adoptive parents.

Recruitment and preparation of prospective adopters

Since openness within the adoptive family, and openness to the possibility of contact, clearly emerged from this study as helpful to all participants, agencies should recruit and prepare adopters in the expectation of openness, and perhaps contact, explaining that the evidence suggests this will enhance, rather than detract from, their identity as adoptive parents and is likely to reduce the risk of placement breakdown. Because the wish for contact (or an adoptive parent's perception that contact would be beneficial) may arise in any adoption, it is important that all adoptive parents accept this possibility, irrespective of the wishes of the birth relatives and/or the child at the time of placement and adoption.

It is important to emphasise that in many placements agency philosophy and support, over time, were significant in the development of these positive factors. Adoptive parents in 14 families had been influenced at some stage during the process by the agency preparation or by their social worker to consider the potential benefits to their child of contact – it is striking that adoptive parents in 12 of these families had been recruited by four voluntary adoption agencies while the same "excellent" local authority social worker had worked with the remaining two families. Some adoptive parents had initially been anxious about contact with birth parents, particularly where birth parents had been expected to oppose the adoption application. In a few cases, the relationship between the two sets of parents had initially been strained or even hostile. In these situations, helpful social work intervention and a welcoming approach by adoptive parents had enabled birth parents to contribute positively. On the whole, adoptive parents were aware and appreciative of the pressures on birth parents whose child had been placed for adoption and their openness of attitude and capacity to convey this seemed to be the key to a co-operative relationship.

The selection of adoptive parents to take account of contact wishes is essential: adoptive parents in three families who expressed reservations when interviewed in 1987 had reluctantly agreed to contact arrangements set up by the agency. In Stage 1 of the present study, the openness of attitude of the adoptive parents interviewed was assessed, using indicators which have been described in an earlier publication.[53] Briefly, an approach which regards adoption as "gift" rather than "rescue", with prospective adopters who can acknowledge the loss for the child and the birth relatives which adoption entails, is likely to result in a child-focused perspective on contact. People seeking to adopt are unlikely to have this understanding when they first make contact with an agency, while the public perception of adoption continues to be of a "clean break". Involving birth relatives and adopted people in preparation groups may assist prospective adopters to develop greater awareness of the realities of the adoption task.

Maximising benefits for the child

It was important to the adoptive parents and birth parents interviewed that their children benefited, directly or indirectly, from the contact which was occurring or had done in the past. Children seemed most likely to benefit if the plans for contact were child-focused. Until such time as the adopted young people were able to negotiate their own arrangements for contact, the situations which were most satisfactory were those in which adoptive and birth parents were in direct contact, while the least satisfactory were those in which meetings took place on neutral territory supervised by a social worker. In those placements, there were one or more reasons why these arrangements obtained, including lack of openness of attitude on the part of the adoptive parents; birth parents' continuing resentment about the adoption; and a lack of trust between the parents. Neutral territory, such as a place of recreation rather than a social work office, would not have been associated with tension if it had been chosen for practical reasons rather than those outlined above. Several participants expressed the view that adoptive parents and birth parents should be given more opportunity to get to know each other at an early stage and take responsibility for negotiating contact. This suggests that it would be helpful if workers relinquished power to the parties involved, and that even if a pre-placement meeting were not possible, birth and adoptive parents should have control over the information they share with each other.

It is clear from this study that agency policy and practice can increase the likelihood that adoption with some degree of contact will be a positive experience for the participants.

Post-adoption services

There was a limited amount of post-adoption input described by participants in this study. In 1987, only the five adoptive families in which social workers negotiated and supervised contact were currently in touch with the placing agency. These contact arrangements had ended by 1991 and the families were no longer in touch with a social worker. There was some post-adoption input in three families: adoptive parents in one family had been in contact with two social workers to re-establish links with the birth mothers of their two unrelated children; one boy of 13 and his adoptive parents were in touch with a local authority social worker who helped facilitate contact with the boy's brother and sister if his birth mother were unwell; and an adoptive family had approached a voluntary agency to act as a means of their exchanging correspondence with their son's birth family.

Although there was surprisingly little post-adoption input in the study (given that all but two of the children had had special needs at placement), it is generally anticipated by practitioners that contact arrangements will involve more input than would be required in a closed adoption. Burnell, drawing on the experience of the Post Adoption Centre, has described the exploration of mediation services in relation to conflict over contact.[54] Many agencies now have "letter-box" arrangements, whereby news and photographs can be forwarded or exchanged between the adoptive and the birth family. However, it is easy to anticipate circumstances in which an agency will need to do more than forward letters and photographs, for example, if distressing news has to be conveyed.

Adoption with contact in agency placements has had too limited a history in the UK for any certainty as to how far it will increase the demands on post-adoption services during the childhood of the adopted person. It is possible that the existence of more open arrangements will, over time, reduce the need for the counselling and intermediary work which is offered to adopted adults seeking information or to trace their birth relatives, and to members of birth families who have lost a child through adoption.

III CONCLUSION

As is common with small-scale, exploratory studies, this study has highlighted areas in which further research is needed, particularly the impact on children of birth parents' reluctance to agree to adoption, and indeed of contested cases; and the experience and adjustment of children who lose a brother or sister through adoption. In relation to adoption with contact, there is a need for greater understanding of the significance of differences of ethnic background, culture and class between the birth and adoptive family and, particularly important, of the effects on children into adulthood of a range of contact arrangements, preferably seeking the perspective of the adoptive and birth parents, as well as that of the adopted person. The need for longitudinal studies is confirmed by the preliminary research in the US reported by McRoy: 'family dynamics and openness arrangements change over time and it is critical to continue to study the impact of the changes on each member of the triad'.[55] However, Baran and Pannor, also writing in the US, argue that 'the growth of open adoption must not wait the for the results of long-term empirical studies'.[56]

There were a few examples in the present study of placements in which contact had been, at some stage, a source of stress for at least the adoptive parents, and probably for the adopted child and birth parents also. However, in the majority of placements, contact, in its various forms and in different ways, had been of benefit to the participants and had not undermined the security of the adoption placement. This should prove reassuring to practitioners seeking to place children who wish to remain in contact with birth relatives; to adoptive parents whose child is requesting that contact be initiated or maintained; to birth parents who wish to contribute to their children's well-being after adoption; and to children who should no longer be required to give up contact with their original family in order to have the opportunity of a permanent family placement.

References

1. Bradshaw J, 'The shape of things to come', *Community Care*, 27 January 1994.
2. Dutt R, and Sanyal A, 'Openness in adoption or open adoption – a black perspective', *Adoption & Fostering*, 15:4, pp 111–15, BAAF, 1991.
3. Kirk H D, *Shared Fate: A theory of adoption and mental health*, Collier Macmillan, 1964.
4. Baran A, and Pannor R, 'Open adoption', in Brodzinsky D M, and Schechter M D (eds), *The Psychology of Adoption*, Oxford University Press, 1990.
5. McWhinnie A M, *Adopted Children: How they grow up*, Routledge & Kegan Paul, 1967.
6. Kornitzer M, *Adoption and Family Life*, Putnam, 1968.
7. Triseliotis J, *In Search of Origins*, Routledge & Kegan Paul, 1973.
8. Triseliotis J, 'Identity and security in adoption and long-term fostering', *Adoption & Fostering*, 7:1, pp 22–31, BAAF, 1983.
9. Thoburn J, *Success and Failure in Permanent Family Placement*, Avebury Gower, 1990.

10. Burnell A, 'Open adoption: a post-adoption perspective', in Adcock M, Kaniuk J, and White R (eds), *Exploring Openness in Adoption*, Significant Publications, 1993.

11. Howe D, and Hinings D, *The Post-adoption Centre: First three years*, Research abstracts, University of East Anglia, 1993.

12. Winkler R C, Brown D W, Van Keppel M, and Blanchard A, *Clinical Practice in Adoption*, Pergamon Press, 1988.

13. Brodzinsky D M, and Schechter M D (eds), *The Psychology of Adoption*, Oxford University Press, 1990.

14. See 10 above, pp 85–86.

15. Thoburn J, *Child Placement: Principles and practice*, Community Care Practice Handbook, Wildwood House, 1988.

16. Macaskill C, *Against the Odds: Adopting mentally handicapped children*, BAAF, 1985.

17. Argent H (ed), *Keeping the Doors Open*, BAAF, 1988.

18. See 9 above.

19. Small J, quoted in Winkler *et al*, see 12.

20. Howe D, Sawbridge P, and Hinings D, *Half a Million Women: Mothers who lose their children by adoption*, Penguin Books, 1992.

21. See 17 above.

22. Hill M, Hutton S, and Easton S, 'Adoptive parenting – plus and minus', *Adoption & Fosterting*, 12:2, BAAF, pp 17–23, 1988.

23. Fitzgerald J, *Understanding Disruption*, BAAF, 1983.

24. See 17 above.

25. Fox Harding L, *Perspectives in Child Care Policy*, Longman, 1991.

26. Southwell M, 'Terminating parental access against the wishes of parents: court hearings of access applications to children in local authority care', *Social Work and Social Sciences Review*, 2:1, pp 61–76, 1990–91.

27. Weyland I, 'Contact within different legal contexts', *Family Law*, April 1992.

28. Hodgson D, 'Right on', *Community Care*, 10 March 1994.

29. Hinchliffe M, 'Issues of permanence and contact', *Practitioners Child Law Bulletin*, 5:9, 1992.

30. Thoburn J, Murdoch A, and O'Brien A, *Permanence in Child Care*, Blackwell, 1986.

31. See 26 above.

32. See 27 above.

33. Hartman A, and Laird J, 'Family treatment after adoption: common themes', in Brodzinsky D M, and Schechter M D (eds), *The Psychology of Adoption*, Oxford University Press, 1990.

34. *Community Care*, 5 November 1992 and 12 November 1992.

35. *Community Care*, 13 May 1993.

36. Alderson P, *Children's Consent to Surgery*, Open University Press, 1993.

37. See 26 above, p 69.

38. See 36 above, pp 31 and 196.

39. Packman J, Randall J, and Jacques N, *Who Needs Care? Social Work decisions about children*, Blackwell, 1986.

40. Borland M, O'Hara G, and Triseliotis J, 'Placement outcomes for children with special needs', *Adoption & Fostering*, 15:2, BAAF, pp 18–28, 1991.

41. Wedge P, and Mantle G, *Sibling Groups and Social Work*, Avebury, 1991.

42. See 9 above, p 42.

43. *Community Care,* 9 December 1993.

44. Department of Health, *Children Act Regulations and Guidance, Volume 3, Family placements*, HMSO, 1991, para 6.1.

45. Department of Health and Welsh Office, *Children Act Report 1992*: A report by the Secretaries of State for Health and for Wales on the Children Act 1989 in pursuance of their duties under Section 83(6) of the Act presented to Parliament by command of Her Majesty, February 1993.

46. See 39 above.

47. Department of Health and Welsh Office, *Adoption – A service for children*, HMSO, 1996.

48. Tunnard J, *Family Group Conferences*, Family Rights Group, 1994.

49. See 2 above.

50. See 4 above.

51. Ryburn M, 'Contact after contested adoptions', *Adoption & Fostering*, 18:4, BAAF, 1994.

52. See 51 above.

53. Fratter J, 'Adoptive parents and open adoption in the UK', in Mullender A (ed), *Open Adoption – The philosophy and the practice*, BAAF, 1991.

54. See 10 above.

55. McRoy R G, 'American experience and research on openness', *Adoption & Fostering*, 15:4, BAAF, p 109, 1991.

56. See 4 above, p 330.

Appendix I
Una and Keith, adoptive parents of Craig, whose placement disrupted in 1987

When Una and Keith were first interviewed in 1987, Craig was just 14. Like Laura and Hayley, his older sisters by four years and two-and-a-half years respectively, Craig had been admitted to a children's home because of injuries inflicted on him and his two sisters by their stepfather, Mike. He had been placed first at the age of six months; returned to his mother's care when his stepfather was imprisoned; then placed back in the home when he was about 15 months old, his stepfather having re-joined his mother's household. Craig had a different birth father from Laura and Hayley, and was not thought to have had any memories of living with his mother. During the seven years Craig and his sisters lived in the home, their mother, Mary, visited them sporadically, promising (so Keith and Una understood) that they could return home at 16. It was planned that the three children should be adopted, Hayley and Laura by one family and Craig by another (the plan to separate them was based on the assessment that one family would not have been able to meet the emotional needs and cope with the behavioural problems of all three together).

At the time of their application to be approved as adoptive parents, Una and Keith had no children. They had not anticipated an adoption with contact at the outset. The social worker had explained that there was ongoing contact between the children and their birth mother, but the agency planned to limit this to twice yearly. Furthermore, the social worker was 'confident that Mary's interest would fade'. Una and Keith were quite happy to maintain contact with the adoptive family of Craig's sisters and indeed until Hayley started work six years after the placement, the two families met about once every six weeks. When interviewed in 1987, Una and Keith recalled how shocked they had been when they and Hayley's adoptive parents had met Mary during the course of their introduction to the children and realised how strongly opposed she was to the plan for adoption. Una commented: 'I had a gut feeling that she would want to stay involved.'

After placement, as already described in relation to Hayley, the adoption was delayed for almost five years. Mary had wanted the children to remain fostered and a court welfare officer had made a recommendation to this effect at one point. However, Craig was said to have written to her (he was then aged 11) to say he wished to be adopted (Una had recounted with some annoyance in 1987 that the court welfare officer had queried whether Craig had written the letter 'unaided'). When Craig was 13, Mary had eventually given her agreement to adoption, both sets of adoptive parents having offered to continue the twice yearly supervised access.

Keith and Una had been among the six families who in 1987 had described difficulties in relation to contact. They said Craig enjoyed seeing his mother and older sister Laura, but they had found the supervised meetings in a social work office 'full of tension', and Craig's behaviour tended to be more difficult before and after meetings. In their view, Mary 'behaved as if she were still Craig's mother'. Despite this, Una and Keith commented that it would not have helped to terminate contact: 'Craig would have resented this. Contact is essential for him.' At the time of the first interview, Craig had not met his birth mother for nine months. His behaviour then was generally problematic: 'he's going through a difficult teenage phase'. However, Una and Keith believed Craig was quite well attached to them. They did not appear critical of Mary, although they found her attitude unhelpful. They said they talked openly with Craig about his mother's good points – indeed they appeared to be very open in attitude.

About six weeks after the first interview with Una and Keith, Craig had run away, having received a reverse charge phone call which they later learned had been from a birth relative. He had gone to stay with his birth mother and had telephoned them to say: 'You're not my mum and dad'. Subsequently, there were meetings with social workers and Craig, who confirmed his intention not to return. It was only after Craig had run away that Una and Keith had learned that he had been threatened with suspension from school. At the time of placement he had been attending a special unit for children with emotional problems and his attainment had been well below average. However, over the years, Craig had progressed and had been able to attend mainstream school. It emerged after the disruption that Craig had scarcely attended school for the previous six weeks, although the school had not communicated this.

At the time of the second interview, almost four years had elapsed since Craig had left the family and he was then approaching 18. Una and Keith described events during that period. During the first two years there had been very limited contact, but Una had written regularly throughout. Craig had stayed only a very brief time with Mary and Mike, later telling his adoptive parents that he had asked his mother to 'choose between me and him (his stepfather)'. As she had done many years earlier (which was a source of bitterness to Hayley), Mary had "chosen" Mike, and Craig had left to live with various members of the extended family for brief periods, not looking after himself very well, according to Una and Keith. Craig's contact with the adoptive family had become more frequent during 1990 and 1991, although he had changed his name by deed poll to his original family name and referred to his adoptive parents by their first names. He had visited several times with his girlfriend, once bringing flowers for Una and on another occasion sending a fulsome "thank you" note. He telephoned quite often, including on the evening of the interview. Shortly before that, Keith had called in to see Craig (at his request) on his way home from work, and had been surprised to see photographs of the adoptive family and his framed adoption certificate adorning the walls of his room in the hostel in which he was temporarily living!

Una and Keith said they would 'never get over' the loss of Craig as a member of their family. Keith commented, using a phrase commonly used by birth parents: 'It's been like a bereavement.' Nonetheless, they said they had no regrets about having adopted Craig: 'We received a lot from him as well as giving a lot.' They hoped Craig had gained something from the time spent with them. Did they think a different outcome might have been possible, perhaps if there had been no contact? Una and Keith did not believe that ending contact had been a realistic option, because 'Craig definitely had some need for or attachment to his birth family'. Early on in the placement, they had changed their telephone number because Craig had seemed to be upset by the frequent phone calls, and the phone call on the evening Craig had run away may or may not have precipitated this. But both felt that issues to do with identity were the source of Craig's difficulties, not his birth family contact.

Una had telephoned me in 1987 to discuss the fact that Craig had run away and at that time she had spoken of Craig 'having an identity crisis and questioning to whom he belonged.' In 1991, Keith spoke of Craig's identity confusion: in adolescence, the pull of the "genetic bond" had been too strong and he had felt that "his loyalties lay with his birth family". He was 'like a chameleon, even in his speech'. Una added: 'Blood *is* thicker than water'. Furthermore, Craig had only begun during 1987 to attach significance to the fact that he and his sisters had a different father.

Looking back, Una and Keith wondered whether fostering might have been more appropriate than adoption; Mary would have accepted that and Craig, despite his request to be adopted, had found the change of family name difficult. Una thought the difference in social status and educational background of the birth and the adoptive families might have made adoption 'more difficult' for Craig. Una and Keith were reluctant to generalise from their own experience about the impact of contact as they knew of closed adoptions which had disrupted. My impression was of a couple who had remained child-focused throughout the process and who were still ready to be supportive to Craig as he reached adulthood.

Appendix II
The case study families

The adopted children and young people

Antoinette, adopted by Frank and Lorna

Antoinette was aged 20 and living independently when interviewed. Her white Scottish mother, Eleanor, had been living for some years in a long-stay unit for people with psychiatric problems. Antoinette's African-Caribbean father had never had involvement with her. Antoinette had been fostered by Frank and Lorna, a white couple, from the age of six and adopted by them when she was 14. Eleanor's face-to-face contact had been terminated when Antoinette was ten and letter contact had subsequently been maintained by Antoinette and her adoptive parents.

Antoinette was corresponding with her birth mother at the time of the interview.

Janine and Andrew, adopted by Alex and Naomi

Janine and Andrew were 18 and 17 respectively when interviewed. Their birth parents, Paula and John, who were both white, had separated prior to the children being accommodated by the local authority when aged seven and six respectively. Paula had had a diagnosis of depression but had continued to care for the youngest child, Adam. Within ten months of leaving their mother's care, Janine and Andrew had been placed for adoption with Alex and Naomi, a white couple. The prospective adoptive parents confirmed in writing their willingness to maintain face-to-face contact three times a year and on that basis, Paula and John gave agreement to adoption. In 1987, the adoptive mother described the meetings on neutral territory as distressing to her and unsettling for Andrew.

Four years later, Janine and Andrew were making arrangements to see their birth mother and Adam independently of each other and of their adoptive parents.

Paul and Nicola, adopted by Jan and Malcolm

Paul and Nicola were a half brother and sister of African-Caribbean descent, aged 15 and 13 respectively when interviewed. They had been placed with Jan and Malcolm, a white couple, when aged six and four, two years after having been removed from their mother's care and subsequently made subject of a care order. The children's birth mother, Corine, and Paul's birth father, Darren, were said to have felt able to agree to adoption because of the adoptive parents' willingness to maintain face-to-face contact. Jan and Malcolm had previously adopted Maxine, also of African-Caribbean descent, with whose birth relatives they were having contact in 1987.

Family to family meetings, as well as individual visits by Paul and Nicola, were occurring in 1991.

Hayley, adopted by Barbara and Ken

Hayley, a young white woman, was 20 when interviewed and was living with her husband Mark and baby son Aaron. She and her older sister Laura had been placed for adoption with white adoptive parents, Barbara and Ken ten years previously. Their younger brother, Craig, had been placed separately with Una and Keith. The three children had spent almost seven years in a children's home, having been made subject of care orders because of injuries inflicted by their stepfather. Laura left the prospective adoptive family after six months. Five years after they had been placed, Hayley and Craig were adopted, their birth mother, Mary, having delayed giving her agreement. The two sets of adoptive parents had offered to maintain face-to-face contact twice a year. Shortly after the 1987 interview, Craig left his adoptive home. The account of this given by Una and Keith is reported in Appendix I.

Barbara and Ken had expressed dissatisfaction with the contact arrangements in 1987 and later that year, Hayley, having reached 16, decided to end contact.

The birth parents

Beverley, birth mother of Claire

Beverley had been a teenager when she gave birth to Claire, a white child. Beverley's relationship with Claire's father had ended, and Claire was placed with white pre-adoption foster carers, Helen and Chris, via a voluntary adoption agency. Beverley had decided to seek adoption for Claire because of the lack of any good enough alternatives. However, she did not feel able to accept the prospective adoptive parents selected by the agency and asked Helen and Chris to consider adopting Claire. After some initial opposition from the agency, Claire was adopted by Helen and Chris. They negotiated arrangements for contact with Beverley, initially through her visiting but subsequently through other forms of contact.

At the time of the interview, Claire was eight and Beverley was maintaining contact by telephoning occasionally and by sending birthday and Christmas presents.

Eve and Gerald, birth parents of Stephen

Eve and Gerald, a white couple, had three children. At the time of the interview, Louise was 19, Stephen was 14 and Joshua was aged ten. Stephen had Down's Syndrome and his parents had had difficulty in caring for him during his early years However, they were unhappy with the insistence of the local authority accommodating Stephen that he be placed for adoption. When he was nine, Stephen had been placed with white prospective adoptive parents, Doreen and William.

There had been no plan for contact at the time of placement, but following an invitation from Doreen and William, Eve and Gerald and their other two children had visited Stephen, and had continued to do so twice a year.

Ian, birth father of Jamie

Ian and his former wife, Anna, had reached the point of agreeing to Jamie's placement for adoption when their son was seven. Jamie and his two younger sisters, Charlotte and Sophie, were of African/Irish descent,

Ian having been born in Dublin and Anna being Kenyan. Jamie had severe disabilities, and in the absence of extended family, the paediatrician advised a placement away from home because of the strain on the family. Ian and Anna had approached Carol and Rob, a white couple, directly. They all attended the same church and Carol and Rob had already adopted another child with disabilities. Ongoing contact was negotiated from the outset.

At the time of the interview, when Jamie was 12, Ian and the two girls were visiting at least monthly. Anna was maintaining contact by telephone.

Cathy, birth mother of Rachel

Cathy was the mother of four white children, all of whom had spent many years together in a children's home. They had initially been accommodated at Cathy's request, but subsequently the local authority had assumed parental rights. When the oldest child was 15 and the youngest, Rachel, was ten, plans were made to place the children in alternative families because the home was to close. When she was eleven, Rachel was placed with Gareth and Jane, a white couple, on a fostering basis with a view to adoption. Cathy was opposed to adoption, but eventually agreed when she realised that Rachel wanted to be adopted and was not being put under pressure by Gareth and Jane, who were willing for contact to be maintained.

At the time of the interview, Rachel was 19, and visiting Cathy regularly, sometimes at weekly intervals. Cathy was having much less contact with the other three children, none of whom had been adopted.

The adoptive parents

Sally and Alun, adoptive parents of Melanie

Sally and Alun, both white, had initially offered to care for Melanie, whom they knew through their links with their local children's home, for a weekend only. She was a white child, then aged nine, who had had 22 previous placements. Melanie was subject of a care order and maintaining fortnightly contact with her birth mother, Anne. The placement was extended to long term and when she was eleven, Melanie asked to be adopted. Anne was opposed to adoption, but after hearing directly from Melanie, she withdrew her opposition, although she did not give agreement. In 1987, Sally and Alun were taking Melanie to visit Anne twice a year.

By 1991, Melanie, then 17, had chosen to end face-to-face contact with Anne. She was being accommodated by the local authority at the request of Sally and Alun because of difficult, including self-harming, behaviour.

Martin and Joy, adoptive parents of Michael and Sara
Michael and Sara were placed with Martin and Joy, a white couple, when they were aged 18 months and eleven weeks respectively. Their parents, both white, had been diagnosed as having psychiatric illness and both children had been removed from their mother, Shelley, at birth. Care proceedings had not been completed and the children were being taken fortnightly by a social worker to visit Shelley and their father, Sam. Although they had not anticipated adoption with contact, Joy and Martin invited Sam and Shelley to their home as this was less distressing to the children. Eventually, the birth parents accepted the plan for the children to be adopted. In 1987, when Michael and Sara were aged six and five, Sam and Shelley were visiting fortnightly.

By 1991, their visits had become less frequent because of Shelley's health problems.

Sue and Dave, adoptive parents of Anil
Anil, a boy of Indian descent with a life-threatening and disabling medical condition, had been placed with Sue and Dave, a white couple, when he was three. His birth parents had not been able to care for him because of the needs of their other children, and had given agreement to adoption. Nine years later, Anil's birth parents had enquired after him at the office of the social services department which had arranged the adoption. They were relieved to learn he was still alive, and accepted an invitation from Sue and Dave to visit. Subsequently, there had been limited contact by telephone or letter.

In 1991, when Anil was 16, he was wanting contact to be within his control, and planning to correspond via an adoption agency.

Ruth and James, adoptive parents of Peter
Ruth and James, both white, had been open to the possibility of adoption with contact when they first approached the agency. Peter, who was white and 13 at the time of placement, was in regular contact with his birth mother and other family members. He had entered care at the age of ten because of his mother's psychiatric problems and his grandmother's frailty. Peter was able to visit them, via public transport, about once every three weeks after placement. Peter left his adoptive family to stay with an uncle for some months when he was 17, but subsequently returned to live with Ruth and James.

In 1991, when Peter was 20, he was living independently with his girlfriend.

Appendix III
Participants' experience of social work input and suggestions regarding future practice

Birth parents

In considering their involvement with social workers prior to their child's adoption, all the birth parents who were interviewed expressed some criticisms or disappointment about the service they had received.

Eve and Gerald, Stephen's birth parents, and Cathy, Rachel's birth mother, identified inadequate help at an earlier stage in their child's life followed by pressure from the local authority to agree to a placement for adoption.

- According to Eve, there had been little recognition when Stephen was young of the pressures which caring for him placed on his parents and siblings. The family had difficulties in obtaining short breaks and the only alternative was a full-time hostel placement, with Stephen spending some weekends at home. The local authority then explained that the policy was that Stephen be adopted, although this was not what Eve and Gerald had wanted.
- Rachel had spent almost nine years in residential care when Cathy was informed that because of the closure of the home, Rachel and her older three siblings were to be placed with families, with an adoptive home being sought for Rachel. Looking back, and having been caring for 'other people's children' for a number of years, Cathy recognised that lack of family support, her unhappy marriage and low self-esteem had prevented her from successfully resuming care of her children while they were young. She stated that none of the many social workers who had been involved with the children over the years had ever tried to help her in this respect, or even to encourage her contact with the children. Cathy described having felt too devalued to oppose the plan for an adoption placement for Rachel, although she had felt shocked and saddened.

Two birth parents, Ian and Beverley, had found social workers to be critical of their having chosen adoptive parents for their children.

- Ian's emotional support when he and Anna made the decision to place Jamie with another family on a permanent basis was provided by the hospital paediatric team caring for Jamie and not from the local authority. The parents' wish that Jamie be placed with Carol and Rob was initially resisted by the social worker and advertisements were placed to recruit an alternative family before Carol and Rob were considered.
- Beverley's request that Helen and Chris be approved as adoptive parents for Claire was initially refused by the case committee of the voluntary agency.

Both Ian and Beverley highlighted how important it had been for them (and, they believed, for their child) to fulfil their parental responsibility by selecting the most suitable family, yet this had not been understood and acknowledged by the respective agencies.

Birth parents in two families did not find that the agency was supportive of their wish to maintain contact after adoption.

- Beverley had felt that she could not part with Claire without the reassurance of knowing that in the future she would be able to receive news of her. She remembered being advised by the agency worker that she would 'get over' and forget Claire and the guardian *ad litem* had advised Helen and Chris to move in order to prevent her visiting.
- Eve and Gerald had discovered, after the adoptive family had been selected for Stephen, that their request to be kept informed as to his progress had been ignored by the local authority social worker in her negotiations with the voluntary agency through which the placement with Doreen and William had been made. Gerald commented that this attitude took no account of the needs of Stephen's sister and brother, Louise and Joshua, to retain a link with him and to be reassured as to his welfare.

Generally, the birth parents interviewed had not found social workers helpful: Beverley had obtained support informally from a social worker who was not involved with the adoption agency; Ian and Anna had been helped mainly by a clinical psychologist; Eve and Gerald had talked with a friend who was a social worker and had also found the guardian *ad litem* sympathetic to their request for news; and Cathy had derived support from her partner and, when Rachel had expressed the wish to be adopted a year or so after placement, from the local authority adoption worker who had been working with Gareth and Jane (but not from the social worker allocated to her and to the children).

At the time of my interview with them, none of the birth parents was in touch with a social worker and none felt the need at that stage for post-adoption support. Their child's adoption had taken place at least five years earlier and all had been able to negotiate a pattern of contact which they found helpful. However, the parent who had parted with another child for adoption without contact seemed to welcome the opportunity to talk about this.

The suggestions made by birth parents regarding future practice were informed by their good experience of adoption with contact. Eve and Gerald had written: 'We think this should be available for all families if it is appropriate.' They highlighted the importance of the agency communicating the expectations of birth parents to adoptive parents regarding contact – in their case, their concerns that they would never have any information about Stephen or contact with him in the future had led to the adoption hearing being adjourned twice while the guardian *ad litem* discussed their concerns with Doreen and William. Eve and Gerald also felt that their initial meeting with the prospective adopters, after introductions had begun, was 'too far on in the process'.

Ian, drawing on his own experience and his awareness of other cultures, argued that agencies should promote greater openness. Birth parents and adoptive parents should be encouraged to work things out together and adopters should be prepared to let children go and recognise 'the need of the child for flight'.

Both Beverley and Cathy felt it was important to emphasise that in their experience continuing information or contact had proved helpful: 'It is far worse not to know.' Beverley was aware that it was sometimes stated that continuing contact was detrimental to birth parents but she could not imagine this would be so other than in exceptional circumstances.

Adopted children and young people

The adopted children who were interviewed were not asked for their observations on the helpfulness or otherwise of social workers. However, 11 of the 15 young people made suggestions for practitioners about adoption with contact.

Most included the recommendation that social workers should ask and listen to the child. Hayley (who did not feel that her wishes had been sought) commented: 'Social workers should make plans from the child's point of view. The child's view is the one that counts. Ask the child.' Janine felt this equally strongly: 'You should be able to see your birth parents if you want to – it should be the kid's choice.' Andrew estimated that '99 per cent of children would say yes, they want to see their parents' (an interesting view, since his contact with his birth mother had been the source of so much tension in the past for his adoptive mother, Naomi, and he had been aware of this).

Seven young people spoke of being allowed to have contact with birth parents as a right, and four, including the young person whose adoptive parents were unaware of the extent of sibling contact, stressed the importance of contact with brothers and sisters. Some recognised that social workers might need to assist: 'Social workers should make sure parents leave an address for children so they can write to them. And parents should have an address to write to their children.' Anil suggested that birth parents and adoptive parents should 'keep the agency informed of their address. Then it's not forced but the facility is there.'

Antoinette commented on the role of social workers prior to adoption: 'Social workers should give more help to parents – I mean mental help. That's important to the child. There is a very strong bond' (Antoinette had earlier explained that she had not thought her birth mother had received enough support to enable her to care for her).

Adoptive parents

As previously described, most adoptive parents had been influenced to some degree with regard to openness by the agency preparation or by individual workers. Adoptive parents in 15 families also commented on the input of social workers during the period leading up to adoption. Most had found social work input helpful, although some, who had had changes of social worker, found that not all had been helpful, while others' experience was that the adoption worker (whether from the voluntary agency or the local authority) had assisted them more than the child's or birth family's social worker from the local authority. For example, Joy and Martin felt that "their" social worker had been misled about the complexity of the placement of Michael and Sara. And the adoptive parents of Hayley and Craig had been shocked to discover how opposed the children's birth mother was to adoption. Ruth had found social workers helpful overall but too little attention had been given to the details of Peter's contact with his birth mother and grandmother at the outset of the placement. Jan and Malcolm described their experience of social workers as very positive in relation to themselves and their children, but they queried how much help had been offered to the children's (black) birth relatives and felt that too little attention was paid to issues of race when children were admitted to local authority accommodation.

Adoptive parents in three families had had some particularly unhelpful input, they felt, from one or more social workers.

- In one family, adoptive parents, who had maintained contact with their children's birth parents, had been told that they could not apply to adopt because of contact. Eventually they sought independent legal advice and also approached their children's birth mother regarding her agreement. This led to considerable delay in achieving adoption.
- Helen and Chris, Claire's adoptive parents, had initially had their application to be approved as adoptive parents for her refused – not because of their unsuitability but because the case committee believed that only childless couples should be allowed to adopt babies!
- Naomi and Alex were the most critical of agency input from both the voluntary agency and the local authority. They felt that the agencies had been using them as "guinea pigs", having had no idea of the complexities of adoption with contact for "disturbed" children. They felt the support had been too limited: the social workers said they would be there "if needed" but had underestimated the difficulties. After adoption, access meetings had been held in the agency and social work input had therefore continued, but not effectively, according to the adoptive parents. They felt the situation had only improved when Alex had taken responsibility for contact.

Adoptive parents in eleven families had stated that they had not needed social work input after adoption in 1987 or in 1991: one adoptive father commented that he and his wife were 'relieved to be without social workers in our lives'. The meetings on neutral territory which had been occurring in relation to four placements in 1987 had been replaced by visits to the birth parents' home in two instances (negotiated by the young people themselves), while Hayley had ended contact and Craig had left his adoptive family. Thus post-placement input had also ended. There were three families in which adoptive parents were in touch with social workers: in one, it was helpful to adoptive parents whose son was in touch with his birth mother to be kept informed as to her health; in the second, a social worker had helped to re-establish letter contact between a young man and his birth mother; and Melanie's adoptive parents were in touch with their local authority social worker in relation to her being accommodated and not in relation directly to adoption or contact.

When asked to make suggestions to practitioners about adoption and openness, adoptive parents in three families stressed the benefits of meeting birth parents at an early stage: Rachel's adoptive parents, who had not met Cathy until several months after her placement, explained that they had felt more "threatened" before meeting her, but having done so had felt more relaxed. Adoptive parents in another family believed social workers in general 'have not given adoptive parents enough help in understanding the value of openness in the past'. They added: 'Secrecy is unhelpful – the more you know, the less you need to find out.' The importance of grandparents to children was emphasised by an adoptive mother who felt that this was often overlooked by social workers.

When asked what recommendations they would make to other adoptive parents regarding adoption with contact, most adopters would encourage openness, but with the safeguard that individual circumstances would always be important. Jan, the adoptive mother of Maxine, Paul and Nicola, commented: 'It's not fair to deny contact if it can be managed without trauma.' Rachel's adoptive father said: 'You owe it to your children to be as open as possible.' Anil's adoptive mother was more guarded: 'Don't be pressurised by social workers who may over-identify with the birth parents. Sometimes open adoption can be made to sound very straightforward, but it may not be, especially in the case of older, damaged children.' Jamie's adoptive parents pointed out that the relationship between the adults was crucial, but if they worked well together, 'it's a big advantage to be able to ask birth parents direct about the birth and early history.' The comment of Claire's adoptive mother, Helen, was typical of the majority of adoptive parents interviewed: 'I would encourage openness of attitude and keeping the channels open for communication. There has to be more contact, if only through an agency.'

Appendix IV
RELEVANT STATUTES AND CONSULTATIVE DOCUMENTS RELATING TO THE REVIEW OF ADOPTION LAW (ENGLAND AND WALES)

Statutes

England and Wales

Adoption Act 1958
Adoption Act 1976
Adoption of Children Act 1926
Adoption of Children (Regulations) 1939
Adoption of Children Act 1949
Child Care Act 1980
Children Act 1948
Children Act 1975
Children Act 1989
Children and Young Persons Act 1963
Children and Young Persons Act 1969
Family Law Reform Act 1969
Health and Social Services and Social Security Adjudications Act 1983
Local Authority Social Services Act 1970
NHS and Community Care Act 1990